$50.00

S0-ATF-638

FOREIGN AID

Foreign Aid

Diplomacy, Development, Domestic Politics

CAROL LANCASTER

THE UNIVERSITY OF CHICAGO PRESS

Chicago and London

CAROL LANCASTER is associate professor in the Edmund A. Walsh School of Foreign Service at Georgetown University and director of the Mortara Center for International Studies. She is the author of *Aid to Africa*, also published by the University of Chicago Press, a coauthor of *Organizing U.S. Foreign Aid: Confronting the Challenges of the Twenty-first Century,* and a former deputy administrator of USAID.

The University of Chicago Press, Chicago 60637
The University of Chicago Press, Ltd., London
© 2007 by The University of Chicago
All rights reserved. Published 2007
Printed in the United States of America

16 15 14 13 12 11 10 09 08 07   1 2 3 4 5

ISBN-10: 0-226-47043-1 (cloth)
ISBN-13: 978-0-226-47043-6 (cloth)
ISBN-10: 0-226-47045-8 (paper)
ISBN-13: 978-0-226-47045-0 (paper)

Library of Congress Cataloging-in-Publication data

Lancaster, Carol.
    Foreign aid : diplomacy, development, domestic politics / Carol Lancaster.
        p.   cm.
    Includes bibliographical references and index.
    ISBN 0-226-47043-1 (cloth : alk. paper)—ISBN 0-226-47045-8 (pbk. : alk. paper)
    1. Economic assistance. 2. International relations.
3. Diplomacy. 4. Economic development—International cooperation. 5. Economic assistance—Political aspects. I. Title.
HC60.L294 2007
327.1'11—dc22
                                                2006020760

⊗ The paper used in this publication meets the minimum requirements of the American National Standard for Information Sciences—Permanence of Paper for Printed Library Materials, ANSI Z39.48–1992.

To Brian Atwood, Jill Buckley,
Michael Feldstein, and Jennifer Windsor,
from whom I have learned so much

And to Curt,
to whom I owe so much

CONTENTS

PREFACE

The question this book asks is "Why is aid given?" The question may seem odd since, after a half century of aid-giving, aid is a familiar and expected element in relations between states. And yet, in the middle of the first decade of the twenty-first century, foreign aid is much in the news. After major declines during the 1990s, aid levels are again rising. Aid's purposes are still debated, but development aid—apparently headed for extinction in the 1990s—is making an impressive comeback.

"Why is aid given?" is actually two questions. What purposes did governments pursue with their aid? And why did they choose those purposes and not others? The first question remains an important one, but it is not new. It has been asked since the origins of aid-giving in the middle of the twentieth century. Scholars and practitioners have debated whether it was or should be provided for primarily diplomatic purposes—advancing the national security and economic interests of the donor country—or whether it was or should be provided mainly to help better the human condition in countries receiving the aid. This book describes the evolution of aid's purposes over the fifty years of aid-giving. But it goes beyond narrative to dig into the second question of why governments have pursued the mix of purposes they have with aid—whether diplomatic, developmental, relief, commercial, cultural, or others. International events, trends, and pressures are important in answering this question, but they are far from enough. To answer the question, we need to understand the often neglected domestic politics of aid in aid-giving countries—the widely shared ideas and norms shaping aid-giving, the political institutions in which aid decisions are made, the interests competing for influence over aid's purposes, and the organization of governments to manage their aid. This book compares these forces at work in five countries: the United States, Japan, France, Germany, and Denmark. Each has a separate and interesting tale to tell about the influence of domestic politics on aid's purposes, and each has a story about the changing nature of aid-giving.

This book begins by examining the nature of foreign aid and the concepts to be used in the study. Chapter 2 provides a history of aid and also the international context in which governments made key decisions on the amount, country allocation, use, and terms of their aid. Chapters 3 through 7 examine in detail the profiles and domestic politics of aid in the United States, Japan, France, Germany, and Denmark. A final chapter draws comparisons and lessons from these five case studies in aid-giving and peers into the probable future of foreign aid in the twenty-first century.

I should say a word about my own engagement in foreign aid. In addition to a decade of scholarly research on foreign aid, I have spent thirteen years off and on in the US government, working on foreign aid issues from a variety of institutional perches: from the Office of Management and Budget—the only agency in the US executive branch where professionals are rewarded for criticizing policies and programs and for cutting budgets; from the Congress, working on aid issues for a senator and a member of the House of Representatives, both of whom had major responsibilities in this area and who had to balance interests of their home constituencies and of the US government with their own values and proclivities when it came to foreign aid; from the policy planning staff in the Department of State, which tried (not very successfully) to engage all US bilateral aid programs, and later as a deputy assistant secretary of state for Africa, where my job was in part to try to raid the budget of USAID for urgent diplomatic uses; and finally as deputy administrator of USAID, where my job was to manage USAID and the multiple forces seeking to shape foreign aid, to protect the aid budget from being raided by other agencies and departments, and to keep USAID itself from being absorbed by State. In all of these positions, my personal sympathies were with using aid to better the human condition abroad—recognizing that this goal was always experimental and risky, given the limitations on our knowledge of what it takes to support complex changes in foreign lands. But I also recognized the legitimacy and necessity of using aid for other compelling purposes, especially the diplomatic ones where aid was an instrument of US leadership in the world. In all of this experience, I spent much of my time dealing with the domestic politics of aid—inside the bureaucracy and with the Congress, the media, and the many individuals and groups engaged with US assistance abroad. I also observed the role of domestic politics in the work of aid colleagues in other countries. I have mined these experiences over the years to inform this book.

This was not, however, an easy book to write. One of the difficulties is familiar to historians and political scientists: to cover a significant period of time and shape a vast amount of information into a coherent and convincing story and to draw out conceptual and theoretical lessons. But the real difficulty of this project for me was the tension between the complexities of aid's story, which I learned over the years as a practitioner, and the parsimony demanded by scholarly analysis. Even with over a decade's experience working in the "real world" on foreign aid, it is difficult to grasp fully the welter of events and how important apparently small or hidden details can be. The occasional tendency for scholars to miss key factors influencing important policies or events and thereby misinterpret causes and consequences feeds what I have observed as a widespread skepticism of scholarly analysis among aid and foreign policy practitioners. On the other hand, scholars rightly understand that to explain and analyze policies, it is necessary to interpret reality in terms of broad concepts, theories (where possible), and underlying trends—otherwise, comprehending the meaning of events and the fundamental forces shaping them is impossible. I have suffered from this tension in my own writing—the practitioner side of my brain usually rejects the scholarly side as being so conceptual as to be detached from reality; the scholarly side of my brain assails the practitioner side for being too mired in details to understand what has really happened. Comments on various pieces of this book from practitioners and scholars have followed much the same pattern. I can only hope that what follows has struck the right balance between practice and theory and that it will help advance our understanding of the important part of our lives—indeed the lives of much of the world's population—that is foreign aid.

This book could not have been written without the support of many individuals and institutions. I owe the Carnegie Corporation a special note of thanks for awarding me a Carnegie Fellowship that funded much of the research for this study. I wish also to thank the American Council of Learned Societies and the Graduate School of Georgetown University for generous grants to help fund this book. The School of Foreign Service at Georgetown University provided a string of helpful research assistants, including Stephanie Waters, Heidi Arola, Robert Peri, Sujata Thomas, Jennifer Hird, Aliza Pressman, Mollie Richardson, and Ellie Hopping. The Center for Global Development in Washington, DC, offered me a place to do some of my writing. Thanks also to the Japan Bank for International Cooperation for helping to organize my interviews in Tokyo, the Friedrich Ebert Stiftung for helping to organize my interviews in Germany, to Professor Holger Hansen for his invaluable information and help for interviews in Copenhagen, and Serge Michailof and Jean-Jacques Gabas for their advice on interviews in Paris.

I wish also to thank the many people from around the world who read parts and sometimes all of this manuscript: Ann Van Dusen, Kate McNamara, Alene Gelbard, Leslie Vinjamuri, Michael Clemens, JoAnn Moran

Cruz, Steve Radelet, David Ekbladh, David Edlestein, Bill Zartman, Steve Heydemann, William Gormley, Nancy Birdsall, Steve Hook, Mike Feldstein, David Steinberg, Barbara Stallings, Dennis Yasutomo, Kaori Kuroda, Masa Honda, Takao Toda, Juichi Inada, Debra Jewell, a number of anonymous officials at the Japan Bank for International Cooperation, Jeremy Weinstein, Holger Hansen, Serge Michailof, Michel Doucin, anonymous officials at the Ministry of Development in Berlin, two anonymous peer reviewers, and my husband, Curt Farrar, who read the entire manuscript more than once. I have also benefited from the council of too many to mention here. A list of those interviewed appears at the end of the book. The advice and comments have been invaluable. Any shortcomings belong to me.

CHAPTER 1

Why Foreign Aid? Setting the Stage

Foreign aid is among the "real innovations which the modern age has introduced into the practice of foreign policy," according to Hans Morgenthau, one of the fathers of the study of relations between states.[1] Aid is such a familiar and expected element in those relations today that it is often hard to recall just how truly new it is. At the end of the Second World War, foreign aid as we know it today did not exist. There had been a few temporary programs of humanitarian relief in the nineteenth and first half of the twentieth centuries. But the gift of public resources from one government to another (or to an international organization or nongovernmental organization), sizable and sustained over time, an important purpose of which was to help improve the human condition in countries receiving the aid, was unheard of—even unimagined—in policy circles or by the public.[2]

Today, in many of the world's poorer countries, activities funded with aid from foreign governments and international organizations are widespread and familiar. They include billion dollar reconstruction projects in war-torn countries like Iraq and Afghanistan and microenterprise loans of $50 or less to impoverished women in Bangladesh and El Salvador. They comprise international research to find more productive crops and less polluting energy sources, scholarships for PhD economists in world-class universities, and the expansion of primary education in rural Uganda. Aid supports girls' education in Peru, and it helps finance the budget of the Ministry of Education in Ghana. Children in Guatemala, Indonesia, and Ethiopia and in numerous other countries are inoculated with aid-funded vaccines. Couples in Latin America, Asia, and Africa use family planning services subsidized with aid. Aid pays for HIV/AIDS research and prevention and is beginning to finance the distribution of life-saving antiretrovirals. It funds economic reforms in Malawi, debt relief in Mozambique, and enterprise development in Russia. Political party and media training, elections, judicial reform, and civil society development are supported in numerous countries in Africa, Asia, and Latin America with foreign aid, as is humanitarian relief for natural and man-made disasters throughout the world.

The number of organizations and countries involved in providing foreign aid is also large. Several dozen international organizations, like the World Bank, the Asian, African, and Inter-American Development Banks, and the United Nations Development Program (UNDP), plus approximately thirty governments have significant programs of foreign aid, including all the rich countries of North America, Western Europe, and Japan as well as oil-producing countries in the Middle East and "middle-income" developing countries, like Korea, Thailand, and Turkey. Former socialist bloc countries in Eastern Europe are setting up new aid programs, and even relatively poor countries, like India and China, provide aid to other poor countries. And in at least one case, a rich country—the United States— has aided another rich country—the UK (to promote peace in Northern Ireland). Total aid worldwide in 2004 amounted to just over $100 billion.[3] And if we tally up all the public aid provided by governments to other governments, international organizations, and nongovernmental organizations (NGOs) between 1960 and 2004, the total amount exceeds $1.6 trillion.[4]

Foreign aid, though large and commonplace, is not without controversy, especially in major countries providing aid. This controversy centers on the volume of aid that donor governments should provide and the related issue of the impact of aid on development. Aid's critics complain that aid has been ineffective and should be cut. Aid's advocates argue that it has been effective, can with reforms be more effective in the future, and therefore, on moral and practical grounds, it should be dramatically expanded.[5] However, an important part of the debate on aid effectiveness is often missing—the mix of purposes for which aid is provided. Aid has been provided not only to promote growth and poverty reduction abroad. It has been and continues to be provided for a variety of purposes, of which development is only one.

If we are to understand the controversies over foreign aid, if we are to assess fairly aid's past impact and ensure its future effectiveness, if we are to comprehend this important innovation in relations between states, we need to understand why aid has been given over the past sixty years, how and why aid's purposes have differed from country to country, and why and how they have changed over time. It is the intent of this book to answer these questions.

SO WHY AID?

Though we now take aid—especially aid for development—for granted, a moment's thought will remind us that aid is not only a relatively new phenomenon but, in historical terms, a rather puzzling one as well. States are responsible above all for the security and well-being of their own citizens. Why then would they provide their own scarce public concessional resources to promote, among other things, the well-being of people in other countries?

Questioning the purposes of aid is not new among scholars of international relations.[6] Those scholars who interpret relations between states through "realist" lenses—that is, that states operate in an anarchic environment in which power, security, and survival are their predominant preoccupations—answer that aid is, indeed, primarily a tool of hard-headed diplomacy. (Aid's impact on the poor is incidental or instrumental—as a means of increasing the security of the donor nation, for example, through reducing the temptations of communism or terrorism.) Among the early "realists" who argued aid was a tool for enhancing national power and security was George Liska (like Hans Morgenthau, a well-known professor of international relations), who articulated the view that "Foreign aid is today and will remain for some time an instrument of political power."[7] And there are a handful of qualitative scholarly studies illuminating the national-interest motivations in the aid programs of individual countries.[8]

During the 1970s and 1980s, a group of scholars began to use formal modeling techniques to ascertain aid's purposes. Their models tended to rely on correlations between how much aid was provided particular countries and characteristics of those countries to indicate purposes (e.g., low per capita income to indicate development purposes; amount of trade with donor to indicate commercial purposes). The conclusions of most of these studies gave further support to the realist prediction that bilateral aid donors have been driven importantly by their own interests: for example, the United States has been motivated by Cold War concerns; the French by maintaining a postcolonial sphere of influence in Africa.[9]

Marxist scholars and their "dependency," postmodern, and (often) antiglobalization cousins have a different take on the purposes of foreign aid: they regard it as a tool of dominant states at the center of world capitalism to help them to control and exploit developing countries.[10] They can point to plenty of instances of foreign aid being tied to the export of goods and services from donor countries or securing access to needed raw materials imports on the part of those governments.

Liberal internationalists and others of the liberal tradition in international relations would see foreign aid as an instrument or reflection of the tendency of states to cooperate in addressing problems of interdependence and globalization. Growing amounts of aid have been channeled through international institutions and used to expand international "public goods," such as controlling the spread of infectious diseases worldwide or reducing environmental degradation.

Foreign aid has also been interpreted through the lenses of "constructivism"—the newest tendency among international relations scholars—as the expression of a norm that has evolved in relations between states that rich countries should provide assistance to poor countries to help the latter better the quality of lives of their peoples. The principal proponent of this view in the recent literature on foreign aid is David Lumsdaine in his book *Moral Vision and International Politics*. Lumsdaine argues that "economic foreign aid cannot be explained on the basis of donor states' political and economic interests, and that humanitarian concern in the donor countries formed the main basis of support for aid. . . . Support for aid was a response to world poverty which arose mainly from ethical and humane concern and, secondarily, from the belief that long-term peace and prosperity was possible only in a generous and just international order where all could prosper."[11] Several excellent studies of aid from the Nordic countries and the Netherlands have also interpreted that aid through the prism of ideas, norms, and values, especially the social democratic traditions prevailing in those countries.[12]

None of these theories of international politics explain adequately the complexities of aid's purposes. And all of them together lack one important element: the impact of domestic politics on aid-giving. Foreign aid constitutes a public expenditure of significant size, repeated year after year. As such, it is periodically reviewed (and often influenced) by a variety of elements within the executive and legislative branches of aid-giving governments. Further, it is frequently the subject of debate by the public as well as criticism, attack, and pressures from organized groups—representing both public and private interests—in donor countries. All of these groups can and often do influence the purposes of aid. Finally, aid-giving governments themselves must create coalitions of support for foreign aid within their legislatures and publics to sustain aid expenditures over time. The constituents of these coalitions in turn expect their political agendas to be reflected in aid programs. As a result, the purposes of aid are frequently as much the result of what happens inside of a donor government's borders as what happens outside them.

This study offers an analysis of aid's evolving purposes, beginning with an international history of aid-giving (chap. 2). It then provides five case studies of aid-giving in major donor countries: the United States, Japan,

France, Germany, and Denmark (chaps. 3–7). The first four countries have been the largest bilateral aid donors; Denmark was long the largest aid-giving country relative to the size of its economy. Although the narratives of aid's evolving purposes are different from country to country, each of these case studies addresses two basic questions. First, what was the profile of aid's purposes in each country and how did it evolve over time? Second, why did governments choose the particular mix of purposes they did? This second question is answered in a common framework that emphasizes the role of domestic political factors in aid-giving. A final chapter draws conclusions on the nature of foreign aid and on how various elements in the domestic politics of that aid influence its purposes. It ends with several observations on the policy implications of this study and offers conjectures on the future of foreign aid.

ARGUMENT AND FINDINGS OF THIS BOOK

In its narrative of aid's history, this study will show that aid (for purposes other than humanitarian relief) began as a temporary expedient of Cold War diplomacy. It was not primarily an expression of altruism on the part of aid-giving countries. Nor was it driven mainly by commercial interests or a desire to spread capitalism. If there had been no Cold War threat, the United States—the first and, for most years, the largest aid-giving country—might never have initiated programs of aid or put pressure on other governments to do so. While aid commenced as a temporary diplomatic expedient, by the year 2000 it had become a common, and expected, element in relations between better-off and poorer states, with an increasing emphasis on improving the quality of life in recipient countries.

This history reflects the development of an international norm that the governments of rich countries should provide public, concessional resources to improve the human condition in poor countries. This norm can be observed in the discourse on aid, the distribution and use of aid, and the management of foreign aid in donor governments. It did not exist in 1950. By 2000 it was widely accepted and uncontested. It evolved in significant measure because of the domestic politics of aid-giving in donor countries— the imperatives of governments gaining domestic support for annual aid expenditures, the creation and professionalization of aid agencies (which in effect became lobbies within their own governments for aid for development), and the rise of development-oriented NGOs, which created a domestic constituency for aid's development purpose.

Diplomatic and developmental goals, evident in the history of aid, have long been among the most prominent of aid's purposes. However, there have been others: humanitarian relief, commerce, culture, and, after the end of the Cold War, promoting democracy, supporting economic and social transitions, addressing global problems, and preventing and mitigating conflict. Within aid-giving governments, these purposes have always been mixed, even if one has usually been predominant. For example, in the United States, diplomatic and development purposes have predominated. In Japan, commercial and diplomatic goals long prevailed. In Denmark, the priority has been on development and commercial goals. Further, aid's purposes and the priorities among them have differed from government to government, and they have converged over time, with an increasing priority on development evident across governments, as mentioned earlier.

The domestic politics of foreign aid that have had a major impact on aid's purposes include widely shared ideas relevant to aid-giving, a country's political institutions, the interests competing for control over aid-giving, and the way governments organize themselves to manage their aid. "Ideas" are one of the bedrock factors in the domestic politics of aid-giving. The widely shared values and worldviews in donor countries, especially about the appropriate role of the state in society and the role of the donor country in the world, affect public attitudes toward the legitimacy and use of aid and, more indirectly, toward the interests competing for control over aid. Further, while values are slow to change, the way political elites frame aid-giving in terms of those values can have a visible impact on public support for aid. This latter point is demonstrated in the country case studies of aid-giving in Denmark and in the United States.

Political institutions are another bedrock factor in the politics of aid-giving. They determine who has access to decisions, who decides, who vetoes; and they create incentives for action on the part of organized interests. This book will show that the structure of government (especially the role of legislatures and their power to demand accountability from the executive, the access they give to interest groups, and their ability to legislate aid policies) and even electoral rules affect aid-giving by influencing how and when aid issues get on the national political agenda and how they are handled. The rigidities in where and how the United States spends its development assistance, for instance, arise from congressionally imposed restrictions, which reflect, in turn, the power of that branch in the US presidential system and the multiple points of access it provides organized private interests to influence decisions involving foreign aid. The prominence of development as a purpose in German and Danish aid can be traced in part to parliamentary systems based on proportional representation, such that political parties at times have had to offer other parties concessions involving the organization and volume of development aid in order to create and maintain governing coalitions.

Interests are the most dynamic factor in aid-giving. They typically include those private organizations and informal networks as well as government agencies supportive of the diplomatic uses of aid, those pushing for the commercial uses of aid, and those engaged in the development uses of aid. Where one of these interests is weak or lacks access to the political process, as is the case with development interests in Japan and France, the purpose of aid associated with those interests will be weak.

Finally, the way governments organize themselves to manage their aid—whether aid programs and policy-making are fragmented or unified and where they are located in the bureaucratic hierarchy—determines the voice and influence of the interests within government on aid's purposes. Further, organizational arrangements—which institutionalize aid's purposes—are hard to change once in place, as this study will show in the cases of France and Japan.

The findings of this study have implications for scholars, practitioners, and the general public interested in foreign aid. First, aid is with us to stay—at least as long as the challenge of development and the norm that the governments of rich countries should help better the human condition in poor ones continue. This norm does not, however, let us predict the volume of aid provided by donor governments, its allocation to particular countries, or even its uses from one year to the next. Those decisions are not made solely on the basis of this norm. They also reflect budgetary and political conditions at home and external events such as famines, security threats, or conflict, as the historical chapter and the case studies will show. Further, the norm that rich countries should aid poor ones is not without conditions. The publics in aid-giving countries will turn against aid for development and other purposes if they regard it as having been wasted or used corruptly.

Despite the aid-for-development norm, aid continues to be used for multiple purposes by donor governments. New and compelling purposes of aid have arisen since the end of the Cold War (some of which, like dealing with global infectious diseases or environmental degradation, are closely related to development). Diplomatic purposes of aid have undoubtedly had a boost from the terrorist attack of 9/11. For example, aid flows to the Middle East quadrupled between 2001 and 2004 and not just for reconstruction in Afghanistan and Iraq. Foreign aid will likely continue to be used for multiple purposes until the aid lobbies inside aid-giving countries are strong enough to sustain by themselves the sizable transfers now part of aid-giving and can exclude other interests from influencing their purposes. This situation does not seem imminent.

These last two points—that support for aid within donor countries is conditional on aid being effective and that aid's purposes are and promise to continue to be mixed—create a serious and impending problem for aid-giving governments. The recent increase in worldwide aid levels has been justified primarily on the grounds that, with proper reforms in recipient countries, aid will be more effective in promoting development and reducing poverty there. This promise is particularly evident in the expansion of foreign aid in the United States and is the premise behind the creation in 2004 of the Millennium Challenge Corporation—a new aid agency.

But not all aid can be assessed on its contribution to development, because a considerable portion of it serves other purposes—humanitarian, diplomatic, cultural, even still commercial, for example. Thus, to evaluate the developmental effectiveness of aid, one needs to isolate the aid intended for that purpose. But the mix of purposes—including within aid programs for the same country—often makes isolating development-oriented aid difficult. (A further difficulty is the lack of a consensus among aid agencies and aid experts on how best to evaluate aid's development impact and of an agency capable and independent enough to do so for all aid-giving. But that is a topic for another book.) And to add one more difficulty, there have been few efforts on the part of aid agencies or scholars of aid to evaluate the effectiveness of aid for diplomatic, commercial, or cultural purposes—long among aid's major goals, as this study will show.

In a few years, the publics in aid-giving countries will be demanding to know what has been the impact on development from the recent increases in aid. If governments providing the aid have no credible and acceptable answers, we may see a weakening in support for development aid and even an erosion of the aid-for-development norm if publics conclude aid cannot be effective. For those engaged in aid-giving, this is the most serious threat to the future of foreign aid.

A NOTE ON THEORY

By this time, if the reader is a political scientist, he or she will be asking what sort of theoretical model I am using for my analysis of the politics of foreign-aid-giving and, specifically, (with so much emphasis thus far on the domestic determinants of aid-giving) how I conceptualize the relationship between domestic and international influences over foreign aid. First, on the latter relationship, there have been several approaches in international relations theorizing: Some in the realist tradition have ignored domestic political forces, assuming that states are part of an international system, which creates its own strong incentives for policy and behavior, and act primarily in response to challenges and opportunities emanating from that system. A second approach, often drawing on the field of comparative politics, regards domestic political factors—bureaucracies, political institutions, interest groups, and values and identities—as mediating the impact of external events and trends on foreign policy choices. A third approach looks at the impact of external forces on those basic elements in domestic politics—how and when do external forces change a country's political institutions, its configuration of interests, its ideas about itself and the world?[13] None of these approaches is adequate fully to capture the interplay of domestic and international influences over aid's purposes.

In a number of instances, this study will show the mediating role of domestic politics as it shapes aid's purposes. But I will present cases where international events—for example, famines and disasters—and external pressures affected both ideas and interests in aid-giving countries and so, over the long run, influenced the purposes of aid. I will also show where domestic politics, without provocation from abroad, shaped the purposes of aid-giving.

On the broader question of modeling influences over foreign aid, I confess I do not have a model, except at the broadest level where domestic and international factors influence foreign aid's purposes and, in turn, are over time influenced by aid's purposes and uses. There are too many interacting variables to justify a model that would be both parsimonious and insightful. Further, while quantitative data are essential, this study is essentially a qualitative one—an in-depth, case-study approach, appropriate to the complexity of my topic and my intent to deepen our understanding of the politics of foreign aid. I employ concepts from political science to structure my analysis and provide a basis for comparisons across aid-giving countries, but this is not a study in political science theory.

DEFINITIONS

Let me turn to elucidating two terms used frequently in this study whose meaning can be variable and ambiguous—*foreign aid* and *purpose*, along with some associated concepts.

First, Foreign Aid

Foreign aid is a tricky concept. It is sometimes thought of as a policy. It is not a policy but a tool of policy. It is sometimes regarded as including trade and military expenditures abroad or is used to encompass all public transfers among countries. In fact, the conventional definition of aid and the one I use in this study is considerably narrower. Foreign aid is defined here as *a voluntary transfer of public resources, from a government to another independent government, to an NGO, or to an international organization (such as the World Bank or the UN Development Program) with at least a 25 percent grant element,*[14] *one goal of which is to better the human condition in the country receiving the aid.* This definition of foreign aid is close to the one the Development Assistance Committee (DAC) of the Organisation for Economic Cooperation and Development (OECD) uses to define "official development assistance" (ODA), with two important distinctions. First, the definition of ODA used by the DAC involves transfers to low-income countries only. My definition also includes "official assistance" (OA)—concessional public transfers to promote economic and social progress in countries other than low-income ones. These countries include Russia, the Ukraine, Israel, Korea, and others with per capita incomes over $9,200 in 2001 dollars.[15] Including OA in my definition of foreign aid gives a more comprehensive and coherent picture of what is truly innovative about foreign aid—an effort to use public concessional resources from one country to bring about sustained, beneficial change in another. Including both OA and ODA also accords with the way politicians and decision-makers in aid-giving countries tend to regard aid—funding for both of these purposes is typically included in the same budgets and same legislation and usually considered together.

The second distinction involves the phrase "to better the human condition." The DAC uses the term "development" instead of "to better the human condition" but includes a variety of activities within its notion of "development"—for example, providing humanitarian relief, supporting economic and social progress, promoting democratization, addressing global problems, and managing postconflict transitions. I use a more limited definition of *development* here that refers to economic and social progress in poor countries, sustained by economic growth, and leading eventually to a reduction in poverty.[16] The other, related, purposes I distinguish where relevant. I make this distinction because, while all of these activities are aimed at human betterment—the core innovation in foreign aid—these other activities are sufficiently different in their ends, and often in their means, from promoting development as I have defined it to justify their treatment as distinct purposes in aid-giving.[17]

Finally, it is worth emphasizing that the definition of aid specifies that "human betterment" need be *only one* of the functions of intergovernmental, concessional resource transfers for those transfers to be included as aid—and it need not even be the most important one. This study will address not just development but aid's other purposes—especially the diplomatic and commercial ones—as well as the evolving priorities among these various purposes.

Foreign aid is used here to refer to transfers among independent governments and countries. It does not include transfers from a colonial power to its colonies. Further, foreign aid does not include military assistance or military expenditures abroad, government export credits or trade financing, subsidies to promote private investment, intelligence-related expenditures (e.g., to fund covert operations or to subsidize favored organizations in foreign countries), funding to fight terrorism or international crime, government-to-government subsidies, bribes or tributes for purely diplomatic or political ends, the costs of diplomatic representation, or private charitable giving (e.g., contributions from individuals or corporations to NGOs, aid from private philanthropic foundations or corporate entities, or remittances from foreign workers to their home countries). Inevitably, there are gray areas regarding what should be included in the definition of foreign aid. The DAC includes as foreign aid assistance for narcotics control programs when that assistance provides for "alternative development"— that is, making available alternative crops to farmers to replace income lost from ceasing to grow poppies or coca leaves. It does not include the costs of peacekeeping or funding of cultural exchanges. In these judgments, I shall follow the DAC.

Aid can be in the form of cash (grants or concessional loans), in kind (e.g., food aid), or in the form of debt relief. These transfers can fund a diverse set of activities: budgetary and balance of payments needs in recipient countries, investment projects and research activities, economic or political reform programs, technical advice and training, and humanitarian relief. How is the transfer of concessional resources from one government to another supposed to achieve the various purposes of the donor government? Aid can permit a recipient government to *expand activities* that help realize the purposes of the aid. For instance, it can increase investments in infrastructure, provide relief to a suffering population, or ease the budgetary burdens of military expenditures.[18] Alternatively, aid can *expand the capacity* of a recipient government to act in ways that enable it to use all its resources more productively—for example, aid can provide training and advice to government officials in budgeting, auditing, program management, planning, and a host of other technical and managerial areas. Third, aid can *act as an incentive or as a payment* for recipients to act in ways favored by the donor by conditioning it on desired behavior on the part of the recipient (e.g., adopting economic policy reforms or supporting the donor government's positions in international forums) or reducing or eliminating it when recipients behave in ways unwelcome to the aid-giving government.

In addition, especially when it comes from a powerful government or international organization, *foreign aid is a potent political symbol and signal.* As a voluntary transfer, it suggests approbation by the donor of the recipient and vice versa. And rising amounts of aid often signal increasing closeness in relations between donor and recipient, just as falling aid levels can symbolize cooling relationships and disapprobation. Aid can also act as a general signal to other governments, demonstrating that the government providing it is ready to stand behind the recipient government in the face of pressures from hostile or aggressive governments. It can signal that the donor—for example, the World Bank—approves of the policies and economic management of the recipient government. It can signal donor support of particular policies or desired actions on the part of the recipient—for example, expanding democracy. More broadly, aid for development, debated annually in the United Nations and in other international forums, has given the challenge of development a greater international prominence than would have been likely in the absence of its association with sizable resource transfers. Finally, foreign aid often serves several of these functions at once.

Like defining aid, measuring aid can be a tricky business, depending on what one is seeking to understand. For those interested in assessing the increase in resources provided by aid over time, it is important to measure the net flow of resources (i.e., less repayments) in constant terms (accounting for inflation and exchange rate fluctuations). My purposes fall more into the realm of policy discourse. Thus, I need to measure, to the extent possible, the resources policy-makers thought they were transferring abroad. And because policy-makers tend to look at data in current terms in discussing and debating aid (often comparing the aid level of the current year to that of the past year as well as comparing their country's aid levels and increases or decreases with those of other countries), I shall use current data in most of my analysis. Comparability among aid-giving governments is also important in this study. Thus, I will rely on the most common and comparable form of aid published by the DAC—disbursements in dollar terms net of repayments.

One more measurement issue involves comparing the generosity, or aid effort, of donor governments. Annual aid flows are typically compared to the size of a donor's overall economy. The denominator in this ratio has usually been gross national product (GNP—changed to "gross national income," or GNI, in 2001 with little difference in the actual number).[19] There has long been a UN target for rich countries to provide 0.7 percent of their GNP/GNI in foreign aid. Table 1.1 shows the relative amount of aid-giving (ODA only, though adding OA would make little difference) by DAC members. As is clear from the chart, few countries have met the target.

Second, Defining Aid's "Purposes"

Why do governments give aid? In answering that question, some talk about "motivations" or "rationales." But motivations involve individuals and can be difficult to observe, while rationales may not reflect intent. In this book, I shall analyze aid's "purposes"—the broad goals that donor governments

TABLE 1.1. NET ODA IN 2004 AS A PERCENTAGE OF GNI

Norway	0.87	Finland	0.35
Luxembourg	0.85	Germany	0.26
Denmark	0.84	Canada	0.26
Sweden	0.77	Spain	0.26
UN Target	0.7	**DAC Average**	0.25
Netherlands	0.74	Australia	0.25
Portugal	0.63	Austria	0.24
France	0.47	Greece	0.23
Belgium	0.41	Japan	0.19
Ireland	0.39	United States	0.16
Switzerland	0.37	Italy	0.15
United Kingdom	0.36		

Source: OECD, Development Assistance Committee (DAC), table, "Net Official Development Assistance in 2004," http://www.oecd.org/dataoecd/40/3/35389786.pdf (accessed October 2005).

sought to achieve with their aid, evident not only in what they said the goals of their aid were but in the decisions they made on its amount, country allocation, and use.

For much of the period of this study, foreign aid was used for four main purposes: diplomatic, developmental, humanitarian relief, and commercial. Cultural purposes were also present but less prominent. *Diplomatic purposes* involve international security, international political goals, and the management of relationships between governments. (The term *diplomacy* is typically used to cover all types of relations between states, including development, humanitarian relief and intervention, cultural affairs, and so on. *Diplomacy* is also often used to refer to a set of techniques rather than goals. I am taking some license with the use of the term here to refer to only those goals involving a government's international security and political interests abroad.) For example, the use of aid by the United States as a tool of Cold War competition or as an incentive for peace-making in the Middle East has involved international security concerns. French aid in support of the creation and maintenance of a sphere of influence (which may itself be an end or a means to other diplomatic ends) is an example of the use of aid for political ends. Aid has been used by almost all donor governments to ensure high-level access to recipient government officials, and increases in aid have often served as a symbol of successful state visits or international meetings—all elements in the diplomatic purposes of foreign aid.

Development as a purpose of aid—support for economic and social progress and a reduction in poverty—has been both a means and an end of policy. During the Cold War and again with the "war on terror," aid for development has been regarded as a means of dampening the social discontent that can strengthen the temptations of communism or feed terrorist impulses. But promoting development has also been an end in itself—bettering the lives of the disadvantaged abroad, as a reflection of the values of altruism, social justice, and international solidarity on the part of the country providing the aid.

How is foreign aid supposed to contribute to economic and social progress and benefit the poor abroad? Mainstream thinking on this question has evolved over the second half of the twentieth century. In the early postwar period, aid was seen as a tool for easing financial constraints on poor countries and, thus, for stabilizing economies, for stimulating economic growth, and, eventually, for reducing poverty. It was sometimes used to fill budgetary and balance of payments gaps and at other times was provided to finance technical assistance and training, basic infrastructure projects, and the expansion of public services such as education and health. In the 1970s aid for development took on a more redistributive orientation, with much of it used to support activities intended to meet the "basic human needs" of the poor directly, especially in rural areas. In the 1980s views regarding aid and development again shifted to a renewed emphasis on economic growth, with aid (including debt relief) providing the incentive for governments to undertake economic policy reforms. In the following decade, aid took several additional directions—one emphasized the importance of good governance to support economic progress. Poverty reduction also took on a renewed importance, with aid funding more projects intended to benefit the poor directly (e.g., microenterprise lending) while also financing expanded social services.

Aid for *humanitarian relief* has always been the least controversial of all of aid's purposes. Natural or manmade crises often generate large numbers of victims, sometimes producing displaced persons at home or refugees abroad. The governments of poor countries frequently lack the resources or capacity to accommodate the needs of disaster victims. Typically, nongovernmental organizations (NGOs) specialized in relief and rehabilitation deliver assistance, much of it provided by the governments of better-off countries (as well as by private individuals).

Aid's *commercial purposes* include the expansion of a country's exports and securing access to needed raw materials imports, as seen most evidently in the case of Japan but also among Scandinavian governments as well. Aid can be allocated as part of "mixed-credit" schemes (combined with export financing that is usually provided on relatively hard terms) to provide financial incentives for foreign governments to import goods and services from the donor country, usually as part of specific projects (e.g., the construction of airports or dams) or major equipment purchases, such as aircraft. A more passive form of using aid to expand a country's exports is to tie the procurements of goods and services funded by aid (for whatever purpose—including development purposes) to purchases in the aid-giving country. Most aid-giving countries had some form of "tied aid" during the second half of the twentieth century. The use of aid for commercial purposes can also involve helping to secure needed imports, through supporting investments in mines and other raw materials production that is then sold to the donor country. Less directly, aid can be provided to the governments of raw-materials-producing countries (e.g., petroleum producers in times of scarcity and high oil prices) to create close relationships intended to ensure continuing access by the donor government to those raw materials. Finally, aid for commercial purposes can be used to help finance investment opportunities in poor countries or be conditioned on the protection from expropriation of existing investments by the donor country.

Aid for *cultural purposes* usually involves efforts to support the use of a country's language in foreign lands, primarily through funding educational activities in that language. This purpose of aid is often evident in the programs of ex-colonial powers in their former territories, such as France, Italy (in Ethiopia and Somalia), or Portugal. Aid can also be used to strengthen and expand religious communities through funding good works by churches and mosques—a familiar use of aid from Arab governments. This sort of aid is typically channeled through religious organizations for implementation.

Four additional purposes of aid gained considerable prominence in the 1990s. *Promoting economic and social transitions* in former socialist countries involved advice in rewriting constitutions and instituting legal and regulatory reforms; help with reforming the judiciary; advice on privatizing state-owned enterprises, real estate, and land; advice and financing for economic policy changes; financing elections, political party training, and independent media development; and a host of other changes potentially involving all aspects of political and economic institutions in such countries.

Aid has also been used for *promoting democracy* in Africa, Asia, and Latin America, involving many institutional changes in political systems. Here the goal is to spread democracy, not just as a means of furthering development (on the assumption that development is likely to proceed more rapidly in democratic polities) or for promoting international peace and security (based on a view that democratic countries do not wage war on one another) but as a worthy goal itself, reflecting the value placed on political and civil rights by the aid-giving country.

Aid for *addressing global issues* (sometimes referred to as "international public goods issues") has concentrated on international environmental problems such as global warming, loss of the ozone layer, air, water, and land pollution, and protection of endangered species and coral reefs. It has also focused on research, prevention, surveillance, treatment, and blocking the international transmission of disease, especially smallpox, measles, polio, HIV/AIDS, malaria, and tuberculosis. It has addressed the challenge of expanding food production to feed the world's growing population through funding agricultural research and adapting the breakthroughs in agricultural production to the circumstances in individual countries. It has sought to reduce population growth by providing family planning advice and commodities. (Aid for these purposes can also further development in recipient countries, and, indeed, many of the techniques used when planning and delivering aid for development and when addressing global issues are the same, often provided by the same agencies in donor governments. But the end purpose—providing global public goods—is quite different, and the focus of aid-giving for this purpose, which is global in its strategic orientation rather than country-focused, is also different from aid for furthering development in particular countries.)

Aid came to be used increasingly during the 1990s *for mitigating conflicts and managing postconflict transitions*—primarily to help countries recover from war through demining, demobilization and reintegration of soldiers, reconstruction, conflict mediation, and rebuilding political institutions and social relations between communities.

One further point needs to be made with regard to aid's purposes. I have provided a tidy classification of the major purposes of aid-giving. However, reality is seldom so tidy. Sometimes, the mix of purposes can be seen in a government's overall aid program—some aid being allocated, for example, for development while other aid supports commercial goals. Sometimes, the mix of purposes is evident in the aid program for a particular recipient country—US aid to Egypt, for example, serves the objectives both of Middle East diplomacy and of development (evident in the use of aid for agricultural development, infrastructure expansion, microenterprise lending, and so on).

How do we ascertain the purposes of aid-giving? First, there are no precise and definitive metrics for judging purposes; those purposes are often much too intertwined with one another in country aid programs and even in projects to disaggregate and describe them in a single datum or index. Nor do aid donors categorize their own aid in terms of the purposes described here. Rather, one must take a holistic approach to uncovering aid's purposes, using a variety of indicators and sometimes some informed judgment. Quantitative exercises that produce correlations between the value of aid flows to particular countries and the per capita incomes or other indicators of need in those countries—while often a useful first step to understanding aid's purposes—can be quite misleading considered by themselves and in the absence of context. For example, even very poor countries can have diplomatic and commercial value to aid-giving governments, as is reflected in the French aid program in sub-Saharan Africa, which sought, among other things, to maintain a sphere of influence for France. Thus, the prolonged disputes on measurement and methodology in econometric studies of aid-giving, as the primary approach to understanding aid's purposes, can often prove sterile or misleading. An example is the long and inconclusive debate, based on econometric exercises, on whether US aid to Latin America was, in fact, related to the human rights performance of recipients.[20]

Considering aid's purposes holistically involves examining what governments say they are doing with their aid. While public officials do not always fully disclose their purposes, they often give valuable clues to those purposes in their official statements or in government documents. In addition to what they say they are doing, it is important to look at how they are actually distributing and using their aid, as reflected in six major decisions governments must make each year on their foreign aid programs:

- the overall amount of their aid
- the countries and organizations receiving it
- how much aid each of those countries and organizations receives
- what the aid is used for
- the terms of the aid
- the percentage of aid tied to purchases in the donor country

The overall annual value of a donor country's aid is often decided by adding up the planned expenditures for individual countries and programs. However, it is not unusual that when a government wants to send a signal with its aid, for example, that it is a keen supporter of development, the overall amount can be set first (e.g., rising by an agreed amount) and its distribution among recipients decided later. In this case, the amount of aid can be intended as an important political symbol, both at home and abroad, of a government's commitment to particular purposes of aid and should be understood in this way.

The allocation of aid by country also provides clues about the donor's intentions in aid-giving as well as the relative diplomatic importance of the recipient country to the donor government. And increases or decreases in bilateral aid can (though do not always) indicate warming or cooling diplomatic relations between donor and recipient. Additionally, the uses of aid are important indicators of purpose—for example, the more uses are aligned with DAC development norms (e.g., a focus on poverty reduction), the more it is likely that a government is emphasizing development in its aid-giving. The terms of aid can also suggest the importance of development concerns, where those terms correspond to DAC norms of concessionality. The degree to which aid is tied to purchases in donor countries is usually a sign of commercial influences over aid-giving, though it does not necessarily indicate that commercial concerns are driving aid allocations and uses. Businesses in aid-giving countries often press their governments to require that a portion of the aid is spent on domestically produced goods. (Another sign of the influence of commercial purposes of aid is the degree to which aid is used to finance the export of goods and services produced in the donor country, often mixed with commercial financing. But data on this use of aid is frequently unavailable.) And finally and very importantly, the international and domestic political contexts in which aid is given provide important insights into government's intended purposes. For example, has there been an international incident that has intensified security concerns in an aid-giving country or a disaster abroad that has raised public awareness of the need for aid? All of this information is important to fill in the picture of why governments give aid. I shall draw on all of it in this study.

DOMESTIC POLITICAL FORCES AND FOREIGN AID

In my conceptual framework for analyzing and comparing aid's purposes, I have identified four categories of domestic political forces shaping foreign aid: ideas, political institutions, interests, and the aid organization (that is, the way governments organize themselves to manage their aid). Next, I consider in more detail what these categories encompass.

Ideas

There are several types of ideas, shared by significant portions of the public and political elites in aid-giving countries, that can influence aid. Most fundamental are what some scholars have called "worldviews"—widely shared values (based on culture, religion, ideology) about what is right and wrong, appropriate and inappropriate in public and private life. These worldviews themselves are the product of a society's history as well as major events and trends affecting its population. In terms of foreign aid, these might involve a view that all human beings have a right to liberty or a right to minimum subsistence or that individuals (or families) should be self-reliant and responsible to the extent possible for their own well-being.

Worldviews give rise to "principled beliefs," or norms—"collective expectations about the proper behavior for a given identity."[21] An example of a principled belief regarding foreign aid might be that governments of rich countries should provide aid to poor countries. Or, conversely, that individual or collective self-reliance makes public assistance at home or abroad an inappropriate use of public resources. Norms are often framed in terms of fundamental values. I will present a number of cases in which foreign-aid-giving was framed and reframed in terms of different basic worldviews with very different outcomes vis-à-vis aid expenditures. A third type of idea involves causal beliefs—what sorts of policies, for example, lead to effective development.

The term *ideas* in this study is used to refer primarily to the first two of these categories—worldviews and principled beliefs: How do basic values regarding the obligations of the rich to help the poor and the role of the state in fulfilling such obligations affect the purposes of foreign aid in different countries? How do widely shared views about the appropriate role of the state in society affect the existence of civil society organizations which, in turn, can affect the purposes of aid? In the case of the United States, the long prominence of a classical liberal view of the state—that "government governs best that governs least"—has been the basis for sustained criticisms from the political right of government aid (at home or abroad) as inappropriate and (because it is channeled through the state) doomed to be ineffective. In contrast, the norms of social solidarity that underpin the social democratic traditions in Scandinavia and the Netherlands have undoubtedly facilitated the popularity of foreign aid in those countries. The Japanese tradition of strong state–weak society has impeded the development in that country of relief- and development-oriented NGOs that have provided the constituency for development aid in North America and much of Europe.

Institutions

Political institutions shape the rules of the political game[22]—they determine who sets the issue agenda, who has access to decision-makers, who decides policies, and who can veto decisions. The three main aspects of political institutions I shall consider in this study are electoral rules; parliamentary versus presidential systems and, especially, the role of legislatures in both; and the role of local governments and semipublic entities such as advisory committees and state-supported NGOs.

Voting rules affect aid-giving indirectly. Proportional representation tends to produce large numbers of political parties, some of which must join together to form governing coalitions. Minority parties can get their niche issues on national agendas as a price of joining such a coalition. Where those parties have aid for development as one of their issues—as has been the case at key junctures in Germany, Holland, and Denmark—they can get that issue on the national political agenda much more easily than is the case in a political system based on majority voting.

Regarding the impact of parliamentary and presidential systems on foreign aid, the important element is the relationship between the executive and legislature. In parliamentary systems, the executive is drawn from the legislature and typically relies on its party predominance or on a governing coalition in the legislature to remain in power. As a result, legislatures in parliamentary systems tend to support government policies, including aid policies. In contrast, in a presidential system like that of the United States, the two bodies are autonomous and there is a tendency for members of Congress, regardless of the political parties controlling the two houses, to criticize executive branch policies, especially policies that are controversial with their constituents (as has been the case for foreign aid). And those criticisms in turn can deepen public skepticism of the efficacy and appropriateness of foreign aid.

The role of legislatures is important in other ways in influencing aid. They can bring aid issues to public attention and debate and act, as in the case of Denmark, as venues to inform the public and create a national consensus on aid. Where legislators are uninformed or uninterested in aid issues, bureaucracies have much more say over the amount and purposes of aid and much less public accountability for those decisions, as in the cases of France and Japan. A lack of public accountability often leads eventually to scandal and sharp public critiques of aid, even to a collapse in public support. This occurred in Italy in the beginning of the 1990s, when it became known that that country's aid had been involved in government corruption. Legislatures also provide points of access to government decision-making for interest groups supporting or opposing aid and can act as veto players in specific aid-related decisions.

Finally, there are organizations that, because of their access to policymakers, can affect policy-making: for example, local government entities, empowered advisory boards, and semi-independent government supported agencies. In the case of Denmark, an advisory committee to government on aid issues came to wield considerable power over the purposes and uses of Danish aid, because the parliament was reluctant to approve an aid program or policy unless it had the imprimatur of the advisory board. In Germany, the political party institutes acted as "submarines" (this is the way the Germans describe them) within political parties in favor of aid for development and democracy promotion abroad. In other countries, like France and the United States, advisory committees wielded relatively little influence over government decisions on foreign aid.

One final point needs to be made here. Political parties can play a role in determining the amount and direction of aid. It is often the case that more aid, for more development-oriented purposes, is normally associated with left-wing parties and less aid, with more emphasis on security or commercial interests, is associated with right-wing parties in power. However, the ideological orientations of political parties do not always have such an easily predictable effect on aid's purposes, as several of the case studies will show.[23]

Interests

Interest groups are a pervasive and dynamic force in politics, especially where public resources are involved. This is as true of foreign aid as it is of spending on welfare, domestic agriculture, education, and the vast array of other policies and programs governments undertake. With regard to aid, there are three main categories of interests: those supporting the commercial purposes of aid (agricultural, manufacturing, and service producers, who often regard aid as a vehicle for expanding their export markets or who view aid as a means of enhancing their access to needed raw materials imports); nongovernmental organizations and public interest groups that support aid for relief, development, and related purposes (including organizations advocating development, broadly defined, as well as those promoting specific activities within that broad category—almost always those that the organizations themselves undertake—such as family planning and environmental protection); and groups with an affinity for particular foreign countries, ethnicities, or religious orientations that support aid directed to those groups and countries. Specific organizations engaged in aid issues may include agricultural producer groups, chambers of commerce, business associations or individual corporations, trade unions, churches, universities, ethnic diasporas (of which there are many in the United States), linguistic communities (most evident in Canada but also in Belgium), think tanks, and informal networks of influence (most evident in France). Within these categories of interests, there will be different policy preferences and degrees of access and influence (depending in part on the ideas and institutions described in the previous sections) as these groups compete for influence over aid's purposes and uses.

What is the role of public opinion in shaping aid's purposes? Public opinion tends to be passive and permissive—it can influence the general terms of debate on foreign aid and erect broad limitations on the amount and direction of aid. It can also be manipulated by politicians and political activists through "public education" activities (systematic efforts on the part of governments and advocates to explain the need for and successes of aid expenditures) and "framing"—the characterization of aid in terms of widely held norms—which can shape how the public views aid. But public opinion seldom drives aid's purposes—except when a public is aroused. And on foreign aid, public opinion tends to be aroused in two circumstances: when there is a major humanitarian crisis that the public observes in the media (especially on television) or when there is a major scandal involving the use of aid funds. In both cases, public clamor can force government to act—to increase and redirect aid or to decrease and reform it.

Organization

Most of the analyses of the factors affecting public policies stop after considering ideas, institutions, and interests or subsume government organization into the broader category of "institutions." But in the case of foreign aid, this would be a mistake because the way governments organize themselves to manage their aid affects the voice for the development purpose of aid within governments and the extent of encouragement and collaboration by government agencies with groups outside government supportive of development aid. (By *organization*, I am referring to the location within government of the tasks related to a major function or program of government, for example managing foreign policy or welfare programs. It does not refer to the organizational arrangements within government agencies, such as the type or location of bureaus.)[24]

Examining the organization of aid within donor governments as a separate category of analysis is based on two propositions, drawn from the literature of bureaucratic politics as well as my own direct experience. First, government agencies are important political actors in their own right—advocates or lobbyists for their own mission and interests. Sometimes they act wholly within the confines of the executive, but they often work outside those confines, allying themselves with private interest groups at home or international organizations, foreign government agencies, and international NGOs or interest groups with which they share interests. And second, the more functions related to a particular public purpose are unified in a single agency and the more elevated the bureaucratic location of that agency (e.g., cabinet versus subcabinet level), the greater the influence that agency will have over the policies and programs related to its basic mission and purpose.

There is no one formula for organizing aid systems within governments. Some governments, like the United Kingdom's, have unified their aid-related activities in one independent cabinet-level agency, creating a relatively powerful voice within government in favor of the development use of aid.[25] Other governments, like that of Denmark, have located their aid in the ministry of foreign affairs. In Denmark's case, merging aid into the foreign ministry does not appear to have weakened the voice within government for aid. In the United States, on the other hand, there was successful resistance in the mid-1990s inside and outside the government to a proposal to merge USAID into the Department of State based on the fear that the often crisis-driven, diplomatic focus of the State Department would overwhelm the longer term development focus of USAID's programs. Yet other governments, like those of France, Japan, and, increasingly, the United States, have highly fragmented systems in which aid programs are located in a variety of agencies and where policy and implementation are separated.

Even where aid responsibilities are unified, some governments locate their aid responsibilities at the subcabinet level, and others, like Germany, have created a ministry of development. The organization of aid influences the purposes of aid from within government through the unity and status of the competing voices supporting aid's various uses in government decision-making circles. Further, once established, the organization of a government's aid system institutionalizes the interests within government and, thus, the purposes of aid. Even where political leaders wish to change those purposes, the stickiness of government organization makes such changes very difficult, as both Japan and France discovered when those governments sought to impart a greater development focus to their aid in the late 1990s.

NOTE ON SOURCES

This book is a study of aid-giving by governments (*bilateral* aid). It does not include the politics of aid-giving by international organizations, such as the World Bank, the European Union, or the United Nations Development Program (*multilateral* aid). The basic reason for the emphasis on bilateral aid is that both bilateral and multilateral aid originate in donor governments and it is the motivations and purposes of these originators of aid that we wish to understand.

As to sources for the history of aid and country case studies of aid-giving, I have relied on government documents, statements by public officials, legislative debates, DAC publications (especially the annual chairman's reports and country peer reviews), and quantitative data on aid-giving (also primarily from the DAC, which has long provided the most extensive and comparable data on aid-giving), various public opinion polls, and other primary source materials. Many secondary materials—books, journal articles, unpublished studies, news reports, and commentaries— were drawn on for this study. These sources were supplemented by extensive interviews with aid officials, practitioners, and experts in the five case study countries—interviews intended to ferret out the unseen realities of aid-giving, to test ideas, and to understand what was important and what was not. Added to these efforts is my own experience as a government official working on foreign aid, which has given me a sense of how things work (or do not work), what is typically out of sight and what is in full view, patterns of interactions among major political actors, the informal as well as the formal operation of political institutions, and the relative importance of all of these elements in the churning mass that is policy-making. "Being there" has also provided me with direct experience of the way other governments work as well as useful contacts, which I have shamelessly exploited for this study.

CHAPTER 2

Aid's Purposes: A Brief History

Foreign aid as we know it began as an instrument of Cold War diplomacy. Without the Cold War, aid would likely not exist today—or if it did, it would be much smaller than the $100 billion in aid provided by all governments in 2004. Aid is, in short, a child of hardheaded, diplomatic realism.

What began as a temporary diplomatic expedient, however, became a permanent element in relations between states, reflecting a strengthening norm that the governments of rich countries should help poor countries improve the well-being of their peoples. Such a norm was hardly imagined at the beginning of the foreign aid era; it is seldom contested today. The path by which that norm developed involves the domestic political processes of aid-giving countries, international trends and events, and pressures from international organizations that supported the use of aid for human betterment. This chapter describes the history of foreign aid over the past three score years from a global perspective. Succeeding chapters will trace that same history in individual aid-giving countries.

AID'S ANTECEDENTS: BEFORE 1945

Foreign aid has three main antecedents: the use of public resources for humanitarian relief, which in modern times began in the nineteenth century;[1] the small amount of assistance provided by European powers for development in their colonies during the interwar years; and the limited quantity of technical assistance provided by the United States to Latin American countries at the beginning of the Second World War. (Some would include the lend-lease agreements with European governments before and during World War II and even export credits.[2] But lend-lease does not fit the definition of foreign aid I am using here, elaborated in chapter 1: it was not offered on the concessional terms that characterize foreign aid, and it was intended to finance the transfer of military materiel to support the war effort in Europe.)

Aid for Relief

At the beginning of the nineteenth century, providing public concessional resources to help peoples beyond one's borders for any purpose—even to relieve severe human suffering—was almost unheard of and unacceptable to many. For example, on the occasion of the Irish potato famine, a debate took place in the US Congress on whether to provide public relief aid to the victims of the famine. Those against such aid (on the grounds that charity—especially charity to benefit people beyond one's borders—was an inappropriate use of public funds) won the debate. However, toward the end of the nineteenth century, the practice of public assistance for disaster relief abroad had become increasingly common as information about disasters in distant lands increased, as the United States and European countries grew more affluent (and so, more easily able to provide help abroad), and as a more expansive view of what states could and should do with their resources to benefit their own citizens and others became more widespread.

By the end of World War I, public assistance to the displaced and dispossessed from five years of conflict in Europe was clearly necessary. Without it, there would be widespread starvation in a number of the defeated countries. Later, in an extraordinary demonstration of the growing acceptability of using public aid to relieve suffering abroad, the United States and European countries agreed to provide relief to the Soviet Union in 1921 (despite increasingly hostile relations with the Bolshevik regime that had recently seized power there) to reduce widespread starvation resulting from civil war and drought. By World War II, the need to provide significant amounts of public assistance to those in Europe and Asia made destitute by war was taken for granted by Allied postwar planners.

Aid for relief, however, was always regarded as temporary, aimed at returning people to a situation in which they could provide for their own sustenance. It was never intended to bring about "development"—that is, long-term improvements in economic and social well-being in other countries. That purpose of foreign aid had far fewer precursors.

Colonial Development

A second antecedent to foreign aid can be found in the policies of European colonial powers. In the mid 1920s, as the degree of poverty in their colonies became known, the French and British governments began to shift away from their earlier view that those colonies had to be self-financing, with development funded primarily through private investment or public investments by colonial governments. But just as the willingness of the imperial powers to use public funds to expand infrastructure, health services, and education in their territories grew, their ability to do so shrank with the deepening depression followed by the outbreak of the Second World War. Nevertheless, the idea had been planted and would reemerge after the war was over.

US Technical Assistance

The US government, like the European colonial powers, also believed that development in its colonies (the Philippines and Puerto Rico) and in its hemisphere should result from private investment and public investments by the governments of those colonies and countries. However, an exception to this view was made during World War II when Washington agreed to provide Latin American governments with small amounts of publicly financed technical assistance for development purposes. In 1942 two US government corporations were created to manage this assistance: the Institute of Inter-American Affairs and the Inter-American Education Foundation. What motivated these changes was not a new vision regarding the role of public concessional resources to further development in poor countries, but rather, the disruption in Latin American exports to Europe as a result of growing hostilities there plus an effort on the part of Nazi Germany to create closer ties with the governments of the region. Technical assistance, albeit in very modest amounts, was intended to help ease the impact of shrinking markets and to retain the loyalties of governments in the hemisphere.[3]

Though not an antecedent to public aid, during the first half of the twentieth century, there were private organizations beginning to provide assistance abroad that went beyond humanitarian relief. Churches sponsored schools in developing countries; the Rockefeller Foundation set up colleges and universities, especially in the field of public health, and began to fund research into a host of diseases afflicting the tropics. It also sought to further rural reconstruction in China. The foundations (mainly US) and churches and NGOs in North America and Europe had begun to set an example of how organizations in rich countries could help improve the conditions of life in poor countries and territories of the world.

The antecedents to foreign aid were important in setting precedents for the transfer of public resources to other governments, international organizations, and nongovernmental organizations (NGOs) to promote human betterment abroad. But none of them foretold the amount, extent, or purposes of aid that were soon to become common.

ESTABLISHMENT AND SPREAD OF FOREIGN AID: 1945–1970

To meet the need for emergency relief in war-torn countries after World War II, allied planners created the United Nations Relief and Rehabilitation Agency (UNRRA), which began operations several years before the conclusion of the war, and the International Refugee Organization, which commenced operations in 1946. Inevitably, much of the funding for relief came from the United States and was considered to be short-lived. Indeed, the US Congress set terminal dates for this support—1946 for Europe and 1947 for Asia. UNRRA was, in fact, closed down in both regions in 1947.

Postwar planners also created the International Bank for Reconstruction and Development (IBRD, soon to be called the World Bank) to fund reconstruction after the war and to facilitate—primarily through guaranteeing private investment—the flow of private capital to developing countries. However, at this time, no one planned or even imagined that the World Bank, which opened its doors in 1946, would eventually become a major source of highly concessional loans to promote development in poor countries.

Starting with the United States

In 1947 much of Europe was still in ruins, struggling to recover from the war that had ended two years earlier. Deprivation and despair fed discontent with traditional political parties, improving the chances that communist parties in Italy and France could be elected to power. Meanwhile, East Germany, Poland, Hungary, Rumania, and other countries of East and Central Europe were increasingly absorbed into the Soviet bloc, while Moscow was putting pressure on Turkey for territorial concessions and the Yugoslav government was supporting a communist-led insurgency in Greece. Washington's concerns regarding the USSR's expanding influence in Europe further deepened when, in 1947, the British announced they would have to withdraw their support for the Greek and Turkish governments. The US administration felt compelled to act, including providing economic assistance, to help stabilize the regime in Greece and fortify the finances of the Turkish government. Aid for Greece and Turkey was followed by the Marshall Plan, a four-year, $13 billion aid program to help stabilization and recovery in Europe. Foreign aid had commenced.

The United States soon began to provide aid to Asian countries in the wake of the Chinese revolution and the outbreak of the Korean War. And with the death of Stalin and the growing demands on the part of developing countries for aid from both the United States and the USSR, Moscow began providing aid to India and other developing countries. The United States followed suit, and by the end of the 1950s, the United States was aiding most independent, developing countries. Washington began to press Western European governments, now recovering from the war, to establish or expand aid programs of their own.

The Beginnings of Aid in Europe and Japan

US pressure on other governments to create or increase their aid programs had an effect. But the establishment of aid agencies and the increase in the levels of foreign aid by the better-off countries of Europe and Japan were not solely the results of US pressures. Most of these countries had their own antecedents of foreign aid, often quite different from those of the United States. While Britain and France had provided increasing amounts of assistance for their colonies in Africa, Asia, and the Caribbean in the decade and a half after the Second World War, neither London nor Paris intended to continue foreign aid after independence. Once territories were no longer under their control, they considered that their obligations to provide aid would cease. Or at least, this is the way they saw it in the mid-1950s. (The smaller colonial powers, such as Belgium and Portugal, did not even envision independence for their colonies at this time.)

However, these views were to change at the end of the 1950s. In 1958 one of France's African colonies—Guinea—opted for independence rather than association with France. France granted it independence but terminated all assistance. However, it was not long before France's other African colonies sought independence. Recognizing that it had no acceptable alternative, Paris reluctantly agreed and then provided them relatively large amounts of aid—in part to meet their real economic needs and in part to maintain a predominance of French influence in them. In 1958 Britain also backed off its position of no aid after independence, under pressure from its former colonies in the Commonwealth and in the face both of increasing economic problems in India (which, as the largest noncommunist developing country, could not be ignored) and of the extensive economic needs of a number of its former African colonies. Like France, Britain also wanted to preserve its influence in these countries, but more importantly, it wanted independence to proceed smoothly so it could disengage from significant postcolonial responsibilities with its reputation intact, without major claims on its budget, and without a massive influx of British settlers, especially from Kenya, fleeing postcolonial chaos.

Japan's aid grew out of its reparation payments in Asia and its urgent need to secure access to needed raw materials and markets for its exports. Export promotion rather than reparations led Germany into the foreign aid business. As early as 1953, the German government began to provide a small amount of technical assistance to help the importers of German goods to use them effectively. Nordic countries—Norway, Sweden, and Denmark—all set up aid agencies and commenced to provide small amounts of assistance in the early 1960s. Analysts of the motivations of aid-giving on the part of Scandinavian governments often point to their shared values and norms—the social democratic orientation and the Christian heritage, including sponsoring missionary activities abroad.[4] Shared values may predispose governments to initiate programs of foreign aid, but they do not explain what factors trigger that innovation.

The United Nations provided one of these triggers. Like many small countries, the Nordics regarded the United Nations as a valuable organization. With each member state regardless of size or wealth having only one vote, the United Nations created a measure of formal equality among large and small states, providing the latter with a degree of voice and influence they would not normally have in international relations and—so it was hoped by governments of small states—greater protection of their interests in world affairs and a measure of constraint on the behavior of great powers. When it was agreed in the United Nations in 1949 to establish an Expanded Program of Technical Assistance (EPTA), Nordic countries were quick to contribute, in part, as a means of strengthening the UN as a whole. Additionally, during the late 1940s and early 1950s, small amounts of private and public monies were provided to poor countries for occasional good works. For example, these three countries collaborated in financing a hospital in South Korea in the wake of the war there.

However, it was a Cold War issue combined with domestic politics that led Norway to establish a more formal governmental program of foreign aid in 1952. The Storting (the Norwegian parliament) voted to create an Aid Fund for Underdeveloped Countries (which came to be called the "India Fund" because most of the financing went to that country), to be financed by public and private contributions. According to Olav Stokke, Norway's foremost aid expert, the government backed this idea for hard-headed internal political reasons: "After Norway had joined NATO in 1949, the governing Labour Party, with a pacifist tradition in the 1930s, left the aid area to those in the party who had lost the fight on the NATO issue, in a deliberate effort to keep them busy with what might be perceived as a positive way of building peace."[5]

With the close contacts among the publics, organizations, and officials of the Nordic countries, Norway's action was observed and soon imitated by Sweden and Denmark. In the same year, the Swedish government set up a committee of NGOs to manage a small aid program. In 1954 a minister for development assistance was appointed. The Danish government also commenced small aid activities, managed by NGOs during these early years.

Supply often creates its own demand. The supply of Swedish aid, albeit small during the 1950s, created a rising demand on the part of developing countries for more Swedish aid. The expanding demand from poor countries, combined with the rising pressure from the United States on its friends and allies in Europe for greater burden-sharing, contributed to the establishment during the first half of the 1960s of government aid programs in all three of these countries as well as official aid agencies to manage them.

During the first half of the 1960s, other European countries also established aid agencies and expanded their programs of bilateral aid. France created its Ministry of Cooperation in 1961. Germany set up a Ministry for Economic Cooperation in the same year and boosted the size of its aid program. The German government under Chancellor Konrad Adenauer was the first government to establish a Ministry of Development, an initiative driven by the need to create a ministerial-level development portfolio to cement a governing coalition. Had there been no need for coalition building, it is unlikely that there would have been a development ministry—development simply was not a ministerial-level issue, and the Foreign Office and Ministry of Economy did not wish to relinquish the development programs under their control. The exigencies of coalition politics also led the government of the Netherlands to create the position of state secretary for development in 1963, which was later elevated to minister of development (without portfolio, however, since the main responsibilities for managing foreign aid were located in the Ministry of Foreign Affairs).[6]

Japan created its Overseas Economic Cooperation Fund in 1961 and its Overseas Technical Cooperation Agency the following year. Sweden set up its Agency for International Assistance in 1961. The United Kingdom set up the Overseas Development Ministry in 1965. While governments continued to tinker with the way they organized themselves to manage their aid programs over coming decades, by the middle of the 1960s most developed countries had created permanent government agencies to manage their expanding programs of foreign assistance.

Socialist Bloc Aid

During the 1960s, socialist countries became significant aid donors. Both the USSR and the People's Republic of China (PRC) spent $1.1 billion each in aid in 1970, and Eastern European countries provided another $300 million. (For the PRC, the aid level in 1970 was unusually high, to finance the Tanzania-Zambia railroad—a 1,300-mile length of rail from the copper belt in central Africa to the port of Dar es Salaam on the Indian Ocean. The following year, Chinese aid fell to a more "normal" level of roughly half that amount.)

Like much of Western aid, socialist bloc aid was also driven by diplomatic considerations—the Cold War with the West as well as a mini-cold war between the USSR and China as to which was the true representative of socialist aspirations.[7] Three-quarters of Soviet aid went to communist developing countries, including North Vietnam, North Korea, Cuba, and Mongolia, to stabilize and subsidize their economies. In friendly noncommunist countries—primarily India, Egypt, and Syria—the Soviets provided significant amounts of assistance over an extended period of time, usually for projects involving infrastructure, mining, or turnkey manufacturing enterprises and for education in the USSR. The Aswan Dam in Egypt is the best known of Moscow's aid projects.

Unlike Western governments, the Soviets did not attempt to establish a long-term aid presence in developing countries—they simply did not have the resources or personnel to do so. Rather, they often sought to create diplomatic openings in potentially influential developing countries with significant offers of aid credits. Chinese aid was also deployed opportunistically to create diplomatic opportunities and to compete for influence in its various mini-cold wars—with the Soviets, with Taiwan for recognition as the legitimate representative of the Chinese people, including occupying the Chinese seat in the UN General Assembly and on the Security Council (which it achieved in 1971), and, of course, in competition with the United States for influence in Asia and elsewhere. The Chinese, like the Soviets, used their aid primarily to finance major infrastructure projects. The Chinese also became particularly well known for financing sports stadiums in poor countries—intended as highly visible reminders of Chinese generosity.

Developing Countries as Aid Donors

By the end of the 1960s, a handful of developing countries had also become sources of foreign aid to other developing countries. One group included the oil producing countries, primarily in the Middle East. The governments of these countries (primarily Kuwait, Libya, and Iraq) and their multilateral development funds (such as the Arab Fund for Economic and Social Development and the Kuwait Fund for Arab Economic Development) provided modest amounts of concessional funding to countries primarily in Africa and the Middle East. The aid was often motivated by a search for diplomatic support on issues involving Israel and the Palestinians. Israel, as part of this mini-cold war with the Arabs, also provided aid to a number of govern-

FIG. 2.1. TOTAL FOREIGN AID (NET)

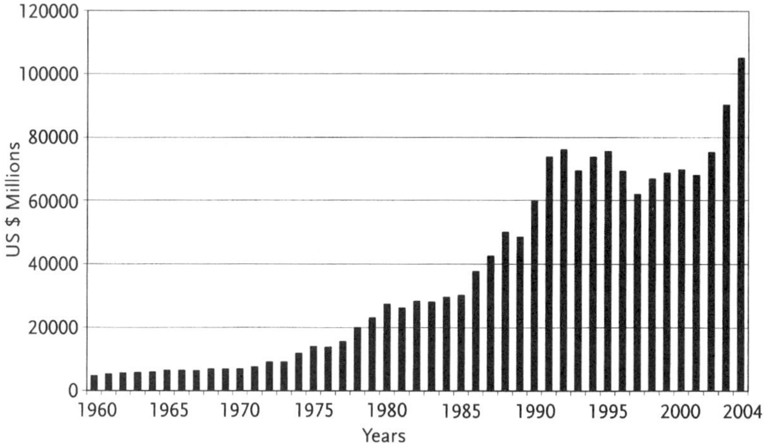

Source: DAC, "International Development Statistics (IDS) Online," http://www.oecd.org/dac/stats/idsonline/ (accessed October 2005).

Note: "Total aid" includes net aid (ODA and OA, expenditures minus repayments) from all donors in current dollars.

ments, especially in Africa. Additionally, South Africa, India, Nigeria, and Brazil provided small amounts of aid in their particular regions to fortify their roles as regional leaders, advance their interests and support linguistic or national diasporas abroad. Few of these governments would have provided foreign aid had it not been for the particular diplomatic purposes they wished to pursue. Development purposes were not absent, but they were clearly secondary in the origins of most of these aid programs.

By 1970 foreign aid worldwide exceeded $8 billion. Most governments were by then either donors of aid, recipients of aid, or, in a few cases (like India or China), both. By that time, aid was no longer an expedient (although it still had much to do with cold wars)—it had become a common element in relations between rich and poor countries and even, in some cases, between poor countries themselves. Figure 2.1 shows the evolution in aid-giving by all donors during the entire period 1960 to 2004.

FOREIGN AID FOR DEVELOPMENT: 1970–1990

In the 1970s the volume of aid rose slowly at first and then increased more rapidly during the second half of the decade. The same pattern was repeated in the 1980s. The decades of the 1970s and 1980s also saw governments of petroleum-exporting countries and their multilateral aid agencies becoming major sources of foreign assistance, as they set aside a portion of their large inflows of petrodollars for aid to developing countries, primarily in the Middle East and Africa.

In these two decades, the development purpose of aid gained in prominence. The profile of aid-giving (including the proportions of aid to the poorest countries, its use for expanding social infrastructure, and the terms of aid) increasingly reflected a focus on development. The policy frameworks for aid for development became more complex and sophisticated. Aid agencies were increasingly professionalized. And a larger proportion of overall aid was channeled through multilateral aid agencies (whose purposes, it was widely recognized, were primarily developmental). But before exploring these changes in more detail, I will present the international political and economic contexts that contributed to the increased prominence of development in aid-giving.

Context: The Upheavals of the 1970s and 1980s

During the 1970s and 1980s, several trends and events within aid-giving countries and outside them combined to elevate the development purpose of foreign aid: a lessening in the intensity of the Cold War competition with moves toward détente between East and West; the quadrupling in oil prices of the early 1970s and the ensuing debt and economic crises in many developing countries at the end of that decade; and two bouts of severe famine, primarily in Africa—one in the mid-1970s and one in the mid-1980s. Also very important was a trend within developed countries: the increasing number and prominence of NGOs, which functioned increasingly not only as service providers but also advocates for aid for development with their own governments and publics.

Toward Détente

By the middle of the 1970s, most of the major battles of the Cold War were over. The communist government in Beijing had consolidated its power and, in 1971, was admitted to the United Nations to replace Taiwan as the representative of China. The war in Korea was a memory even though the North and South Koreans (the latter backed by US troops) still confronted one another across a tense border. The Marxist government in Cuba had consolidated its power but was isolated in the Western Hemisphere. The war in Indochina was over with the US withdrawal in 1975. And there were various efforts at détente between East and West: between the United States and China (which President Richard Nixon visited in 1972), between the United States and the USSR, and between the two Germanys. East-West skirmishes still occurred—in the Horn of Africa and Southern Africa, in Afghanistan, and in Nicaragua—as one side or another sought political or military gains, usually through local surrogates. But the tensions and fears of the 1960s that had influenced the allocation of foreign aid for diplomatic purposes diminished, easing the pressures in the United States, Germany, and elsewhere to direct aid toward Cold War protagonists and creating opportunities for increased priority for other purposes in aid-giving.

Oil and Economic Crises

On October 6, 1973, the Egyptian and Syrian armies attacked the Israelis on the Suez Canal and in the Golan Heights. After an initial surprise and retreat, the Israelis fought back and took the war into Egypt and Syria. A ceasefire was called after several weeks. Thereafter, the members of the Organization of Petroleum Exporting Countries (OPEC) imposed an oil embargo against governments supporting Israel that led to a quadrupling in petroleum prices. Those prices stayed high for the rest of the decade until they doubled again at the end of the 1970s with the war between Iran and Iraq, both of which were large producers of oil. The surge in oil prices made those countries exporting oil—a number in the Middle East, plus Indonesia, Nigeria, Gabon, Cameroon, Mexico, Venezuela, and several others—suddenly flush with petrodollars. On the other hand, it produced rising foreign exchange outlays for those developing countries (as well as industrialized countries) that had to import petroleum. Most of those countries exported other primary products—minerals, food and fiber, beverages—and the prices of many of these products rose at around the same time oil prices increased, thus partially (and temporarily) offsetting their increased oil import bills.

High prices for their exports led many developing country governments to go on a spending spree, using their increased foreign exchange earnings to expand government employment and services, finance a variety of ambitious investment projects, and, in some cases, borrow against expected future export earnings. The go-go days of the early and mid-1970s soon gave way to a collapse in the prices of primary products toward the end of the decade. Inflation in industrialized countries, in part a result of increases in oil prices, raised the cost of manufactured goods, adding to the import bills of poor countries. The governments of those countries that could borrow internationally often did so to ease the need to adjust to a decrease in their real income vis-à-vis the rest of the world. Soon enough, however, international commercial lending dried up and governments in Latin America and Africa found they could not service their external debts. The debt crisis that broke in the early 1980s and the balance of payments crises faced by many developing countries at this time—even those without burdensome external debts—led them to appeal to Western governments, international organizations, and commercial lenders for debt relief and additional aid.

Food Crisis and Famine

The 1970s also brought the world a food crisis as the prices for major world grains—wheat and corn in particular—rose as a result of several years of drought in the beginning of the decade, particularly in the USSR, and the decision by Moscow to purchase grain on the world market rather than compress domestic meat and grain consumption. The United States, whose large grain reserves served in effect as a food reserve for the world, decided to sell a major portion of those reserves to the Soviets. That sale raised fears that an extended global food crisis was at hand and drove up prices further. Concerns about world hunger were further heightened by two major famines in the mid-1970s. There already had been several years of drought in the Sahelian region of Africa during the first part of the decade. In 1974, however, there was a famine both in Ethiopia and Bangladesh (the former caused by drought; the latter by floods). These crises, which received worldwide attention, helped boost overall aid levels as temporary responses to famine relief. But aid levels continued to rise after the famines were over. Aid from DAC countries rose by two-thirds between 1973 and 1975, one of the largest increases ever over a two-year period, and continued to increase significantly for the rest of the decade. In 1984 there was another major famine in Ethiopia, which gained even more international attention than the one a decade earlier, with several internationally known rock stars hosting benefits in Europe and the United States to raise money for relief in that country. The 1984 famine called attention to the deepening economic crisis in sub-Saharan Africa generally. Aid levels again rose, first to meet the needs of the stricken Ethiopians and then continued to increase, in particular to fund development programs and projects throughout sub-Saharan Africa.

Nongovernmental Organizations

Thus far, I have recounted the international trends and events contributing to the prominence of the development purpose of aid during the 1970s and 1980s. But there was also a movement within many developed countries that played a key role in boosting the priority of development as well as the overall volume of aid—the growing number and political activism of nongovernmental organizations (NGOs)[8] involved in relief, development, and associated issues. These organizations added their voices to those of church groups in articulating the public's concern with humanitarian crises and world poverty and amplified demands that their governments respond generously with aid.

NGOs engaged in private relief activities have a long history. In the nineteenth and twentieth centuries, those few relief NGOs that existed (e.g., the Red Cross, founded in 1863, and Save the Children, created in 1919) began to use public as well as private funds to assist refugees and displaced persons fleeing from war, famines, or other natural disasters. Much of their work was done in Europe, but during the 1940s and 1950s, many new NGOs were established which, as postwar relief efforts wound down, extended their activities to promoting long-term development in poor countries. As early as the 1940s and 1950s, several developed-country governments were beginning to draw NGOs into aid-funded development work, recognizing their potential value as service providers (especially in places where governments might not be easily able to operate) as well as educators of their own populaces on the importance of relief and development abroad. The US government had long channeled its relief aid through NGOs and in 1946 created a committee of NGOs to advise government agencies in relief work. The United States also made public subsidies available to these organizations to enable them to expand and strengthen their capacities. The Swedish government went even further in the 1950s by creating a committee of forty-four NGOs to manage Swedish aid (albeit still very modest in amount). In Germany, both the Catholic and Protestant churches established their own influential development arms—MISEREOR and Brot für die Welt, respectively.

In 1960 NGO involvement in development issues got a boost from the Food and Agriculture Organization (FAO), a specialized agency of the United Nations, which initiated a high-profile Freedom from Hunger Campaign, establishing a number of antihunger committees in European countries that encouraged the creation of NGOs working on hunger and poverty reduction. (It was this campaign that popularized the old Chinese saying, often applied to aid-giving, "Give a man a fish and you feed him for a day. Teach him to fish, and you feed him for a lifetime."[9]) Meanwhile, in the late 1950s, the World Council of Churches—an NGO in its own right—issued a call for governments to dedicate 1 percent of their GNP to helping poor countries develop. This target was adopted by the UN in the early 1960s and eventually evolved into 0.7 percent of GNP as a target for aid-giving—a standard against which aid-giving governments are still judged.

At this time, NGOs in a number of countries began to act as advocates with their own governments for development aid. The War on Want and Oxfam in the UK were among these early activist organizations. The civil war in Nigeria in 1967 and the prospect of massive starvation in the secessionist state of Biafra there further galvanized NGOs in the United States and Europe to press their governments to provide relief aid.[10] This growing NGO activism, evident in the 1950s and 1960s, was, in the words of one student of NGOs, "part of a movement cutting across several levels of society, including labor, professional, religious and political groups that were beginning to act at the time as a political lobby on behalf of those in need abroad, especially in those societies of Africa, the Middle East, and Asia where European colonial ties were strong."[11]

The 1950s and 1960s also saw the emergence of NGOs with a focus on particular international problems, often related to development, one of the earliest examples of which was population growth. The pioneer organizations concerned with the worldwide increase in population and attempting to address it through family planning were the International Planned Parenthood Foundation, established in Bombay, India, in 1952 with branches in a number of Western countries, and the Population Council, established in the United States in the same year. The Ford and Rockefeller Foundations in the United States were also involved in family planning research. In the late 1950s, the government of Sweden had begun to provide the first aid for family planning—a small amount of assistance to support research in this area in Sri Lanka and, later, Pakistan. But most other governments—both developed and developing—were reluctant to deal with this sensitive issue.

As concerns about population growth increased, especially in the United States, new NGOs were established in the field of population and family planning—for example, Population Action International in 1965 and the Alan Guttmacher Institute in 1968. Pressure from NGOs, major foundations, prominent individuals in the United States, and key members of Congress, together with a world food crisis (especially severe in India, one of the world's most populous countries), led President Lyndon Johnson, in his 1965 State of the Union address to announce that the US government would support family planning efforts in developing countries. By 1968 Congress was writing earmarks in USAID's budget for family planning programs.[12] Later, in the 1970s and 1980s, NGOs' activism extended to additional international issues, especially human rights and the environment.

Another set of development-oriented organizations arose in the 1960s and 1970s: research institutes in aid-giving countries, which produced policy-relevant research supportive of aid for development. The Overseas Development Institute in London, established in 1960, was a model. In the late 1960s, the Overseas Development Council was set up in the United States. Similar organizations were established in Denmark, Germany, Canada, and elsewhere.

Church-based NGOs, development and relief NGOs, organizations associated with particular issue areas related to development, trade unions, universities, and think tanks together made up a diverse, sometimes fractious, but increasingly important constituency for development aid at this time in a growing number of aid-giving countries.

Consequences: Elevating Aid's Development Purpose

The increasing priority of development in aid-giving is evident in a variety of trends in the 1970s and 1980s. First of all, the distribution of aid during this period tilted toward the poorest countries, rising from just over 10 percent of total aid in 1970 to 25 percent by a decade later (see fig. 2.2). Much of the increasing proportion of aid to the poorest was for the large number of countries in sub-Saharan Africa, where famines and civil conflicts were most numerous and where the development challenge appeared most intractable.

During these two decades, the terms of aid also softened significantly, with the average grant element of aid from DAC countries rising to nearly 90 percent by the early 1990s along with a modest increase in the proportion of bilateral aid devoted to what the DAC calls "social infrastructure," especially in the areas of education and health (generally regarded as essential to development and poverty reduction).

Experience during the 1960s helped to give greater shape and sophisti-

FIG. 2.2. PERCENTAGE OF TOTAL AID GIVEN TO THE LEAST DEVELOPED COUNTRIES

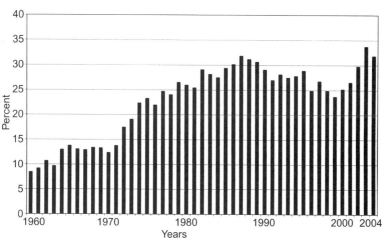

Source: DAC, "International Development Statistics (IDS) Online," http://www.oecd.org/dataoecd/50/17/5037721.htm (accessed October 2005).

cation to the broad policy frameworks for using aid to further development in later decades. New thinking on aid and development in the 1970s emphasized helping the poor in the poorest countries. During the 1960s, aid had been used to fund balance of payments and budgetary needs of developing countries, to finance investment projects, especially in infrastructure and industry (with some in education), and—in the case of the United States—aid was used as an incentive for governments in Latin America to adopt economic and social reforms. Although growth in developing countries during the 1960s was relatively healthy—exceeding the rate of population growth in all developing regions—this was not as fast as had been hoped. And poverty showed little sign of rapid decline. As one commentator declared: "the unparalleled economic growth rates achieved by most developed countries during the 1960s had little or no effect on most of the world's people, who continue to live in desperate poverty."[13] Thus, at the beginning of the 1970s, even as aid programs were becoming well established in aid-giving countries, there was a sense of malaise with foreign aid. DAC reports at this time speak of "donor fatigue" and a "crisis of development."

What eventually emerged from this period of criticism and debate on the way aid should be used to promote development was a focus on "basic human needs" of the poor. Rather than emphasizing aid interventions aimed at stimulating long-term growth that, it was assumed, would eventually eliminate poverty, aid donors, starting with the World Bank and United States, adopted aid policies that would provide immediate and direct benefits to the poor—especially in rural areas of the least developed countries, where the poor were concentrated—through funding primary education, primary health care, rural roads, clean water, and other projects that would eventually permit the poor to lift themselves from poverty. One popular approach to aid interventions during the 1970s involved "integrated rural development" projects—clusters of interrelated aid-funded projects intended to improve basic human needs in specified regions in poor countries. These usually included activities to help expand agricultural production as well as health, education, and infrastructure improvements. Governments of poor countries typically tolerated but did not embrace the basic human needs approach to development—their priorities tended to be rapid growth, in particular in urban areas (where most elites supporting them as well as the potentially politically troublesome masses likely to threaten them lived). Nevertheless, the emphasis on meeting basic human needs provided the intellectual basis for directing aid to the poor in the least developed countries—one element in the increasing focus on development as the central purpose of aid.

The Professionalization of Aid Agencies

Yet another sign of the growing seriousness and sophistication of the development purpose of aid was the professionalization of aid agencies themselves. By the early 1970s, major aid-giving governments and international organizations began to produce official policy statements and white papers setting out their development thinking and strategies. Additionally, realizing that theirs was a long-term task involving strategic interventions in recipient countries' economies, aid agencies began to put into place systematic programming arrangements to increase the relevance and effectiveness of their aid. A typical "country programming" process would include an overall assessment of the economic conditions in individual recipient countries, development of a strategy for aiding that country, usually over a multiyear period, and a plan for how much aid would be provided and for what purposes. By 1973 the World Bank, United Nations Development Program (UNDP), the European Development Fund, most major aid-giving governments (including the United States, United Kingdom, Germany), and a number of smaller donor governments had such programming processes in place.

In 1971 USAID introduced a new method for designing and evaluating its projects called the logical framework, or "logframe." This methodology, which was based on an input/output model of analysis that included assumptions about causal relationships between aid interventions and desired outcomes, added a measure of rigor and detail to the management of aid projects.[14] This programming technique was quickly picked up by the Germans, Canadians, and British and by the UNDP and applied to the design of their aid projects. Many other aid agencies eventually adopted it as well, providing them all with a more systematic approach to planning aid interventions.

Because the logical framework identified desired outcomes and how they would be achieved, it also offered a useful basis for project evaluation, contributing to the adoption by a variety of aid agencies in the early 1970s of formalized evaluation systems and the establishment or upgrading of evaluation services. By the late 1970s, there was an "explosion of interest" in aid evaluation, according to Basil Cracknell, with most of the European aid agencies establishing their own evaluation departments.[15] In 1982 an evaluation committee was created in the DAC for aid agencies to share their experiences and establish standards for evaluation. Since that time, most aid agencies have adopted many of the DAC evaluation norms, though often with rather different methodologies and varying degrees of rigor. In the 1990s evaluations broadened to include not only project and program performance, but the impact of aid on entire sectors and overall country development as well.

The Rise of Multilateral Aid

A final manifestation of the increasing priority of aid for development in the 1970s and 1980s was the rise in importance of multilateral aid agencies, especially the World Bank and the European Development Fund (EDF, the principal aid agency of the European Union). Aid from these agencies was regarded as among the most developmentally oriented of aid programs, because multilateral agencies, unlike governments, did not have diplomatic, commercial, or cultural motives that typically influenced the country allocation and use of bilateral aid.

When Robert McNamara became president of the World Bank in 1968, he announced that "the Bank Group should during the next five years lend twice as much as during the past five years."[16] And he set about vigorously pursuing that goal to good effect. World Bank aid (that is, lending from the International Development Association, or IDA, the World Bank's soft loan[17] window) enjoyed a sustained rise during the 1970s, from $162 million in the first year of the decade to $1.6 billion ten years later. In fact, McNamara was pushing on an open door. There was already considerable sympathy in the United States and other countries for expanding the proportion of aid channeled through multilateral organizations.[18] This sympathy was based on a widely shared view that these funds would have a greater impact on economic and social progress in poor countries than those provided through bilateral channels. In smaller aid-giving countries, governments also favored multilateral aid agencies, like the World Bank, the regional development banks, and UN development agencies because these governments often lacked the expertise or capacity to manage a far-flung aid program abroad on their own.

In addition to the multilateral development banks and UN agencies, such as the UN Development Program, the members of the European Community committed themselves in the Treaty of Rome in 1958 to set up a joint aid program (in addition to their bilateral aid programs). The European Development Fund became a sizable source of grants to developing countries, concentrating on the African and Caribbean countries that were former colonies of EC member states, rising from $160 million in 1970 to $1.5 billion in 1980.[19] (In the year 2000, aid from the European Union reached nearly $5 billion.) Figure 2.3 shows worldwide multilateral aid as a percentage of total ODA from 1960 to 2004.

The increases in the relative amount of multilateral aid during the 1970s were reversed later as multilateral aid dropped to just over a quarter

FIG. 2.3. MULTILATERAL AID AS A PERCENTAGE OF TOTAL ODA

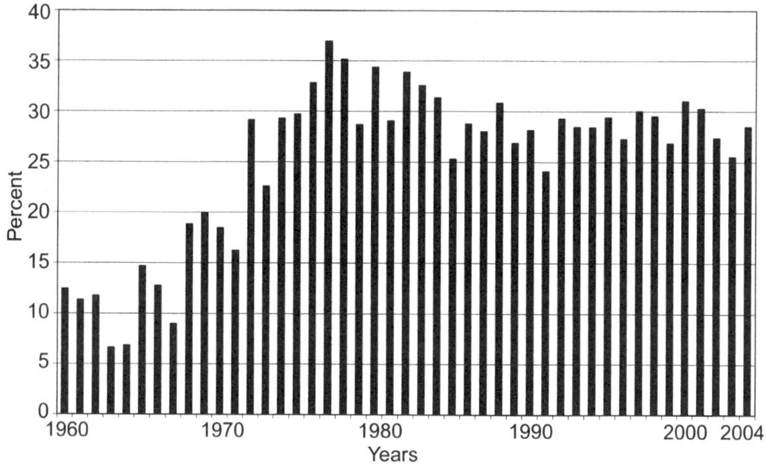

Source: DAC, "International Development Statistics (IDS) Online," http://www.oecd.org/dac/stats/idsonline/ (accessed October 2005).

of total aid by the 1990s. The main reason for this decrease was the growing resistance in the United States (especially during the administration of Ronald Reagan) to funding multilateral aid and particularly increases in the replenishments of IDA. And because the United States balked at increases in IDA funding, other member states of the World Bank held back in their contributions to maintain the same percentage relationship with that of the United States.

To Sum Up

Over the decades of the 1970s and 1980s, aid for development came of age. This did not mean that all donor governments put development at the top of their foreign-aid-giving priorities. The United States and France in particular continued to deploy significant amounts of their assistance for a variety of diplomatic purposes; the Japanese still pursued commercial and diplomatic interests with their aid, and other governments continued to use their aid for a mix of purposes.

Nor did the coming of age of development as a priority in aid-giving mean that there was a broad consensus on how aid should be used for development. Indeed, beginning in the 1980s, there was another shift in mainstream thinking about aid for development, away from basic human needs and redistributive goals. With the debt and balance of payments crises in many developing countries, the emphasis in aid-giving was now on "structural adjustment"—aid tied to economic reforms, such as currency devaluation, trade liberalization, deficit reduction, elimination of controls on prices, wages, and interest rates, and a host of other economic policy changes intended to reinvigorate economic growth in developing countries. The World Bank and IMF, supported by the United States and other governments, took the lead in shaping and negotiating economic reform programs with developing countries. However, there were those—many of whom were in the NGO community—who argued that economic reforms were making poverty worse and that aid should be focused as much as possible on activities aimed directly at reducing poverty and empowering the poor. These differences continued and sharpened as the decade wore on without the debate being resolved. Despite these caveats, this was the period in which development gained a preeminence in foreign-aid-giving it had not enjoyed before. "Development," observed Robert Asher as early as 1971, "is now the name of the game."[20]

THE 1990S: A DECADE OF CHANGE

The decade of the 1990s was one of great changes in the world as well as important changes in foreign aid. The end of the Cold War lessened the diplomatic relevance of aid-giving for some governments but also led to the emergence of new purposes for aid, including supporting economic and political changes in former socialist countries, addressing global problems, promoting democracy, and postconflict rehabilitation. These new purposes, plus increasing doubts about aid's development effectiveness, challenged the prominence of the development purpose of aid. Coincident with these changes was the rise in the overall volume of aid to its highest level ever at the beginning of the decade, followed by a rapid decline during the middle of the 1990s and a slow increase during the latter part of the decade. Within these changes, particularly striking was the drop in aid to sub-Saharan Africa by one-third between 1994 and 2000. Long-term observers of foreign aid began to wonder whether they were watching the beginning of the end of aid for development.

Context: The New World of the 1990s

The major world event in the early 1990s was the end of the Cold War, marked definitively by the collapse of the USSR in 1991. Globalization, the spread of democracy, prolonged civil conflicts in a number of poor countries, and economic problems within aid-giving countries also played a role in changing the amount and purposes of aid during this decade.

The Cold War's End

The collapse of the Soviet Union in 1991 marked the end of the Cold War, with two important consequences for the purposes of aid. First, the disintegration of socialist regimes in Eastern Europe and the USSR (and the breakup of the USSR itself into fifteen independent countries[21]) began a transition in most of these countries from command economies to free markets and from authoritarian regimes to democracies. They sought advice and assistance in transiting these difficult economic and political passages—assistance that the West was eager to provide to help make the transitions both smooth and permanent.

Second, while the end of the Cold War made it possible for aid-giving governments to reduce or terminate aid to repressive and corrupt regimes that had been assisted only because of East-West maneuvering, it also permitted Western governments to ignore threats of conflict or the outbreak of violence in developing countries, often leaving such conflicts to drag on to cause destruction, destitution, and death for large numbers of civilians. Some long-running conflicts, fed by Cold War competition, ended in part as a result of the collapse of the USSR—for example, the wars in Ethiopia and, eventually, in Angola. In other cases, however, civil violence may have been unintentionally encouraged or provoked by the withdrawal of aid and Western engagement, as in the former Zaire and Liberia. Altogether, throughout the 1990s, there were fifty-seven major armed conflicts in forty-five locations, the bulk of which were in Africa and all but three of which were conflicts within states rather than between states.[22] Their number, prolongation, and destructiveness and the humanitarian crises they provoked—the most horrendous being the genocide in Rwanda in 1994—led aid-giving governments to consider what could be done to prevent conflicts and support recovery and rehabilitation after them. (Experience had shown that in countries that had suffered civil conflicts, civil violence was most likely to erupt again when postconflict rehabilitation was weak.) Several aid agencies, including USAID and the World Bank, set up offices and programs specifically addressed to postconflict recovery and rehabilitation.

The end of the Cold War also eliminated a key rationale for aid-giving and thus lessened the relevance of aid among foreign policy elites in countries—above all, in the United States—where the Cold War had long been one of the main justifications for providing aid (even if it had for some time ceased being a major driver of where that aid went and how it was used). There was now more political space for other purposes for aid, but the rationales for that aid were less compelling than in the past. Thus, aid was vulnerable to being cut in times of economic recession and budgetary stringency.[23]

Globalization

The intensification of the process of globalization in the 1990s was a second important element in the new context of aid-giving. The ease and affordability of international travel made even the most remote areas of the world accessible to businesspeople and tourists; the revolution in information technologies brought knowledge and real-time news about distant places to many millions of people. The rapid expansion of international trade and investment also made economic conditions in one country increasingly sensitive to those in other countries. These changes, in turn, called the world's attention to problems in distant lands, including civil conflict, poverty, environmental challenges, and problems of disease, especially the spread of HIV/AIDS and, more recently, the threat of an avian flu pandemic. In short, globalization facilitated the spread of problems across borders, while contributing to a heightened awareness of their existence. Reinforcing the emphasis on global problems (as well as their association with development) was a series of UN summits focusing on several of those problems, including the UN Summit on the Environment and Development in Rio de Janeiro in 1992, the UN Conference on Population and Development in Cairo in 1994, the UN Summit on Women in Beijing in 1995, the World Food Summit in Rome in 1996, and the Global Climate Conference in Kyoto in 1997. Each of these summits produced negotiated statements and a plan of action (often involving foreign aid).

Globalization brought with it a backlash. Antiglobalization groups and organizations formed and held large demonstrations against various international organizations and activities identified with global capitalism—against trade negotiations hosted by the World Trade Organization in Seattle in 1999 and large and sometimes violent demonstrations against the World Bank on the occasion of its annual meetings. Antiglobalists argued that the World Bank used its aid to further international corporate interests and should be abolished. While the noisy demonstrations discomfited many (especially those attending the World Bank meetings), they did not have a significant effect on the functioning of that institution or on foreign aid generally.

Democratization

A third element in the context of aid-giving in the 1990s was the pace of democratization, which picked up momentum across the developing world. What is often called the "third wave" of democracy commenced with a military coup in Portugal in 1974 and subsequent democratic reforms by the new government there.[24] In the late 1970s and 1980s, one after another Latin American country shifted from authoritarian to democratically elected regimes (even if, in a number of cases, the military still played a major role behind the scenes in national politics). The collapse of totalitarian regimes in Eastern Europe in the late 1980s encouraged demands for democracy in sub-Saharan Africa. "National conferences" (with representatives of various groups and segments of the population) were held in Benin, Congo (Brazzaville), Mali, and elsewhere, many of which rewrote their countries' constitutions and set national elections. Multiparty democracies were also established in Kenya, Zambia, and Tanzania. The newly elected regimes that were put in place in response to demands for political liberalization were often only minimally democratic, but most were more open and less repressive than their predecessors. Foreign aid promised to be a useful tool in promoting democracy, especially in sub-Saharan Africa—both as an incentive for governments to implement political reforms and a source of financing for activities related to democratization, such as elections, technical assistance, and training, supportive of those reforms.

Economic Problems in Aid-Giving Countries

A final factor in the context of aid-giving in the 1990s related more to the amount of aid than to its purposes—the economic problems within aid-giving countries themselves. At the beginning of the 1990s, most Western economies faced recessions and significant fiscal deficits. For the Europeans intending to join the planned EU monetary union, the Maastricht agreement of 1992 required that budgetary deficits exceed no more than 3 percent of gross national products. In preparation for membership, a number of governments had to cut overall spending. In most countries, foreign aid was one of the "discretionary" programs whose expenditures were not mandated by law and so were vulnerable to such cuts, and especially so in the wake of the end of the Cold War. In the United States, both the first Bush and the Clinton administrations sought to reduce the federal budget deficit and slashed aid levels substantially. And when the Republican Party gained control of the Congress in 1995, foreign aid was further cut as part of the efforts to reduce the overall size of government. The Japanese government, in the face of slow growth and worsening economic problems at home (together with the example of falling aid levels in the United States and other countries), also began to compress its aid levels in mid-decade. As a result, foreign aid worldwide dropped by 20 percent between 1995 and 1997—the largest decrease in aid since the 1960s—and while it began to rise again toward the end of the decade, by 2000, aid was still below its level in 1995.

Consequences: Aid's "New" Purposes in the 1990s

As a result of changes in the world and in aid-giving countries, by the end of the 1990s aid had acquired four "new" purposes: promoting economic and political transitions, addressing global problems, furthering democracy, and managing conflict. (In fact, apart from supporting economic and political transitions in former socialist countries, these purposes were not really new—but each gained a prominence in the 1990s they had not enjoyed previously.)

What types of activities did aid finance as part of these new purposes? Promoting economic and political transitions in former socialist countries included assistance for the drafting of new constitutions and laws (e.g., property law and commercial law); for the reform of the judiciary (e.g., establishing a jury system); for reforms in the regulatory and financial systems; for training for political parties and the independent media; and for strengthening civil society organizations. The best known (and most controversial) aid in former socialist countries was support for privatizing state-owned enterprises, the largest effort being in Russia.

Aid to address global problems included a variety of environmentally oriented activities such as coral reef preservation, the reduction of ozone-destroying gases, the reduction of air, water, and soil pollution, the collection and preservation of endangered plants, and community wildlife management programs. Toward the end of the decade, the emphasis in addressing global problems shifted to the international transmission of infectious diseases, above all, HIV/AIDS.

Aid for democracy promotion (outside of former socialist bloc countries) was focused primarily on sub-Saharan Africa where, during the decade of the 1990s, demands for multiparty elections and democratic reforms were most widespread. Aid financed the (often very expensive) first election, which required voter registration and the creation of procedures and capabilities for campaigning, voting, and vote counting. It helped fund the drafting of new constitutions, political party and media training, judicial reforms, and strengthening of civil society organizations, especially those engaged in human rights and civic education.

By the late 1990s, postconflict aid was provided from various aid agencies, including the United States, the World Bank, the UN Development Program, and the Scandinavians, to the Balkans, Guatemala, Haiti, Angola, Mozambique, Sierra Leone, Liberia, and a host of other countries. So extensive did this type of aid become in the 1990s that, in 1997, the DAC member states signed on to a common policy statement on conflict, peace, and development cooperation.[25]

How much aid was in fact allocated to aid's new purposes? It is difficult to say for sure, because governments do not classify their aid in all of these categories of purposes, so the DAC has limited data in this form. And in any case, aid's purposes are, as I noted in chapter 1, often difficult to disentangle. We can make a very rough estimate of a breakdown among these purposes in 2000. Bilateral aid commitments from DAC countries ascribable to specific sectors totaled $50 billion that year. Of that total, $4 billion was used to support economic and political transitions in former socialist countries. Aid for relief was $3.6 billion. Aid for supporting government and civil society amounted to $2.2 billion. The remaining $40 billion was divided among three purposes: furthering diplomatic goals, supporting development, and addressing global problems. With regard to the latter purpose, bilateral aid from DAC countries to promote health and the environment totaled $3 billion, but only a portion of this sum would have been used primarily to address these problems in a global context rather than as part of a country development program. The best we can say is that by 2000, it appeared that the amount of bilateral aid for the new purposes was certainly less than $13 billion (of a total of $51 billion in bilateral aid) and probably closer to half that amount—a small proportion of overall bilateral aid but still a significant sum.[26]

Aid for Development Revisited and Reformed

The 1990s began with two competing approaches to using aid to further development, as noted earlier. One, associated with the World Bank (and often criticized as "top down"), emphasized economic policy reform as a means of stimulating growth. The other, most associated with NGOs, emphasized poverty reduction through small-scale, community development activities targeted directly at the poor and engaging their participation in planning aid-funded activities as a means of empowering them as well as encouraging them to assume responsibility for the success and sustainability of the activities. Some official aid agencies, like USAID, leaned more toward the World Bank approach (though a portion of its aid was channeled through NGOs). Others, like those in Scandinavian countries, sympathized with the NGO approach.

By the middle of the decade, a truce had evolved between these competing visions of aid and development. The World Bank, under the presidency of James Wolfensohn, began to emphasize the importance of "putting the recipient government in the driver's seat" in shaping aid interventions, of poverty reduction as the end goal of development, and of funding projects with a more direct effect on poverty.[27] And a number of NGOs began to acknowledge that little economic and social progress would be possible in poor countries in the absence of a supportive policy environment and of effective economic policy management.

But no sooner had a degree of consensus been achieved among development practitioners than a major challenge erupted to the overall effectiveness of development aid. Concerns about aid effectiveness were not new in development discourse, but they gained particular prominence during the 1990s for several reasons. One was the end of the Cold War, which reduced the national security justification for aid-giving that had also served as a shield against attacks on aid's developmental effectiveness. Second was the improvement in economic data that made new assessments of aid's impact possible. Much more information on macroeconomic conditions as well as household well-being, for example, facilitated time series and cross-country statistical analyses on aid effectiveness. Third, and perhaps most importantly, was the dismal economic performance of most of sub-Saharan Africa. Since the late 1970s, aid to this region had been rising, both in absolute and relative terms, reaching one-third of bilateral aid by 1989, and for many African countries, aid represented a significant portion of their gross national product annually. Yet economic performance in sub-Saharan Africa had been poor over several decades. Growth rates were often below the rate of increase in population. Investment was low, savings were low, and shortages of medicines, books, and other essentials continued. Further, the region had more than its share of corrupt and repressive governments, further impeding growth. As a result of these problems, together with droughts, pests, disease, and an often adverse international economy, the average real incomes for Africans in 1990 were little better than those at the beginning of the independence period in 1960. Africa's problems were seen by many as compelling evidence for the inability of foreign aid to promote development.

Several reports on aid effectiveness by the World Bank gave further credence to arguments that aid had been far less effective than had been previously assumed. The first was a 1992 internal study (that was soon much quoted publicly) entitled *Report of the World Bank Portfolio Management Task Force* (also called the "Wapenhans Report" after the Bank vice president who led the study). The report pointed to disappointing results of World Bank loans and criticized a number of Bank practices—especially the absence of local commitment to aid projects, the standalone nature of project lending, and the absence of coordination among multiple donors—as contributing to poor outcomes. *Assessing Aid: What Works, What Doesn't, and Why*,[28] published in 1998, focused on the shortcomings of recipient countries, finding that aid was ineffective in furthering growth where economic policies were poor—for example, where there was high inflation or barriers to trade. And while aid was effective where there was a supportive policy environment, it had not been effective in causing governments to create such an environment. The findings of the World Bank report and others criticizing aid were contested by scholars and practitioners, but they nevertheless had a major impact on the way many in the policy community thought about aid effectiveness.

Other criticisms of aid arising at this time were aimed at the practices of aid agencies. They included the lack of "ownership" of aid-funded activities on the part of recipients, often because donors had made the decisions on what aid would fund without taking into account the views and preferences of those intended to be the beneficiaries of the aid. (A senior official in the French aid establishment once told me, reflecting on his country's aid to Africa during much of the second half of the twentieth century, "We asked the questions and we gave the answers.")

Another critique applied especially to aid in sub-Saharan Africa was the proliferation of aid donors and their various projects, absorbing the attention and energies of overstretched African government agencies and often disrupting their planning and budgetary processes (which were none too strong in any case). Further, aid was attacked as involving too many stand-alone projects that were not part of an overall strategy for poverty reduction and growth supported by recipient governments and their publics. Finally, aid agencies were criticized for a lack of selectivity in the governments they aided—too much aid had been provided to governments that were corrupt, managed their economies poorly, or lacked the capacity to use the aid effectively.

These criticisms—not just from aid's traditional critics but increasingly from its traditional supporters—combined with the drop in aid levels in the middle of the decade to deepen concerns about the long-term prospects of aid for development. They also led aid agencies rapidly to adopt a series of reforms in the way they did business—not only to enable them better to achieve their development missions but to protect themselves from further cuts and eventually to expand again the scope of their operations abroad. Those reform initiatives, described below, include results-based management, selectivity, poverty reduction strategy papers (PRSPs) and sector-wide assistance programs (SWAPs) to aid-giving. Also occurring at this time were several international agreements restricting the use of aid for commercial purposes. Finally, a worldwide agreement on Millennium Development Goals for the reduction of poverty and a New Partnership for Africa's Development (NEPAD), proposed by African governments, rounded out the international aid reform movement of the 1990s. While each of these innovations had both advantages and disadvantages, they did enable officials and development advocates to argue that development aid in the future would be significantly more effective than it had been in the past and thus helped to refresh support for it.

Results-Based Management. Even before the impulse the World Bank report gave to the debate on aid effectiveness, the US government had embraced results-based management, which had become popular in the private sector—an effort to identify strategic objectives, indicators of progress toward those objectives, and measurable results expected within a given time period (often covering several years). In 1993 the US Congress passed a law—the Government Performance and Results Act—requiring that all government agencies adopt this process in managing public programs and expenditures. Results-based management was embraced by USAID during the first half of the decade and spread from there to a number of aid agencies in other countries, including those of the United Kingdom, Denmark, Canada, the World Bank, and the UNDP, as they tried to improve the effectiveness of their aid interventions. (This approach, while useful in focusing aid agencies' attention on strategic goals and measurable targets, had several serious limitations when applied to foreign aid. The data used for indicators were sometimes unreliable, and attributing changes in the indicators themselves to aid interventions—especially after a short period of time—was problematical. More basically, aid for development, in particular, was often experimental, applying technologies that were sometimes new and unproven to bring about change in complex and poorly understood societies over an uncertain period of time. The most important result—learning how to be effective in a particular kind of aid intervention in a particular place and time—was typically not included as an indicator of results.[29])

Selectivity. A policy of selectivity in the choice of aid recipients was not new in the aid business in the 1990s. Aid-giving governments had long assumed that if the countries chosen to receive aid had policies in place that supported development (e.g., significant investments in education and health, equilibrium exchange rates to encourage exports, trade policies that encouraged competition and economic efficiency, prices and interest rates that encouraged investment, fiscal and monetary policies that contained inflation), aid would be effective in hastening growth and poverty reduction. Scandinavian countries, for example, favored developing country governments with a social democratic orientation similar to their own—above all, Tanzania. The United States and Germany, at least at the level of rhetoric, tended to favor countries with policies that supported the expansion of the private sector. But diplomatic, commercial, and cultural purposes of aid-giving during the decades preceding the end of the Cold War made implementing a policy of selectivity based on development criteria difficult. With the end of the Cold War and especially with the findings of the World Bank study *Assessing Aid*, which found aid to be more effective in countries with supportive economic policies, the notion of selectivity got a boost. By the early years of the twenty-first century, discussions of selectivity included not only macroeconomic policies pursued by recipient governments but the quality of governance (and degree of corruption), political openness, and the relative amount of government expenditures on social services and on the military. And there were signs during the 1990s that donors were becoming more selective in their allocation of aid, with aid flows to the most corrupt and incompetent governments decreasing.[30] The US government even sought to institutionalize the notion of selectivity in its creation of a new aid agency—the Millennium Challenge Corporation—which was required to disburse its aid funds only to countries qualifying on the basis of sixteen criteria involving just governance, free markets, and investment in their own people.

Sector-Wide Assistance Programs. Following the criticisms of the World Bank in the Wapenhans Report and the attacks on its structural adjustment lending as often being imposed on unwilling recipient governments, the Bank began to develop a new lending instrument called a sector-wide assistance program (SWAP) that delivered development aid through a program of budget support for sectoral investment plans—for example, in health, education, or agriculture. The plans are drawn up by recipient government ministries (in consultation with relevant domestic groups) and financed with domestic resources and pooled development assistance from a variety of aid donors. SWAPs thus addressed the criticisms that aid was too "donor driven" and that aid donors needed to better coordinate the delivery of their aid. A number of aid agencies, primarily in Europe, embraced this new approach to providing aid. Between 1995 and 2004 an average of $1.5 billion per year in aid worldwide was in the form of SWAPs.[31]

PRSPs. Poverty reduction strategy papers, or PRSPs, are another innovation adopted by the World Bank in 1999 to improve the effectiveness of development aid. These strategy papers, according to the World Bank, "describe a country's macroeconomic, structural and social policies and programs to promote growth and reduce poverty, as well as associated external financing needs."[32] PRSPs are, in effect, broad development planning documents. But they differ from those that aid donors required from recipient governments forty years earlier in that they are supposed to be developed by a government in consultation with its people—thus engaging its public, its civil society, and the poor in a national conversation on development and poverty reduction. PRSPs, approved by the boards of the World Bank and IMF, were required by those institutions for debt relief and concessional lending—creating incentives for developing countries to produce the strategy papers. By April 2005, fifty-six countries—thirty in sub-Saharan Africa—had produced PRSPs or interim PRSPs (preliminary documents). These documents were increasingly used by aid agencies worldwide as guides to development financing in poor countries, thus providing a broad basis for more coordinated donor aid interventions. However, an evaluation of the PRSP process by the World Bank was lukewarm in its conclusions, remarking that "Countries have understandably focused more on completing documents [i.e., the PRSP] that give them access to resources, . . . often . . . at the expense of adaptation of the PRS process to unique country circumstances."[33] Nor was it clear that the World Bank had yet adjusted its lending operations in individual countries to reflect the contents of the PRSPs.

This unusually large number of reforms in the management of foreign aid, adopted by a wide range of donor governments and international organizations, were intended to increase the developmental effectiveness of aid. And even with their many weaknesses, the new approaches provided a rationale for renewed increases in development assistance.

Constraining the Commercial Use of Aid

One of the explanations for aid's ineffectiveness in furthering development was that it had, in fact, been used to further the commercial interests of the donor country. And those interests not only frequently collided with development concerns, they could also undercut development by funding overpriced, inefficient, and low-priority projects that left behind little development but lots of debt. The 1990s saw two international agreements among aid-giving governments limiting the commercial orientation of foreign aid. One involved mixed-credit schemes. The mixing of concessional aid with commercially priced loans in export packages (e.g., in bids for contracts with foreign governments to construct large infrastructure projects) to make the overall package financially attractive was significantly limited by the "Arrangement on Guidelines for Officially Supported Export Credits," also known as the Helsinki Arrangement, negotiated under OECD auspices in 1991. This agreement significantly constrained the use of concessional financing for projects only to the least developed countries, only for projects that could not attract commercial financing, and only if the concessional financing had at least a 35 percent grant element.

A second agreement involved "tied aid"—assistance that had to be spent in the country providing it. A number of donor governments had strongly resisted limits on tied aid in the past, regarding it as a means of maintaining domestic support for aid from important commercial interests. In 2001 a high-level meeting of the DAC endorsed a recommendation to untie aid to the least developed countries. This agreement did not cover technical assistance and food aid, however, and thus excluded a sizable amount of total aid. But it was the first international agreement to untie aid—a sign that governments were amenable to changing their policies on this long-debated issue.

The Millennium Development Goals and NEPAD

Two further international initiatives were part of an effort to revive aid for development. During the 1990s, a number of efforts had been made to establish goals for the achievement of development and development-related activities. The UN conferences mentioned earlier proposed goals for their particular areas. In 1996 the DAC published its report *Shaping the 21st Century: The Contribution of Development Cooperation*, with seven development goals to be realized. When the UN convened its special Millennium Assembly in 2000, it incorporated these various programs into the Millennium Development Goals (MDGs), to be achieved by 2015.

Millennium Development Goals for the Year 2015
- Halve the proportion of people whose income is less than $1 per day and those living with insufficient food.
- Achieve universal primary education.
- Eliminate gender disparities at all levels of education.
- Reduce child mortality by two-thirds and maternal mortality by three quarters.
- Halt and reverse the spread of HIV/AIDS, malaria, and other diseases.
- Ensure environmental sustainability and reverse the loss of environmental resources.
- Halve the proportion of people without sustainable access to safe drinking water.
- Achieve by 2020 a significant improvement in the lives of slum dwellers.
- Develop a global partnership for development.[34]

Whether these ambitious goals could be realized or not (and many thought they were not likely to be achieved in the time frame agreed, especially in sub-Saharan Africa), the international agreement on them represented a renewed commitment to development on the part of the world's governments and created a standard of performance and a focal point for discussions for many in the development community on foreign aid. Realizing these goals was estimated by the World Bank to require an additional $50 billion per year or more above existing aid levels.[35] As part of a strategy for advancing these goals, the United Nations organized the Conference on Financing Development in Monterrey, Mexico, in 2002. World conferences, attended by heads of government, had long been a way of raising the international visibility of particular issues and pressuring governments to announce policy initiatives on them. The Monterrey Conference was no exception, where a number of major governments, including the United States and many European governments, announced significant increases in their aid for development. Data on worldwide aid flows in the years after the Monterrey Conference show that those flows have increased substantially (see fig. 2.1 above).

An effort to bolster development in Africa, proposed by African governments, was the New Partnership for Africa's Development (NEPAD), adopted by the African Union in 2001. NEPAD was intended to reduce poverty in the region, consistent with the Millennium Development Goals. It emphasized good governance, peace and security, regional integration, and capacity building. Its innovation was a periodic peer-review process, undertaken by Africans, of the performance of African governments. These innovations were to be combined with increased aid and debt relief in support of faster growth in the region. This was the implicit compact at the core of the "partnership" notion in NEPAD—better governance in exchange for more aid. At the time of this writing, NEPAD was still evolving, including the peer review process itself.

These reforms in aid processes and management in the 1990s were even broader than those of the 1970s, when aid agencies began to professionalize their operations. While not developed by aid agencies as a comprehensive package of reforms, they did become the basis for those agencies to claim in the twenty-first century that they were much better positioned to manage aid more effectively and to handle substantially more aid as well.

Aid's Revival

In fact, aid did begin to rise again modestly in the late 1990s, initially for emergency assistance, debt relief, and education. Setting aside the emergency aid, which was temporary, the two other areas of increase were ones that had been subject to "aid campaigns"—concerted, internationally coordinated efforts led by NGOs within aid-giving countries to raise aid levels for specific purposes. These increases signaled the beginning of a resurgence in the amount of foreign aid provided annually.

A Word on Aid Campaigns

The campaign approach to aid advocacy was not new—campaigns for famine relief in the 1970s and 1980s had helped elevate aid levels on those occasions and not just for relief alone. In the 1990s aid advocacy campaigns continued, but none was more prominent than Jubilee 2000 for debt cancellation. Jubilee 2000 was a worldwide campaign, originating in the United Kingdom in 1997, in support of eliminating the debt owed by poor countries to rich ones and to international organizations. The name was taken from the Old Testament, in which periodically (roughly every fifty years), slaves were to be freed and debts annulled. In the Middle Ages, the Catholic church began to celebrate jubilee years at the turn of the century.

Many developing countries carried into the 1990s high levels of international debt, contracted from private and public lenders during earlier decades. Heavy debt burdens could discourage potential investors, and high debt service ratios could drain resources from already cash-strapped governments. Demands by indebted governments and lobbying by NGOs in a variety of capitals (spurred in the second half of the 1990s by the worldwide Jubilee 2000 campaign to Drop the Debt[36]) encouraged governments and international organizations to cancel public debts of the poorer countries and led the World Bank to create a process for debt reduction for countries owing it large debts. The World Bank adopted a debt reduction initiative for the heavily indebted poor countries (HIPCs) that, while rather restrictive and slow to be put into operation, did help some of those countries reduce their debts to the World Bank for the first time.[37] Debt forgiveness from DAC member states rose from $650 million in 1990 to $3.7 billion in 2004.[38] Not all the debt of poor countries was eliminated during the 1990s, but the Jubilee campaign in particular was successful in mobilizing NGOs, in helping to sensitize the public in Western countries to the problems of developing country debt and poverty in general, and in getting creditor governments to cancel an increasing volume of debt to poor countries.

The rise in aid for education was also assisted by a campaign, though a much less prominent one than Jubilee 2000. NGOs had actively supported expanded aid for basic education during the 1990s, arguing that it was most beneficial to the many poor in developing countries. There had also been considerable advocacy of girls' education—girls typically enjoyed less access to education than boys even though the social payoff to educating girls was very high. Better educated girls became healthier, more prosperous women and had healthier children (and smaller families)—a major boost not only to the well-being of girls and women but to a country's economic and social progress in general. A further source of advocacy for expanded education came from human and labor rights groups concerned about child labor in poor countries. Children in the workforce seldom attended school. Those NGOs and unions opposing child labor were also advocates for expanded basic education.

In 1990 the UN Conference on Education for All was held in Thailand. That conference agreed on a goal of providing primary education for all children by the end of the decade and created an Education for All Campaign of NGOs to lobby for expanded education and increased foreign aid to further that goal. In 2000 the World Forum on Education, sponsored by five UN agencies, was convened in Dakar, Senegal, to assess progress over the past decade and give further impetus to primary education worldwide. This conference gave greater international visibility to the importance of primary education and helped reenergize national and international networks of NGOs advocating more aid to education. The increase in aid funding for education was in part spurred by the continuing Education for All campaign, led by the United Nations Educational, Scientific and Cultural Organization (UNESCO).

INTO THE TWENTY-FIRST CENTURY

Several events and trends at the beginning of the new century had a major impact on the volume of aid, elevating its use once again to further economic development. At the UN Conference on Financing Development held in 2002, President George W. Bush promised to increase US aid by $5 billion, or by half, by 2006 and to make that increase permanent. In 2003 the US president promised $15 billion in foreign aid over five years to fight HIV/AIDS (roughly $10 billion of which was additional to existing levels of aid). In addition, prior to the Monterrey conference, member states of the European Union promised to raise their aid to an average of 0.39 percent of GNP by 2006, and each member state undertook to raise its aid at least to 0.33 percent of GNP—implying an increase of at least $7 billion by 2006. Together, the United States and European commitments promised a major boost in foreign aid—largely for development purposes—within five years. In 2003 worldwide aid flows rose by $10 billion over the previous year, as governments began to implement their commitments. In the United States alone, foreign aid (without supplementals for war reconstruction and emergency relief) was set to rise by 25 percent between 2001 and 2005— one of the largest increases in several decades.[39] Furthermore, all three of the largest aid donors—the United States, Japan, and France—sought to reorganize their aid agencies to elevate the development purpose of their aid. In the United States, an entirely new aid agency was created, focused exclusively on development aid—the Millennium Challenge Corporation (MCC). In Japan and France, efforts were already underway to coordinate their fragmented aid agencies better, to engage NGOs more in advising and implementing government aid programs, and to align those programs more with DAC norms for development assistance.

Aid levels had already begun to rise again before 2001. But the UN Conference on Financing Development in Monterrey, Mexico, that year triggered a big boost to aid increases. But international conferences generally succeed only if the environment is favorable for positive action. In this case, the economic and fiscal constraints that had led to a drop in aid in many countries during the 1990s had eased. The United States, for example, had gone from a budget deficit to a surplus by the early years of the twenty-first century. And, as noted, there had been a number of reforms in aid aimed at making it more effective.

The terrorist attack on the United States in September 2001 played a role in predisposing political elites and publics in the United States and Europe to support higher levels of aid for development.[40] The attack was interpreted by many in the media and among the public as a consequence of the poverty and gross inequalities in the world. In fact, few of the terrorists came from poor families or the poorest countries (many were from Saudi Arabia), and social justice was not what motivated them. But perceptions are important, and the connection between poverty and terrorism was one that was made particularly in the European media. A more subtle and accurate connection between the terrorists and weak or failed states (which were usually in the world's poorer countries) argued that such states could become havens for terrorist organizations and therefore it was in the interests of the world community to help prevent state failure. No one was sure just how to do this, but poverty as well as poor governance clearly played a role in the turmoil in these unfortunate countries. They could not be ignored by the rich countries, and aid was a potentially useful tool for preventing civil conflict and state collapse. In the words of the World Bank president in 2001:

> Poverty in itself does not immediately and directly lead to conflict, let alone to terrorism. . . . And yet we know that exclusion can breed violent conflict. Careful research tells us that civil wars have often resulted not so much from ethnic diversity—the usual scapegoat—as from a mix of factors, of which, it must be recognized, poverty is a central ingredient. And conflict-ridden countries in turn become safe havens for terrorists. . . . Our common goal must be to eradicate poverty, to promote inclusion and social justice, to bring the marginalized into the mainstream of the global economy and society. . . . What should be our agenda? First, scale up foreign aid.[41]

In addition to these enabling and triggering events were two other, more fundamental, factors. First was an international norm that rich countries should help further development in poor countries, with foreign aid as the principal tool for implementing that norm. This norm—which did not exist a half-century earlier—was widely accepted by developed country governments and significant portions of their publics as early as the 1970s, reinforced by international organizations such as the DAC, the World Bank, the European Union, and elements of the United Nations and supported by a growing relief and development lobby of NGOs within aid-giving countries. But albeit norms are permissive, they do not cause action themselves. The cuts in aid during the mid-1990s mobilized NGOs to call on their governments and publics to stop further cuts in development assistance and instead to support increases in development support. In the United States, the campaign called "Just 1%" (referring to the volume of aid as a percentage of the federal budget) was in reaction to the sharp decreases in aid during the mid-1990s. In Germany, it was called the "Pro-0.7%," referring to the UN target for aid as a proportion of gross national product. Development-oriented NGOs began to collaborate across borders in aid-for-development campaigns and in supporting the expansion of NGOs in countries, like Japan, where they were weak. Beginning in the 1990s, they initiated the annual publication of *The Reality of Aid*, a review and assessment of the aid programs of their governments (modeled on the annual DAC reports but intended to provide an NGO perspective on development aid).[42] The United Nations secretariat, in consultation with member states and NGOs, also used the Millennium Assembly in 2000 to gain international acceptance for the Millennium Development Goals, which were intended to be, among other things, a vehicle for mobilizing international action on development aid. All of these factors, plus others specific to individual countries (some of which are described in succeeding chapters), combined in the early years of the twenty-first century to revive and boost foreign aid for development and appeared likely to sustain continuing increases in development aid.

And so, the history of foreign aid is the story of a new tool of foreign policy that began as a temporary expedient in a spreading Cold War in Europe and Asia. At its core was an innovation: to promote human betterment in recipient countries through economic stabilization, long-term growth, and poverty reduction. Promoting human betterment was not initially an end in itself for most aid-giving governments, but a means to diplomatic ends having to do with national and international security. However, promoting human betterment carried a political logic of its own: it proved to be a long-term project that required a cadre of specialized professionals to accomplish, leading to the establishment of aid agencies within donor governments and, in a number of countries, the creation and strengthening of

NGOs to deliver a portion of the assistance. Thus, a constituency for aid—especially development aid—took shape inside and outside governments, reinforced by a variety of international organizations that discussed, debated, and pressed the governments of rich countries to expand the quantity and quality of their aid. Foreign aid also needed to be sold to the public in aid-giving countries, much of which proved supportive of providing public assistance abroad to relieve suffering and hunger and to reduce the poverty that led to both. Thus it was that the widely shared norm in both rich and poor countries that the governments of the former should provide concessional public resources to better the human condition in the latter abroad gradually took shape and gathered strength in the second half of the twentieth century. By the end of the twentieth century, foreign aid was no longer an innovation but a common and expected element in relations between rich and poor countries.

However, the aid-for-development norm was neither unconditional nor uncontested in major aid-giving countries, and aid never became a single-purpose tool of foreign policy in those countries—at least not during the period covered in this study. Aid that was ineffective, wasted, or used for corrupt purposes provoked public criticism of aid, and economic stresses generally in donor countries exerted powerful downward pressure on aid levels. Nor were the constituencies supporting development aid powerful enough by themselves to carry sizable amounts of foreign assistance through the annual political and budgetary processes of major aid-giving governments. Aid usually needed a broader base of support, and with that broader base came a mix of purposes for foreign aid. Where presidents and prime ministers needed aid for diplomatic purposes, these purposes often trumped aid's other purposes. And where compelling new purposes for aid arose, driven by emerging problems abroad, especially those that resonated with the publics and domestic interests in donor countries, these were added to the mix of aid's purposes. But from the perspective of 2005, it appeared that aid's development purposes—reflected in the increasing volume, country allocation, and use of aid, as well as in the policy statements and commitments of the leaders of major aid-giving countries and worldwide attention to aid and poverty issues—had achieved a greater prominence than at any time in the past.

CHAPTER 3

The United States: Morgenthau's Puzzle

This book opened with a comment by Professor Hans Morgenthau in the middle of the twentieth century that foreign aid was one of the "real innovations of the modern age." He went on to complain that "none has proven more baffling to both understanding and action."[1] Morgenthau, talking about US aid, was frustrated by its mix of purposes. Was it an instrument of Cold War containment? Was it an expression of American altruism? Shouldn't it be one or the other?

The fact is that US foreign aid has long been both and much more besides. The combination of diplomacy and development as the most prominent purposes of US aid was no accident of history. It was the result of the peculiarities of US domestic politics: the especially controversial nature of foreign aid, both on the right and left of the American political spectrum, and its usefulness to both; the struggle between diplomatic and development interests over the purposes of aid—the latter strengthening over time but never strong enough alone to carry forward aid appropriations year after year; and the nature of American political institutions, which tended to amplify controversies involving foreign aid. By the time of this writing (2006), it appeared that domestic political support for aid for development was strengthening with the growing engagement of the evangelical movement in development and related activities abroad. But the War on Terror had also elevated the prominence of diplomatic purposes in aid-giving. Thus, the tensions between these two purposes of US aid seemed set to continue in the twenty-first century.

A HISTORY OF US FOREIGN AID

Before 1945

The antecedents to foreign aid in the United States and elsewhere were described in the previous chapter. They include, first, relief for humanitarian disasters abroad. In the early decades of the American republic, the idea of such relief was actively and often successfully opposed in Congress as inappropriate and not permitted by the Constitution. But by the end of the nineteenth century, public aid for relief was widely accepted and provided. Further, through its army, the United States provided some assistance to improve public health, public works, and education to countries which it occupied militarily, such as Cuba after the Spanish-American War and, later, Haiti, the Dominican Republic, and Nicaragua. What was not funded through the military was for the most part financed through customs collections. These transfers resembled those from colonial metropoles to territories over which the metropole had assumed control and responsibility. Small amounts of technical assistance were provided to Latin American countries just before and during World War II, as mentioned in the previous chapter. But the idea that the US government should provide sizable amounts of public resources to independent countries to promote sustained economic and social progress there remained in the future.

Origins: From Diplomatic Expedience to an Enduring Dualism

Foreign aid as we know it today began in the United States as a diplomatic tool to respond to the nascent Cold War in Europe. We can almost pinpoint the moment of its inception. On a Friday late in February in 1947, the British ambassador, Lord Inverchapel, informed the Department of State that the British government would no longer be able to support Greece in resisting a communist-led insurgency or to assist Turkey to modernize its military in the face of pressures from its Soviet neighbor. It was clear immediately to Secretary of State George Marshall and President Harry Truman that the United States would have to act to help these countries maintain their independence and territorial integrity. And because the problems confronting Greece and Turkey were as much economic as military, the United States would need to provide economic assistance to stabilize and expand their economies if their populations and their governments were to resist the pressures of communism. The major challenge in providing such aid was to persuade a fiscally conservative Congress with strong isolationist tendencies to support the needed funding.

Dean Acheson, at that time undersecretary of state, describes the meeting called by President Truman on Wednesday, February 26, 1947, to brief leaders of Congress on the need for aid for Greece and Turkey:

> When we convened the next morning in the White House to open the subject with our congressional masters, I knew we were met at Armageddon.
> . . . No time was left for measured appraisal. In the past eighteen months, I said, Soviet pressure on the Straits, on Iran, and on northern Greece had brought the Balkans to the point where a highly possible Soviet breakthrough might open three continents to Soviet penetration. Like apples in a barrel infected by one rotten one, the corruption of Greece would infect Iran and all to the east. It would also carry infection to Africa through Asia Minor and Egypt, and to Europe through Italy and France, already threatened by the strongest domestic communist parties in Western Europe. The Soviet Union was playing one of the greatest gambles in history at minimal cost. It did not need to win all the possibilities. Even one or two offered immense gains. We and we alone were in a position to break up the play. These were the stakes that British withdrawal from the eastern Mediterranean offered to an eager and ruthless opponent.
> A long silence followed. Then Arthur Vandenberg [Chair of the Senate Foreign Relations Committee] said solemnly, "Mr. President, if you will say that to the Congress and the country, I will support you and I believe that most of its members will do the same."[2]

And so they did, agreeing to the president's appeal for $400 million for Greece and Turkey. Later that same year, the administration announced the Marshall Plan—a $13 billion, four-year program to help spur economic stabilization and recovery in Europe. Like the aid for Greece and Turkey, this program was driven by diplomatic concerns—the fear in Washington that Europe's faltering recovery from the war would bring communist parties to power in France and Italy. Humanitarian and commercial concerns also played a role in the rationale for Marshall Plan aid. But neither commerce nor human empathy would have been enough to persuade Congress (or, for that matter, the administration itself) to support these two aid programs. It took the gathering threat to US security represented by the beginning of the Cold War to move Congress and produce the "real innovation" that became foreign aid.

There was yet a third aid initiative during the Truman administration. In his 1949 inaugural address, President Truman proposed a "bold new program for making the benefits of our scientific advances and industrial progress available for the improvement and growth of underdeveloped areas."[3] What came to be known as the "Point Four" program of technical assistance was the forerunner of a more development-oriented aid program. But it was not at the time intended to signal a significant elevation of the development purpose of aid. It was to be small and, like the other aid initiatives, it was presented as a temporary program and justified primarily as a means of stopping the spread of communism.

Two events near the turn of the decade led to the prolongation and geographic spread of US foreign aid. The successful communist revolution in China in December 1949 and the invasion by North Korea of South Korea in June 1950 greatly heightened concerns in Washington about further communist gains. In 1951 President Truman moved to establish a "Mutual Security program" to include the final installments of aid from the Marshall Plan as well as additional aid to help the Europeans rearm and to persuade countries along the perimeter of the USSR and the PRC to join Cold War pacts or alliances with the United States. Without the Cold War imperative, US foreign aid would likely have been drastically cut or terminated at the end of the Marshall Plan. As one scholar of US aid observed, "The demise of development assistance was forestalled by its use in the security arsenal."[4]

President Dwight Eisenhower came to office in 1953 intending "to curtail" foreign aid.[5] He and several of his senior officials were unconvinced about both its appropriateness and effectiveness. The overall amount of assistance was declining in any case from the extraordinarily high levels of the Marshall Plan. However, aid soon proved too useful to eliminate. It was still needed to help the Europeans ease the economic burden of rearmament; to continue to support the establishment of a network of communications facilities, military bases, alliances, and relationships around the borders of the USSR and the PRC;[6] and to stabilize and expand the economies of key allies—for example, South Korea, which was recovering from war.

Several trends eventually forced the administration to rethink the heavy emphasis on using its aid to create Cold War alliances and pump funds into those countries directly exposed to communist pressures. First was the increasing importance in world affairs of developing countries generally. And second was the growing view among US policy-makers that supporting economic and social progress in those countries was much more important in shaping the outcome of the Cold War than simply providing their governments with aid to help stabilize their economies.

Elevating the importance of poor countries to the United States was the interest in them shown by the Soviets after the death of Stalin in 1953. Outside Moscow's allies in China, North Korea, and Vietnam, Stalin had had little time for the developing world. The USSR's new rulers—Nikita Khrushchev and Nikolai Bulganin—shared a more positive view of the importance of poor countries in Soviet diplomacy. In 1956 they visited India, Afghanistan, and Burma with offers of aid and technical assistance. Khrushchev told the Indians, "We are so near that if ever you call us from the mountain tops we will appear at your side."[7] (One can only imagine the alarm bells that remark set off in Washington.) The extension of Soviet aid to countries not already in Moscow's orbit signaled that the competition between the United States and the USSR for influence would now be worldwide. And the successful launch in 1957 of Sputnik—the first artificial satellite—intensified that competition, as the Soviets demonstrated that the communist system could produce spectacular technological and economic results and offered a real alternative to the capitalist West.

Also boosting the importance of developing countries were their own efforts to create political space for themselves between the United States and the USSR—to avoid being absorbed by either camp (and to be able to play one off against the other for maximum influence and advantage). The first "nonaligned" conference of developing countries was held in Bandung, Indonesia, in 1954. One of the movement's early demands, which developing countries began also to raise in annual United Nations debates and elsewhere, was for greatly expanded aid to further their development.

Just as the Cold War competition appeared to be spreading to the developing world generally, elements of the US policy community—including both liberals on the left, as well as conservatives on the right of the US political spectrum—began to criticize the apparent ineffectiveness thus far of foreign aid. Prominent members of Congress argued that using aid to "buy" Cold War alliances had proven to be a failure. In many cases, those allies, once bought, failed to stay bought. And in any event, the Cold War had spread, not diminished, despite US efforts to contain it. Many political conservatives argued that, because of these failures, aid should be cut back or terminated. Political liberals (like Senator William Fulbright, a powerful member of the Senate Foreign Relations Committee) urged that what was really needed was for economic assistance to be reoriented toward furthering the long-run development of poor countries so that at least their poverty would not drive them into the arms of the communists.

One of the people who promoted the idea of using aid to support long-run development was Walter Rostow of MIT. He had floated a theory of development and modernization—relatively straightforward and highly accessible to politicians and policy-makers—that proceeded through a series of stages, beginning with traditional societies and subsistence economies reliant on low-level technologies, which then moved to a period of "preconditioning" (rising aspirations and commitment on the part of the society and government to achieve modernization and growth), then through a period of economic "take off" to an era of sustained growth, followed by a drive to maturity, and, finally, arrival at a high mass-consumption society.[8] Where growth and modernization were lacking, argued Rostow, discontent and despair could lead to support for radical doctrines, including communism. Even where modernization did occur, the stresses of fundamental social and economic changes could also make radical ideologies attractive. Foreign aid could play a key role both in spurring modernization in developing countries and in reducing the stresses associated with that process.

Rostow not only had a theory of development and a justification for aid; he also had the access that enabled him to promote his ideas with senior officials in the Eisenhower administration from the early 1950s and in the mid-1950s to influential Democrats such as Senators William Fulbright and John F. Kennedy. (He later served on the National Security Council in the Kennedy administration.) With his ideas and access and his energy and perseverance, Rostow was the most successful intellectual entrepreneur of his day in influencing aid policies.[9] His ideas (which seem simplistic a half-century later) provided the policy world of the 1950s and 1960s with a reason for focusing aid on economic and social progress in poor countries and a rationale for a long-term policy of aid-giving since development and modernization would clearly not take place in a few short years.

The beginning of a reorientation in US aid became evident in the late 1950s. In 1957 the administration (with congressional support) separated economic from military assistance and created a Development Loan Fund (DLF) to provide concessional credits to developing countries worldwide (i.e., not, as in the past, just those in areas of potential conflict with Moscow) to promote their long-term growth. One year later, the administration supported the establishment of the International Development Association (IDA), a soft loan window of the World Bank.

The establishment of IDA grew out of an idea of Senator Mike Monroney, who proposed transferring to the World Bank the large quantity of local currencies, generated from repayments of earlier US aid loans, then in the accounts of the US Treasury, to be lent by the World Bank on "soft," or highly concessional, terms. It soon became apparent that loans in local currencies had many potential problems, including feeding inflation and balance of payments deficits in borrowing countries. But loans from the World Bank in hard currencies on soft terms did make sense, given the poverty of many of the poorer developing countries, the mounting international debts of others, and the absence of a soft loan window at the Bank. Further, developing countries in the UN had been pressing vigorously for nearly a decade for a Special UN Fund for Economic Development that would also make soft loans for development. Successive US administrations had resisted such an idea, not wishing to see another fund placed in the UN, where, on the basis of one state, one vote, developing countries would have a predominance of votes and control. (This was not the case with the World Bank, where voting power was tied to the amount of member states' contributions and where the United States, because of the proportion of votes it had, in effect had a veto.) With administration support, the Senate passed a resolution in support of the new World Bank lending facility, and the administration proceeded to negotiate it with other members of the Bank. The International Development Association of the World Bank began operations in 1960.

Another aid initiative at this time involved the establishment of the InterAmerican Development Bank (IADB). This regional development bank, a large proportion of the funding for which was to be provided by the United States, would make loans to countries of Central and South America and the Caribbean for development purposes. Such a bank had long been something countries in Latin America had wanted. But it took open manifestations of anti-American sentiment (including the violent demonstrations against Vice President Nixon when he visited the region in 1958) and the political and military gains by Fidel Castro in Cuba to persuade the administration to agree later that year to the establishment of the Inter-American Development Bank.

These new initiatives were added to a program of food aid (also known as Public Law 480, or PL480) created in 1954. This program involved transferring US agricultural surpluses abroad on concessional terms, to provide relief, spur development, support diplomatic goals, and, at times, to expand markets for US agricultural exports. (Food aid can provide additional food in emergencies or for food-for-work programs, as well as for school feeding programs and other nutrition interventions. It can also provide balance of payments and budgetary support for recipient governments where food replaces imports that would otherwise have been made or where it is sold— or "monetized"—by the government in the local market.[10]) In contrast to other programs of foreign aid, food aid proved relatively uncontroversial at home, having the strong backing of US farm organizations (especially the powerful commodity producers' groups whose products were being exported as food aid) as well as NGOs (many of which managed food-aid programs) and antihunger advocacy groups. The PL480 program also provided a model that, in ensuing decades, would be replicated by Japan and Europe as they set up their own food-aid (and agricultural surplus disposal) programs in the late 1960s and led to the creation of the World Food Program in 1963, which provided food aid for humanitarian emergencies.

Finally, toward the end of the Eisenhower administration, foreign aid began to rise modestly. It had begun in the late 1940s as an expedient to deal with short-term diplomatic crises arising from an expanding Cold War. But with the increasing emphasis on furthering long-term development as a means of achieving Cold War objectives, it had begun to move from being an expedient to an increasingly permanent element in the toolkit of US diplomacy. Indeed, President Eisenhower, after having announced at the beginning of his administration that he wanted to curtail aid, is reported to have offered toward the end of his time in office "to give up part of his own salary to 'meet the pressing need of adequate funds for foreign aid.'"[11]

The Kennedy Administration—A Focus on Development as Diplomacy

John F. Kennedy became president in 1961, bringing with him an enthusiasm for foreign aid that was replicated by no other twentieth-century president. In a special message to Congress shortly after taking office, Kennedy warned, "There exists, in the 1960s, an historic opportunity for a major economic assistance effort by the free industrialized nations to move more than half the people of the less-developed nations in to self-sustained economic growth. . . . we are launching a Decade of Development on which will depend, substantially, the kind of world in which we and our children shall live."[12] It was in Kennedy's administration that promoting development became an established priority of US foreign aid, although, for Kennedy and others in his administration, development was still primarily a means to the end of Cold War containment.

The president undertook several important initiatives involving US aid: he launched the Alliance for Progress for Latin America, and he offered aid to the burgeoning number of newly independent African countries. He put pressure on governments in Western Europe and Japan to take up the burden of aiding development abroad. And in what was arguably his most lasting legacy in foreign aid, Kennedy reorganized the way the US government managed its aid programs.

The Alliance for Progress

The Alliance for Progress was inspired in part by the fear that, with a Marxist government installed in Havana since 1960 under the leadership of Fidel Castro, the temptations of communism might become more immediate and compelling to other countries in the Western Hemisphere. Foreign aid to spur reforms (e.g., land reform and tax reform) and to finance new projects in education and infrastructure would, it was hoped, promote modernization, development and democracy and diminish radical impulses.[13] Between 1960 and 1964, US aid to Latin America (which had been small in the past) rose fivefold—from $157 million, or 5 percent of US aid, to $989 million, or 25 percent of US aid overall.[14] Also in the early 1960s, much of sub-Saharan Africa gained independence. The Kennedy administration offered aid to most of these new countries, increasing assistance to the region from $38 million in 1960 to nearly $220 million in 1964. Additionally, the president created the Peace Corps to send Americans to developing countries to help in technical assistance, training, and managing small aid projects. With these and other increases, overall US aid levels rose roughly by one-third during this period, from just under $3 billion in 1960 to just over $4 billion in 1964. Figure 3.1 shows US aid from 1946 to 2003.

The Kennedy administration also put pressure on other governments—especially the Germans and Japanese (now well on their way to recovery from the Second World War) to expand their own aid programs. Persuading the Germans, in particular, to commit to a major increase in foreign aid was not just a means to expand overall aid levels worldwide but also a tactic of the Kennedy administration to encourage the Congress to raise US aid significantly on the understanding that other governments were also raising their aid. (Kennedy used the prospect of increases in US aid to persuade the Europeans to expand their aid as well—a case of "double-edged diplomacy" if ever there was one.[15]) The administration took an active role in the Development Assistance Committee (DAC) of the OECD—the international club of aid-giving governments created a US initiative to exchange views, coordinate aid, and, most importantly, to exert pressure on one another to expand their aid programs.[16] Finally, the Kennedy administration proposed that the UN proclaim the 1960s as the first Decade of Development and

FIG. 3.1. TOTAL US AID (NET)

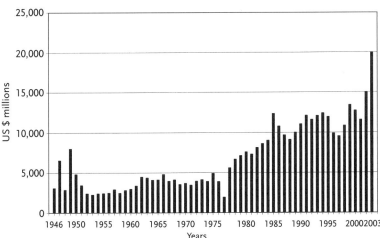

Sources: USAID, *Greenbook,* http://qesdb.cdie.org/gbk/; http://www.usaid.gov/policy/budget/cbj2006/pdf/fy2006summtabs1_150acct.pdf (both sites accessed October 2005).

Note: The large increase in aid in 2003 is in part because of reconstruction expenditures in Iraq and Afghanistan.

support the establishment of a target of 1 percent of GNP in financial flows (private and concessional) from rich countries to poor countries. All of these efforts were made to encourage other countries to raise their aid levels.[17]

While the efforts of the Kennedy administration produced an expansion in US aid, the willingness of Congress to support such an increase did not last long. By 1962 aid's critics complained that USAID was too slow and had too few results to show for its efforts, particularly in Latin America. That year, Congress slashed the administration's request for aid by 20 percent.[18] Behind these criticisms (which were rather hasty given the time it takes to set up both a new agency and to start a major new program) were conservatives in Congress who continued to challenge the appropriateness of the United States providing aid at all and who were skeptical of its ability to bring about beneficial economic and social change abroad. One particularly well-placed member of Congress—Otto Passman, a Southern Democrat who was chairman of a key foreign aid committee (the Foreign Operations Appropriations Subcommittee of the House Appropriations Committee) and in charge of getting aid appropriations through the Congress—attacked aid as "ill-conceived, badly executed, unrealistic, wasteful and expensive."[19] Others feared that foreign aid would lead the United States into protracted engagements throughout the world that could prove costly and difficult ever to shed. The new aid programs started in Africa especially fueled these fears where, it was felt, the Europeans should take primary responsibility for development in their former territories. In 1963 a blue-ribbon committee of private notables, chosen by President Kennedy to study and (he hoped) recommend increased aid, instead gave voice to these fears, concluding that "we are trying to do too much for too many too soon, that we are over-extended in resources and under-compensated in results and that no end of foreign aid is either in sight or in mind."[20] These criticisms and opposition to aid in Congress and among elements of the public led to a decline in US aid during most of the remainder of the decade. Foreign aid may have become a permanent tool of US foreign policy, but it remained a highly controversial one.

Organizing US Foreign Aid

One of the most important of Kennedy's foreign aid initiatives was to unify two existing aid agencies, the Development Loan Fund and the International Cooperation Agency (ICA) (part of the Department of State and responsible for technical assistance), into a single new one—the Agency for International Development (USAID)—that would be semi-independent from the Department of State. (Responsibilities for US contributions to the World Bank and regional development banks would remain in the Department of the Treasury.) He announced his intention to reorganize US aid with the following critique of existing arrangements (which is still heard today):

> no objective supporter of foreign aid can be satisfied with the existing program—actually a multiplicity of programs. Bureaucratically fragmented, awkward and slow, its administration is diffused over a haphazard and irrational structure covering at least four departments and several other agencies. The program is based on a series of legislative measures and administrative procedures conceived at different times and for different purposes, many of them now obsolete, inconsistent and unduly rigid and thus unsuited for our present needs and purposes. Its weaknesses have begun to undermine confidence in our effort both here and abroad.[21]

There was an extended debate in the administration, in Congress, and among policy analysts on how a new aid organization should be organized and where it should be located bureaucratically. A number of studies, for example, those done by the Brookings Institution (a Washington think tank) and the International Cooperation Agency, urged the establishment of a new, cabinet-level agency that would combine existing aid programs. Some, like the Ford Foundation, suggested instead that existing aid programs be merged and placed in the Department of State under the direction of an undersecretary. Aid planners resisted putting the new agency within the State Department for fear that its development mission might be overwhelmed by diplomatic imperatives. They were also reluctant to create a cabinet-level agency that would be fully independent of other agencies, because they wanted to ensure that the new agency would be to some extent supervised by the State Department and its aid would continue to serve diplomatic purposes. In the end, it was decided to create a semi-independent, subcabinet-level aid agency whose administrator would report to the secretary of state and the president. They decided, in effect, to institutionalize aid's emerging dual purposes of diplomacy and development, giving both an organizational voice within the US government.[22]

It was also decided at this time that assistance managed by USAID would be conditioned on the recipient government having a plan for its country's long-term development. This was the beginning of a country programming process (in contrast to ad hoc funding of aid projects and programs as opportunities arose), in which the overall needs of a developing country were considered in decisions on how to program foreign aid—specifically, what to finance and where to finance it. USAID was further professionalized in the 1970s as it adopted the "logical framework"—a structured approach for planning aid projects—and created an evaluation service. From the beginning, USAID was a highly decentralized agency, with field missions responsible for proposing projects and programs and for overseeing their implementation. (Projects themselves were increasingly implemented by consulting firms and NGOs during the 1970s as USAID moved from being a "retailer" to a "wholesaler" of foreign aid.) Over the years, field missions gained the authority to allocate funds as well, albeit within budgetary and programmatic limits set by Washington. USAID officials also put a strong emphasis on basing the allocation of aid on the development performance of recipient governments—an early effort to be selective in providing aid. It was here that the diplomatic and development purposes of US aid most frequently collided. The good performers—those governments that were capable, clean, and committed to development—did not always carry much importance diplomatically, and the diplomatically important countries were often "poor performers." Perhaps the best-known example of the latter was the Democratic Republic of the Congo (formerly Zaire), which was regarded in Washington as diplomatically important (receiving $1.1 billion in aid from the United States between 1960 and 1990) but was so corrupt and poorly led that the aid produced little of lasting development value. As was intended, it likely helped strengthen the government of Mobutu Sese Seko in the face of internal and external threats (and Mobutu's own assertions that the country might fall apart or turn toward Moscow should he be overthrown) by signaling US support for his regime. This tension between the developmental and diplomatic purposes of aid has produced a long-term problem in US aid: its effectiveness is assessed on the basis of its achieving its development goals, but where it is provided primarily for diplomatic purposes, the ability of aid to be effective developmentally may be impaired by the nature of the regime receiving it.[23]

By the mid-1960s, the organization of US foreign aid for much of the remainder of the century was nearly complete. It turned out to be one of the more complicated arrangements of any aid-giving government. The three major bilateral aid programs were Development Assistance (DA), Security Supporting Assistance (SSA, later renamed the Economic Support Fund, or ESF), and food aid (also called PL480). Development Assistance was allocated and managed by USAID, with some negotiations on the country allocation with the Department of State. Its main purpose was funding development-oriented activities. But it was sometimes provided for diplomatic or security purposes. SSA/ESF was allocated primarily by the Department of State (often with some consultation with USAID). USAID managed the implementation of SSA/ESF. Initially intended as balance of payments support to ease the cost of security-related expenses in recipient countries, it eventually came to be used to fund development-oriented projects and programs as well.

For food aid, whose budget was located in the Department of Agriculture but which was managed primarily by USAID, country allocations for most of the period of this study were determined by an interagency group made up of the Department of Agriculture, Department of State, Treasury Department, USAID, and Office of Management and Budget (OMB). In the 1990s the interagency group was disbanded and both the allocation and management of the humanitarian and development-oriented elements of this program were located in USAID, which still consulted, however, with the other agencies, especially with the Departments of State and Agriculture. Food aid's main purpose was furthering development and providing emergency relief. But it was sometimes allocated in support of diplomatic purposes, especially in Indochina, where it was used to ease the import costs of the governments of South Vietnam and Cambodia while the US was involved in the war there. And in its early decades, it was used to develop markets abroad for US agricultural exports.

The Treasury Department was in charge of US participation in the multilateral development banks (like the World Bank) and, later, debt relief, while the State Department managed voluntary contributions to most UN development agencies, such as the UN Development Program (included in International Organizations and Programs, or IO&P) and later set up and managed its own sizable fund to support refugees, especially those settling in the United States, as well as programs associated with drug control in cocaine- and heroin-producing countries. (The role of foreign aid in drug-control programs was to provide coca farmers with alternative crops to grow in place of coca—called "alternative development" programs. These programs were concentrated in Andean countries, where most coca was grown, but they had spotty success. Carrots just did not bring the same income as coca.)

The Peace Corps was an independent agency and managed programs of volunteers working in schools, community projects, and governments in developing countries. In the 1970s the InterAmerican Development Foundation—a small government agency—was set up to fund community-based activities in Central and South America. An African Development Foundation was set up in 1980 to finance similar activities in that region.

The relationship between the organizations participating in aid decisions and the several aid programs that they governed and managed in 1965 are set out in figure 3.2. The ovals represent the agencies, the squares rep-

FIG. 3.2. THE ORGANIZATION OF US FOREIGN AID, 1965

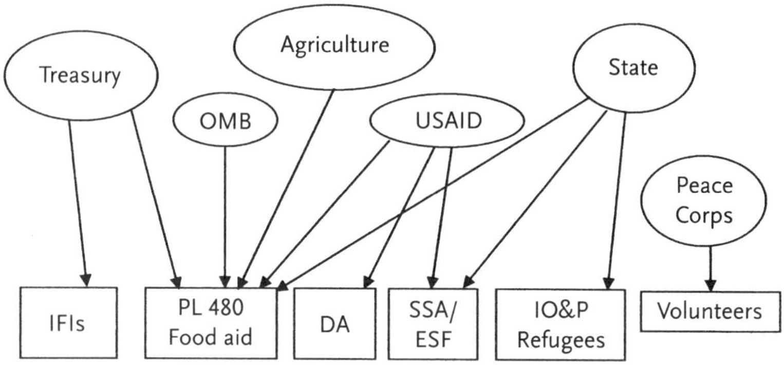

resent the programs, and the arrows represent the direction of decision-making and implementation responsibilities.

Development Becomes an End: Aid under Presidents Johnson, Nixon, and Ford

Criticisms of foreign aid continued through the Johnson administration (1963–67). Aid for Latin America diminished as the threat of communist revolution abated. Aid to Africa fell as fears of an expansion of Soviet influence there also diminished and hopes for democracy were overturned by a spate of military coups. Additionally, criticisms of too extensive US engagement worldwide led the administration to close a number of its aid missions abroad (especially in sub-Saharan Africa) during the second half of the 1960s. While aid for Vietnam, Cambodia, and Laos rose with the intensifying war and the deepening US involvement in Indochina, overall levels of aid drifted downward from the mid-1960s to the mid-1970s.

As had been the case with President Kennedy, President Johnson, facing serious criticisms of aid, created a committee to study foreign aid and make recommendations for its reform. The General Advisory Committee on Foreign Aid (called the "Perkins committee," after its chairman) produced a report that recommended that a larger portion of US aid be channeled through multilateral development banks as a means of reducing the diplomatic element in aid allocations. This report came too late in the Johnson administration to be the basis for action. It was followed in 1970 by a report requested by President Nixon (and called for by the Congress) that was known as the "Peterson Report," which also recommended that US multilateral institutions become the "major channel" for development assistance.[24] The recommendations of the Peterson Report formed the basis for a plan by President Nixon to undertake a fundamental reorganization of foreign aid, intended by its supporters to put greater distance between the diplomatic and developmental uses of aid and to upgrade the latter. President Nixon proposed to Congress that USAID be eliminated and three separate US government agencies be created to replace it: an International Development Bank to manage aid loans; an International Development Institute for research and technical assistance; and an International Development Council to coordinate trade, finance, and investment policies vis-à-vis developing countries. Congress declined to act on such a radical reorganization, and Nixon, lukewarm about the idea and with many other pressing issues to deal with, did not push it strongly.

Congress did enact an important change in US aid policies, however, that strengthened the developmental focus of that aid. In 1971 political liberals—unhappy about the war in Indochina and the large amount of military assistance the United States was providing abroad—joined with conservatives who disliked aid in any case to vote down for the first time an aid authorization bill.[25]

Congressional refusal to pass aid legislation led the administration and key members of Congress to search for policy initiatives that would restore at least liberal support for foreign aid. At that time, research purported to show that economic growth during the previous decade had not "trickled down" to benefit the poor and may even have made some of them worse off. These findings coincided with an increasing emphasis within the US development community on growth with equity, participation by the poor in development decisions, and the use of aid directly to help the poor improve their quality of life and income-earning capabilities.[26] With the advice of the Overseas Development Council (a Washington think tank specializing in development issues) and the support of the administration, in 1973 the Congress passed new aid legislation that mandated a shift in the use of US aid toward funding projects for the "basic human needs" of the poor in developing countries, in effect, underlining the development purpose of aid both in its country allocation (emphasizing poor countries) and its use for such things as primary education, primary health care, and agricultural development (since most of the poor were in rural areas).

President Nixon also sought to "emphasize the humanitarian aspect" of foreign aid in the rationales for providing it. For example, in his message to Congress on foreign aid in 1969, the president declared, "There is a moral quality in this nation that will not permit us to close our eyes to the want in this world. . . . We have shown the world that a great nation must also be a good nation. We are doing what is right to do."[27] Whether Nixon, despite his hard-headed realist image, was also motivated by altruistic concerns for helping the poor abroad or whether (as seems likely) he was simply trying to balance an aggressive military posture in Indochina with more humanitarian policies involving development aid to garner political support from liberals at home sufficient to pass aid legislation, his remarks, together with increased US aid to multilateral banks and his emphasis on basic human needs, served to elevate the development purpose of aid as an important end in itself as well as a means of fighting the Cold War. This change in emphasis did not immediately lead to a sustained increase in the overall level of US aid. But several events later in the decade did.

Meanwhile, another indication of the rising importance of development as a purpose of US aid was the increasing percentage of that aid allocated to multilateral aid agencies, in particular, the World Bank, as shown in figure 3.3. During the Nixon administration, a variety of official reports and individuals (including Robert McNamara, the president of the World Bank) urged that more US aid be channeled through these institutions as a means of increasing the developmental purpose and impact of that aid.

Gerald Ford became president in 1974 after President Nixon was forced to resign. That was the year in which the drought in the Sahelian region of Africa that had begun in the early 1970s culminated in serious suffering and starvation in Ethiopia. In the same year, there were floods in Bangladesh, also leading to famine and suffering there. Both were widely reported in the US media and led to a quick jump in emergency aid. Between 1974 and 1975, US food aid more than doubled and aid to one of the most affected countries—Bangladesh—tripled. Thereafter, the overall volume of US aid began

FIG. 3.3. MULTILATERAL AID AS A PERCENTAGE OF TOTAL US AID

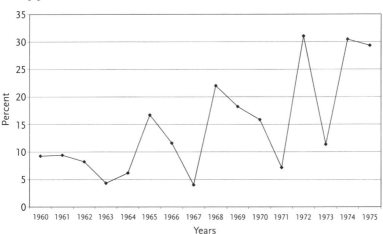

Source: DAC, "International Development Statistics (IDS) Online," http://www.oecd.org/dac/stats/idsonline/ (accessed October 2005).

Note: The variations in levels on this rising trend reflect the cycle of replenishments to the International Development Association of the World Bank.

to rise steadily. It seems quite likely that the well publicized problems of famine and human suffering and the broader specter of world food shortages during the first half of the 1970s encouraged the administration to begin a multiyear expansion of aid, predisposed the US public to support an increase in aid (framed as part of the fight against world hunger), and eased for a time congressional resistance to such an increase. Several public opinion polls sponsored by the Chicago Council on Foreign Relations during the 1970s support this observation. In 1974 only 8 percent of those interviewed thought "world hunger" (which was often regarded as both starvation and the poverty that contributed to it) was one of the two or three important foreign policy problems facing the United States, while 18 percent thought that cutting foreign aid was a high priority. By 1979, 16 percent thought hunger was one of the most important problems facing the world and only 1 percent thought cutting foreign aid was a priority. Another poll done in 1978 found that 59 percent of those interviewed thought that combating world hunger should be among US foreign policy goals.[28] A further reflection of the increased concern about world hunger was the creation during this decade of a number of NGOs dedicated to fighting that problem: Food for the Hungry (established 1971), Bread for the World (1972), Institute for Food and Development Policies (established 1975, later renamed Food First), and Action against Hunger (1979). Several of these NGOs—especially Bread for the World—became active advocates of aid to help the "hungry" (an emotive term used by many to refer not only to a shortage of food but to poverty and human deprivation generally).

The second event that affected US aid during the administration of President Ford involved its use for diplomatic purposes. It had its beginnings before Ford moved into the Oval Office. In 1973 the Egyptians and Syrians attacked the Israelis in the Yom Kippur War. After some gains, the Egyptians and Syrians were pushed back by the Israeli army. A ceasefire was called as Israel was threatening to surround Egypt's Third Army and the Soviets were threatening to intervene to protect it. In the aftermath of that war, the Ford administration sought to bring about a comprehensive peace settlement between the two adversaries, and aid—first to Israel and then to Egypt— became a tool of this "peace-making" diplomacy. Such a settlement was important to the United States in part because of Cold War concerns regarding Soviet influence in an unstable, strategically located region with large amounts of oil (making it, in part, an element in US Cold War diplomacy) and in part because of ties of affinity with Israel felt by many Americans (and not solely Jewish Americans). President Ford did not achieve a settlement, but he did gain an interim agreement between the two countries that reaffirmed the ceasefire of 1973 and committed them to settle their differences peacefully in the future. US aid to both governments was a support and incentive to their keeping the agreement. In 1975 the United States provided Israel with $350 million, up from $50 million the previous year, and in the following year, the administration provided Egypt with $245 million, up from $80 million in 1975. These commitments caused Egypt and Israel to become the largest recipients of US aid in the world. Combined with rising aid in response to emergency needs, a diplomacy of peace-making in the Middle East also helped to boost overall US aid levels.

Foreign Aid from Carter through Reagan

President Jimmy Carter brought two important things to US foreign aid: an emphasis on human rights and negotiation of the Camp David Accords between Israel and Egypt, formalizing a peace agreement between the two governments. Shortly after he took office in 1977, President Carter described a commitment to human rights as a "fundamental tenet of our foreign policy."[29] US aid, including US support for loans made by international financial institutions like the World Bank, would be conditioned on the human rights performance of recipient governments. This policy was applied with some flexibility, especially to bilateral aid, depending on US interests in particular countries. But the overt emphasis on a government's human rights performance as a criterion for aid represented a departure from the past as well as from the practices of most other donor governments.[30]

The Camp David Accords were signed in 1978. Albeit there was no reference to foreign aid in the Accords,[31] it was generally understood in Washington that sizable aid programs, both to Israel and Egypt, would be important to sustain them. And while the annual levels of economic aid to these two countries varied somewhat, they were expected normally to be authorized at $800 million for Egypt and $1.2 billion for Israel annually. The approximately $2 billion per year for these two countries equaled a quarter of US bilateral aid annually through most of the remainder of the century and solidified "peace-making" as a prominent diplomatic purpose of US foreign aid.

Thus, by the end of the presidencies of Kennedy, Johnson, Nixon, Ford, and Carter, the United States had a truly dualistic aid program—with a strong diplomatic orientation (including both Cold War containment and, now, peace-making objectives in the Middle East) combined with a significant development purpose. The diplomatic purpose was most evident in the choice of the major recipients of US aid, but development also played a role in that choice, particularly in sub-Saharan Africa. Development purposes played the key role in decisions on the use of aid, in both diplomatically and developmentally important countries. To illustrate this complicated mixture of motives, consider the twenty countries that received the largest amount of US bilateral economic assistance in 1980 (listed in descending order):

1. Egypt
2. Israel
3. India
4. Turkey
5. Indonesia
6. Bangladesh
7. Sudan
8. Philippines
9. Jordan
10. Somalia
11. Sri Lanka
12. Pakistan
13. El Salvador
14 Dominican Republic
15. Kenya
16. Peru
17. Honduras
18. Zambia
19. Nicaragua
20. Cambodia[32]

Aid to Israel and Egypt was associated with peace-making and regional security, as was aid to Jordan, Sudan, and, to an extent, Turkey. Aid to Cambodia involved postconflict recovery in a diplomatically sensitive region. Aid to the Philippines was influenced by the presence of US military bases there. Development concerns were strongly reflected in the levels of aid to Bangladesh, Sri Lanka, and Bolivia. Aid to most of the rest of these countries was influenced both by diplomatic and developmental purposes—for example, in Kenya, Somalia, and Zambia, where problems of poverty and/or Cold War regional strategic considerations played a role in their relatively large amounts of aid for these countries—as was aid to El Salvador, Nicaragua, Honduras, and Peru (where left-wing politics and insurgency were on the rise). Aid to India and Pakistan involved diplomacy (specifically, a degree of Cold War balancing and regional peace-making) as well as development. Many of the smaller aid programs not listed here—those, for instance, in Burkina Faso, Botswana, Benin, Mali, Nepal, and numerous others—were motivated far more by development than by diplomatic purposes. And although limited in their individual sizes, the smaller programs, together with aid to multilateral institutions, added up to half of US foreign aid in 1980.

Finally, there was another effort to reorganize US foreign aid during the Carter administration—this time, originating in the Congress. Senator Hubert Humphrey, frustrated by the fragmentation in US foreign aid, proposed the creation of an International Development Cooperation Agency (IDCA) to replace USAID and have significant responsibility for US aid to multilateral development banks, international development organizations, the Peace Corps, and the Overseas Private Investment Corporation. The source of this initiative may, in fact, have come from USAID staff to preempt what seemed like an attempt on the part of the State Department to seize control of USAID's budget. Early in the administration, the policy planning staff of the Department of State, in an unusual move, decided to review and revise USAID's budget proposal to the White House for the coming fiscal year. In theory, USAID's budget always went first to the secretary of state for transmission to the White House. In practice, the budget had typically been negotiated at a lower level between USAID and State Department officers, and the review by the secretary was perfunctory. This sudden change in process by the State Department appeared to USAID as a form of takeover.[33] The IDCA director would report only to the president. This was an effort to move toward a more unified, more autonomous, and more powerful development aid agency—in effect, upgrading the priority of the development purpose of aid. It provoked considerable opposition from affected government departments and agencies and did not pass in Congress. But it did lead President Carter to issue an executive order creating a much less powerful IDCA to "coordinate" all the programs included in the congressional bills. Little coordination actually took place, however, because IDCA had no real authority over any of the programs, personnel, or budgets in its purview. And, not surprisingly, none of the agencies with responsibilities for aid programs—which included the Treasury Department, the Peace Corps, the Overseas Private Investment Corporation, and USAID—were willing to cede IDCA any of their authorities. IDCA eventually became moribund and was finally eliminated by President Bill Clinton.

The Reagan administration came to office in 1981 as one of the most ideologically conservative regimes in recent memory and was expected to reform and reduce US aid. One of its first actions was a proposal from David Stockman, the new director of the powerful Office of Management and Budget, to terminate completely US contributions to IDA and the soft loan windows of the regional development banks.[34] I was just leaving my post as deputy assistant secretary of state for Africa as this incident occurred. I had the impression that all the country-desk officers in the Africa Bureau had called US ambassadors in their capitals to inform African governments of this policy and informally to encourage them to ask their ambassadors in Washington to make a démarche at the State Department in opposition to the proposal. I understand that such a démarche was in fact made. This is a case of *gaiatsu*—a technique common in Japan, in which Japanese officials ask foreign government officials to lobby the Japanese government on issues favored by the Japanese officials— which I will discuss in the next chapter of this book. Opposition to such a drastic change from the Department of State, from US allies, and from developing countries led the administration to back off and instead to cut its IDA contribution significantly, producing a drop in replenishments for IDA by a quarter as other governments reduced their contributions accordingly. From averaging one-third of US aid in the years 1978–80, aid to multilateral institutions fell to an average of 22 percent during the years 1986–89.[35] However, the administration soon found the World Bank useful in promoting what President Reagan called "the magic of the marketplace"—specifically, the importance of economic reforms that promoted free markets and reduced government's role in the economy—and the fervor to reduce the aid provided by the World Bank and other international financial institutions waned.

Despite the Reagan administration's initial skepticism toward aid, bilateral US assistance during its eight years in office increased steadily, elevated by a humanitarian crisis in Africa and a Cold War skirmish in Central America. The suffering resulting from a drought and famine in Ethiopia in 1984–85 was brought to the world's attention by a film of emaciated and dying children, broadcast first on the BBC and later on US evening news programs. The film provoked a public outcry and demands that the US government act immediately to boost humanitarian aid. This it did, increasing aid to sub-Saharan Africa by 60 percent between 1983 and 1986—or from $900 million to $1.4 billion. (Private contributions to relieve suffering, stimulated by rock star Bob Geldof and his "Live Aid" concerts to benefit those affected by the drought in Ethiopia, also reached record levels in the United States and elsewhere.) In the years after the drought was over, the United States continued to aid sub-Saharan Africa at around $1 billion per year. The humanitarian emergency in that region again sensitized the American public and elites to the deepening economic crisis there and supported a sustained increase in aid for African countries.

A second factor supporting an increase in US aid during the 1980s arose out of the last major Cold War clash, this time in Central America. It involved the Marxist-oriented Sandinista revolution in Nicaragua and the civil war in El Salvador that pitted a Sandinista-supported guerilla group against a conservative government. The Reagan administration used aid to fortify existing governments in the region against leftist challenges and rewarded those governments, like Honduras, that supported US policies (including giving refuge to the "Contras"—a US-backed guerilla movement challenging the Sandinista regime). Between 1980 and 1990, US aid to Central America and the Caribbean rose from $250 million per year to just over $1 billion. (By 1996, in the aftermath of the change of regime in Managua and the end of the Contra war, US aid to this area dropped back to just $175 million.) Thus, the combination of a diplomatic crisis in Central America and a humanitarian emergency and deepening development crisis in Africa combined to support a continual increase in the overall volume of US aid in the 1980s. By 1989 US aid was nearly $10 billion and 30 percent higher than it had been in 1980.

Aid in a Time of Transition: Presidents Bush and Clinton

The 1990s saw the end of the Cold War and, with it, the loss of a major rationale for foreign aid. It was also a decade when the development rationale appeared to weaken, with an erosion of confidence in the effectiveness of aid in furthering development, while a number of new purposes for aid emerged. These changes coincided with efforts on the part of the Clinton administration to cut the federal budget and efforts on the part of militant Republicans to cut the size of government, all resulting in the greatest decrease in aid since the end of the Marshall Plan. However, a reaction to further deep cuts and a mobilization to advocate a halt to such cuts on the part of development-oriented NGOs, a number of business groups, and elements in the foreign policy community, plus an easing in budget constraints, brought an end to cuts in aid in the latter half of the decade and a gradual increase in overall aid levels.

Aid for Political and Economic Transitions

George Herbert Walker Bush was sworn in as president in 1989 just as the Cold War was ending. In June of that year, the first noncommunist government since the Second World War took power in Poland; in October, the Hungarians adopted a new, democratic constitution; in November, the Berlin Wall came down; December saw the Velvet Revolution in Czechoslovakia and the execution of Rumanian communist dictator Nicolae Ceauşescu and his wife. The Bush administration moved quickly to support the transitions in these countries and later, in 1991, to aid the new countries emerging out of the collapse of the USSR. By 1994 aid for transitions had risen to over $2.5 billion for twenty-six countries in Eastern Europe and the former Soviet Union. After the spike (mainly in aid for Russia) in 1994, aid for transitions declined during the middle of the decade and remained below the levels of the early 1990s. Within these changes, aid was shifting from the more successful countries, such as Poland, Hungary, the Czech Republic, Slovakia, and the Baltics, to those with weaker economies and more challenging political transitions, like Russia, the Ukraine, the Caucasus, and countries of Central Asia. Aid for transitions continued to decline during the early part of the new century, dropping by just over one quarter between 2000 and 2004. Figure 3.4 shows the total amount of US aid to countries in transition.

FIG. 3.4. US AID TO COUNTRIES IN TRANSITION

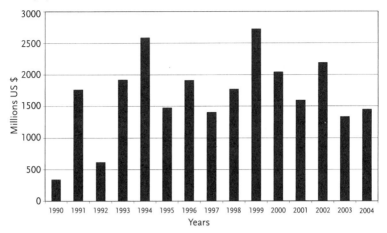

Sources: 1990–2004: USAID, *Greenbook,* http://qesdb.cdie.org/gbk/.

Note: The spikes in 1994 and 1999 were in response to economic crises in Russia.

Aid for Democracy Promotion

Also in the early 1990s, demands for multiparty elections and greater democracy spread throughout sub-Saharan Africa. The Bush administration began to allocate funds for this purpose, for example to finance elections, strengthen of the rule of law, support civil society, and improve governance. To anchor the prominence of this purpose, both the Department of State and USAID created democracy centers or bureaus in the early 1990s. For the diplomats, democracy promotion was a natural outgrowth of the human rights policies that gained prominence in the Carter administration. President Clinton, echoing scholarly discourse of the time, declared that democracy strengthened international security because democratic governments were believed disinclined to war against one another. For the development community, it was increasingly asserted that democracy was a precondition for development—where governments were not transparent and accountable to their population, corruption, mismanagement, repression, and conflict could impede economic and social progress.

Aid to Address Global Problems

Similarly, what I have termed "global problems" also gained in priority at that time as a purpose of US aid, especially with the establishment in the early 1990s of a Global Affairs Bureau in USAID and an undersecretary for global affairs in the Department of State.[36] In the early 1990s, it was the issue of the environment that engaged the attention of US policy-makers, especially in the wake of the UN Conference on Environment and Development in Rio de Janeiro in 1992. However, by the end of the decade, issues of international health—especially the devastating impact of HIV/AIDS in Africa and its spread to other parts of the world—gained in importance, with the United States taking the lead in funding programs of prevention and research from the early part of the decade.

Aid and Conflicts

Finally, the numerous and prolonged civil conflicts of the 1990s led the United States (along with many other aid-giving governments) to support postconflict recovery and avoid the slide back into conflict that often occurs after civil wars. Sometimes, aid was offered both as an incentive for peacemaking (which I have classified as a diplomatic purpose of aid) and a means of funding for postconflict reconstruction, such as the $500 million fund for the Balkans, an incentive for peace-making at the negotiations on the Dayton Accords and later a source of funding for postconflict reconstruction.[37] To address the increasing need for postconflict aid, USAID created the Office of Transition Initiatives in 1994, with the capacity to move rapidly into postconflict areas as soon as is feasible, with funding for quick-impact projects at the community level, for national reconciliation efforts, and for support for media campaigns against nationalist propaganda, as well as for the more common aid-funded postconflict activities mentioned above. By 2000 this office had an annual budget of $50 million and had worked in Haiti, Cambodia, the Balkans, Colombia, Sierra Leone, Liberia, Sri Lanka, Indonesia, Angola, East Timor, and a number of other postconflict areas.

The end of the Cold War did not bring an end to the diplomatic uses of US foreign aid. A considerable amount of that aid was still deployed for peace-making in the Middle East, the Balkans, and elsewhere. But without the Cold War rationale, the priority of aid diminished considerably in the foreign policy community. I base this statement on my experience in a senior position in USAID in the Clinton administration. There was opposition in the White House to even mentioning aid in the president's speeches, there was no one in the National Security Council in the Clinton administration responsible for aid issues, and there was little attention paid to aid issues in the foreign policy think tank community (e.g., the Council on Foreign Relations)—all manifestations of a lack of interest in this instrument of foreign policy. The two exceptions to this generalization among the senior officials of the Clinton administration were Vice President Al Gore, who had a particular interest in aid for the environment, and First Lady Hillary

Clinton, who supported aid for development purposes. Mrs. Clinton played a quiet but very important role in issues involving the amount of US aid and even the existence of USAID as a separate agency.

Within the development community, there was the continual conflict over the relative importance of economic reform (centered in the World Bank) and more direct interventions to reduce poverty (primarily the NGO community). There was also a growing sense that aid had not been as effective as hoped, especially in Africa—a concern that was deepened by a number of publications, both by aid's traditional critics (such as the Heritage Foundation) and its supporters and practitioners (such as the World Bank).[38] Finally, a number of US NGOs, including human rights groups and environmentalists, attacked the World Bank for neglecting or damaging the environment and human rights, especially with its large infrastructure projects, and hurting the poor with its structural adjustment programs. Some of these groups, in the past usually among the supporters of foreign aid, appealed to Congress to cut or eliminate US contributions to the World Bank and thus began to undercut the Bank's supporters there (who were never many in number in any case). While the new president of the World Bank, James Wolfensohn, who took office in 1995, sought to address the problems raised by the NGOs and thereby restore support for the institution, the attacks by influential groups inevitably contributed to the malaise in development aid during this period.[39]

While these changes made foreign aid vulnerable to cuts, it took two elements in the US political scene to make cuts a reality. One was the efforts on the part of the Clinton administration and Congress to reduce the federal deficit, which was nearly 5 percent of GNP at the time he took office. Foreign aid was a "discretionary program"—one where expenditures were not mandated by law—and so the president could propose to reduce it without going to Congress for changes in the authorizing legislation. Added to the president's cuts in aid in the 1994 and 1995 budgets were the additional cuts made by the new Republican-controlled Congress, beginning in 1995. In the 1994 election, for the first time in forty years, Republicans gained control of the House of Representatives. As part of efforts to reduce the budgetary deficit and the size of government itself (and reflecting open hostility felt by many of the newly elected and often militant conservatives), the Republicans slashed aid further. Overall US aid fell from over $12 billion in 1993 to $9 billion in 1996. And because several of the largest country programs were protected from cuts—the $2 billion annually for Israel and Egypt—the decreases fell disproportionately on development aid. Thus, aid in the Development Assistance program (the most developmentally oriented bilateral aid program) as a portion of total US bilateral aid declined from nearly one-third in 1991 to one-quarter in 2000. In addition, there were numerous congressional "earmarks" and "directives" involving bilateral aid.

In the annual appropriations process, the Congress has the power to impose legislative earmarks on how aid is to be used or what countries or organizations receive it. Congress can also write "directives" into appropriations legislation and reports that, while not legal requirements, are no less politically compelling. Earmarks and directives are common in many other US government spending programs. For members of Congress and their staffs dealing with foreign aid, however, earmarks and directives are especially important—often functioning as the "price" of their support for unpopular aid legislation. And for many in Congress and among NGOs who do not trust the administration to carry out congressional priorities, earmarks are also a way of ensuring that it does so. The scope and specificity of the earmarks and directives have increased over time. In the 1970s they consisted largely of sectoral accounts, as in agriculture and health and family planning. By the year 2005, they were often quite specific as to how the aid should be used. Table 3.1 lists the types of earmarks and directives in Development Assistance and Child Survival (separate accounts for purposes of congressional action but usually combined into "development assistance") and ESF for the year 2005. Each involved a minimum amount to be spent on the particular use.

One additional indication of the declining priority of development in US foreign aid was the effort on the part of the Department of State to absorb USAID. In 1994 the secretary of state proposed that the vice president lead a study on the issue of merging USAID into the Department of State. Behind the secretary's proposal was a desire on the part of senior State Department officials to gain greater control over foreign aid resources, with a particular interest in applying them against global problems.[40] USAID resisted a merger on the grounds that its development mission would likely be overwhelmed by diplomatic concerns and crises if it were made part of the much larger and more powerful State Department. The agency sought support against a merger from within the administration, the Congress, in the media, and among NGOs. After considerable internal debate and political maneuvering on the part of USAID to gain maximum support for its continued existence, Vice President Gore decided against a merger. However, the issue continued, as Senator Jesse Helms, chairman of the Senate Foreign Relations Committee—long unfriendly to foreign aid and to USAID—began to exert considerable pressure on the administration to merge USAID into the State Department. USAID continued to resist, and the president opposed a merger. The merger debate was a near-death experience for USAID, because it found lukewarm support for its continuing existence from other agencies within the administration, from members of

TABLE 3.1. CHILD SURVIVAL, DEVELOPMENT ASSISTANCE, AND ECONOMIC SUPPORT FUND, FISCAL YEAR 2005, CONGRESSIONAL EARMARKS

Child Survival (CS): $1.5 billion, $1.6 billion of which is earmarked*

Child survival/maternal health	$345 million
of which Polio	32
Vulnerable children	30
HIV/AIDS	350
of which, AIDS vaccine	27
Microbicides	30
of which, International Partnership for Microbicides	2
HIV/AIDS Vaccine Fund	65
Other infectious diseases	200
Family planning	375
Global Fund to Fight HIV/AIDS	250
Haiti	20

Development Assistance (DA): $1.4 billion, $1.7 billion of which is earmarked*

Basic education	$300 million
Biotechnology research	25
International Fertilizer Development Institute	4
World Food Program	6
American schools and hospitals	20
Clean energy	180
Biodiversity	165
Plant biotech research	25
Orphans	375
Trade capacity building	194
Women's leadership capacity	15
Clean drinking water	100
Water treatment	2
Haiti	25

Additional Earmarks for Child Survival or Development Assistance: $87 million

El Salvador	27
Guatemala	11
Honduras	22
Nicaragua	27

Economic Support Funds: $2.8 billion, $2.5 billion of which is earmarked

Israel	$360 million
Egypt	535
Jordan	250
Cyprus	35

(continued)

TABLE 3.1. *(continued)*

Lebanon	35
Pakistan	200
Timor Leste	22
Indonesia (media)	3
Cambodia	4
Haiti	40
Afghanistan	980
Reforestation	2
Human rights commission	2
Women and girls	50
Women-led NGOs	8
Burma	12
Tibet (NGOs)	4
Cambodia (democracy promotion)	4
Reconciliation among warring groups	12
Wheelchairs in developing countries	5
Help for disabled	3
Democracy promotion in Muslim countries	15
Iran	3
Journalists' training	3
National Endowment for Democracy Work in Africa	5
Democracy, Human Rights Bureau in Department of State	37
Labor, environment capacity building in CAFTA	20

Additional Earmarks from Any of the above Programs: $436 million

Sudan	$311 million
China and Hong Kong (human rights, rule of law)	19
Cambodia (endowments for two NGOs)	6
Basic education	100

* The earmarks are greater than the total appropriation because some of the funds can be double-counted.

Note: Child Survival Programs, Development Assistance, and Economic Support Funds are three of several major US bilateral aid programs. In addition to the earmarks listed above, some of which overlap with one another, there may be "directives" (mentioned in the committee reports from the Congress but not written into legislation). These carry the political if not legal weight of earmarks. Some of the earmarks and directives reflect administration proposals; most originate with members of Congress.

Source: US House of Representatives, *Making Appropriations for Foreign Operations, Export Financing and Related Programs for the Fiscal Year Ending September 2005 and for Other Purposes*, conference report to accompany H.R. 4818, November 2004, 163–233, http://www.thomas.loc.gov/home/omni2005/index.htm (accessed March 2006).

Congress, and among NGOs, based not so much on the merits of its development mission as its reputation of being a "difficult agency." Efforts at fundamental reform in the way the United States organized its aid had in the past been intended to elevate the importance of development as a purpose of aid-giving and had failed. This effort was intended to elevate the influence of the Department of State over aid-giving; it, too, failed.

Backlash

The decline in the overall volume of aid during the mid-1990s provoked a reaction in the development community, one that resonated beyond that community and suggested that there was a broader acceptance of the appropriateness and importance of aid-giving among the public and political elites than had been evident in the recent efforts to cut aid. The reaction against further aid cuts appears analogous to the reaction against the closure of government that the Republican Congress provoked in late 1995 by refusing to appropriate adequate funds to keep federal offices open. The hostility to government that many newly elected representatives brought to Washington proved to be unpopular with the public once government was closed for an extended period and federal services not provided. This experience reminded people that government was useful, even essential, to their lives and provoked a backlash against Republican antigovernment militancy. Similarly, sharp cuts in aid energized many of its advocates to take action to halt the cuts and awakened passive supporters among political and business elites and the public to act in favor of maintaining foreign aid levels, including both those favoring aid for development and those who regarded aid as an essential instrument of US leadership in the world. All of this suggests that the acceptance of aid-giving as a norm was broader than it seemed from the heated debates on foreign aid at the time.

In 1997 InterAction, the umbrella organization for relief and development NGOs, launched its "Just 1%" campaign to inform the US public on the real amount of US foreign aid (which was considerably less than 1 percent of the federal budget, even though the public thought it to be between 10 percent and 20 percent[41]) and to persuade Congress and the administration to halt and reverse the cuts in development aid. Other aid advocacy groups took up the issue too, for example, the US Global Leadership Campaign, made up of 350 business leaders, framing the drop in aid as threatening US leadership in world affairs. The Business Alliance for International Economic Development was established with an aim of lobbying for increased aid. Groups of universities, energy enterprises, and other groups formed to lobby for more aid. Influential individuals in the foreign affairs community also spoke out against the cuts in foreign aid.[42] And while the pressures for more development aid did not immediately result in a significant increase (though aid for emergencies and for political crises abroad did rise), they likely played a role in stopping the cuts by bringing to the attention of members of Congress that there was in fact a significant base of support for foreign assistance among the American public, organized groups, and segments of the political elite.

INTO THE NEW CENTURY

In the early years of the twenty-first century, several dramatic changes occurred in US foreign aid. In March 2002, President George W. Bush announced a $5 billion annual increase in aid for development to be achieved by 2006, called the Millennium Challenge Account (MCA). The MCA was described by the president as "a new compact for global development, defined by new accountability for both rich and poor nations alike. Greater contributions from developed nations must be linked to greater responsibility from developing nations."[43] This new program was specifically focused on funding development alone. Also, the aid was to be provided only to governments that "govern justly, invest in their people, and encourage economic freedom." The funds would be managed by a new aid agency called the Millennium Challenge Corporation (MCC).

In September 2002, the White House published a *National Security Strategy for the United States of America*.[44] The element in this strategy that gained most public attention was the assertion that the United States would use force preemptively to counter threats to its security. But another important element in this document was the elevation of development as one of the three priorities of US foreign policy, along with defense and promoting democracy abroad. Finally, at the beginning of 2003, the president announced an additional $15 billion boost in aid, over three years, to fight HIV/AIDS. As of 2005, the president had fallen short by about $6 billion in realizing the commitments he had made to increase aid. But even with the shortfall, since the beginning of the Bush presidency, US aid (not including aid for the emergencies in Afghanistan and Iraq) had still risen over a period of several years at one of the fastest rates in the history of US aid-giving, expanding by roughly 40 percent between 2001 and 2005. And, assuming the Congress goes along with the president's proposed budget for foreign aid in 2006, aid will have increased by half between 2002 and 2006.[45]

What led President Bush—a president even more conservative than President Reagan—to commit to such a dramatic boost in US aid and to create an entirely new agency to manage part of it? First was the terrorist attack on September 11, 2001, which led to US military intervention in Afghanistan against the Taliban government, which was sheltering Al Qaeda terrorists. The 9/11 attack appears to have raised the consciousness of the US public of the potential for problems abroad to harm US security at home—making the public more supportive of larger aid flows. Congressman James Kolbe from Arizona (chairman of the key Subcommittee on Foreign Operations of the House Appropriations Committee) stated, "Since 9/11, there is an opportunity to do more. There is a plurality in my district who favor increasing foreign aid. We have never had that before."[46] This new willingness to support aid did not, however, make a commitment by the president to more aid inevitable.

Several things played a role in that commitment. One possible motivation harked back to the Nixon administration: the president may have wanted to balance his assertive military posture and tendency toward unilateralism (e.g., dismissing the Kyoto Protocol on global warming, withdrawing from the Anti-Ballistic Missile Treaty, and opposing a treaty limiting small arms transfers and other treaties and international accords) with a generous act of providing help for those in need abroad. Another apparent element was the increasing pressure from the Christian right to use aid abroad for an expanding circle of good works, including humanitarian relief, debt reduction, and fighting HIV/AIDS.

The political right in the United States had long been the source of most of the criticisms of foreign aid as an inappropriate and wasteful use of public monies. But part of the political right—Christian groups and, in particular, elements of the evangelical movement—had become increasingly engaged in foreign aid–related issues during the 1990s, regarding it as a Christian duty to help the innocent victims of oppression, disease, and deprivation abroad. This growing engagement came from the experience of evangelical missionaries in Africa and elsewhere, where they observed firsthand widespread poverty and disease. They brought those impressions back to their home churches. It was also part of a broader engagement on the part of conservative Christians during the last decade or so of the twentieth century in public policy, an engagement that included reframing issues involving foreign aid and its uses.[47]

Emblematic of this reframing was the way HIV/AIDS was now regarded by major conservative politicians. From being viewed earlier as primarily a consequence of sin (drug use, homosexuality, or promiscuous sex), HIV/AIDS was reframed as a tragedy inflicted above all upon innocent women and children and something that demanded a response from Christians in the spirit of the Good Samaritan. For example, Senator Jesse Helms, long an outspoken conservative opponent of foreign aid, did a 180 degree turn and in 2002 urged a major aid effort to fight HIV/AIDS with the following comment, "I know that, like the Samaritan traveling from Jerusalem to Jericho, we cannot turn away when we see our fellow man in need."[48] Senator Bill Frist, a conservative Republican from Tennessee who became majority leader of the Senate in 2002, also, along with Senator Helms, introduced legislation that year to increase spending for HIV/AIDS in Africa and continued to press the administration to support it. Earlier, a number of political conservatives, including Senator Helms, also reversed their opposition to debt relief for poor countries. Senator Helms redefined the debt problem from one arising out of irresponsible behavior on the part of foreign governments to one depriving poor children of access to food. In an article on international debt in the *Los Angeles Times,* the senator was quoted as saying that "he'd be willing to quit the Senate to aid starving children 'if the Lord would show me how.'"[49])

Finally, the president described himself as a "compassionate conservative," suggesting that his own sympathies with human deprivation and suffering may have played a role in his decision to increase aid for development and to fight HIV/AIDS. And, in contrast to many of his predecessors, President Bush proved willing to lobby Congress himself—phoning key members of Congress to urge their support for the increases he had announced. This pattern of changes in US aid in the early years of the twenty-first century—an increased priority for development in US national security doctrine, a major increase in development aid, the creation of a new aid agency, the commitment to increase aid to fight HIV/AIDS, and the president's willingness to lobby for support for these proposals with Congress—all suggest that something more than the threat to US security represented by 9/11 was influencing these decisions, that the politics of US foreign aid may have begun to change fundamentally.

POLITICS OF AID-GIVING

The history of US aid has been a marriage of multiple purposes. What explains that pattern? And to what extent does the dramatic increase in aid for development in the early years of the twenty-first century mark a change in the politics and purposes of US aid? I begin my analysis of the politics of US aid with an examination of the ideas, some of which go back to the establishment of the American republic, that have shaped US aid-giving. Thereafter, I examine the nature of US political institutions and their impact on US aid. I then turn to the interests, broadly defined, inside and outside government, that have competed for control or influence over the allocation and use of foreign aid. Finally, I explore the organizational context within the US government for aid-giving and that context's influence on the purposes of US foreign aid.

Ideas

The major ideas shaping US aid reflect a fundamental tension in US history and society between those whose worldviews were informed by classical liberalism's preference for limitations on the role of the state in society and those who looked to the state as a major vehicle for redistributive policies at home and, eventually, abroad. In no other aid-giving country has the debate on foreign aid between these two traditions been as evident and enduring. Other important ideas shaping aid involved the appropriate role of the United States in the world.

State and Society

The first debate in the United States on foreign aid took place in the Congress in 1794, and it tells us much about the ideas that have influenced aid-giving since the early days of the republic. At that time, three thousand French refugees from a slave revolt in St. Domingo (then a colony of France) had fled to Baltimore and were near destitution. It was proposed in the House of Representatives that the US government provide $10,000 to the government of France for their relief. One member of Congress argued the humanitarian case: "By the law of Nature, by the law of Nations—in a word, by every moral obligation that could influence mankind, we were bound to relieve the citizens of a Republic who were at present our allies, and who had formerly been our benefactors."[50] Not everyone agreed. Congressman James Madison objected that "Charity is no part of the legislative duty of the government" and that the US Constitution did not authorize an appropriation of funds for such purposes.[51] This exchange took place between what we can call the "humanitarians," who made an argument for public relief aid on the grounds of moral obligation, and what we might call the "libertarians" or "classical liberals,"[52] who argued that it was inappropriate and illegal to use public funds to aid the needy (especially abroad). This argument was repeated at considerably greater length in a debate in the US Senate on the occasion of the Irish potato famine in 1847 and raised all the fundamental ethical and philosophical considerations involving aid that are debated in university classrooms today. Senator John J. Crittenden of Kentucky argued that "The very abundance with which we are blessed increases our obligation to act generously, as well as charitably and justly, and to render obedience to the great law of humanity. . . . Tell me now of mere private and individual charity, when a whole nation [i.e., Ireland] is asking for assistance. In such a case, let a nation answer the imploration. . . . There are no other means by which all can alike contribute for the relief of a nation's suffering and privations."[53] Senator John Fairfield of Maine responded that "he could not permit his generous impulses to blind his judgment and lead him to disregard his solemn obligations to support the Constitution. . . . The money in the treasury was not ours—it belonged to the people, whose servants and agents we were. We had no more right to appropriate it to purposes not contemplated in the Constitution, than we had, as private individuals, to lay our hands upon the property of our neighbors."[54] The libertarians won this argument, with the vocal support of President James Polk, who threatened to veto any public aid to the Irish on constitutional and libertarian grounds. But nothing is ever simple in aid-giving. While no public relief was provided to relieve hunger in Ireland, it was agreed that two US Navy ships could carry privately funded relief for that purpose.[55]

During the nineteenth century, the arguments for publicly funded relief aid gradually gained currency. By the twentieth century, it had come to be widely accepted that government relief aid, for example, in the wake of the First World War, was appropriate—indeed, indispensable—if massive starvation was to be avoided among the many displaced and dispossessed in Europe at that time. But perhaps the most definitive demonstration that public funds for international relief had become a broadly acceptable norm in the United States was the government relief effort in 1922 to help reduce starvation in the USSR in the wake of civil war and drought there. This effort for a foreign country and government whose ideology was anathema to much of Washington was led by Herbert Hoover, a conservative Republican, later to become president.

But the libertarian argument still had considerable currency; it resurfaced in the aftermath of World War II when it was proposed to create an aid program for stabilization and development abroad—a much more ambitious set of goals than aid for relief. For example, in his 1960 book, *The Conscience of a Conservative*, Barry Goldwater declared, "The American government does not have the right, much less the obligation, to try to combat poverty and disease wherever it exists. . . . *the Constitution does not empower our government to undertake that job in foreign countries,* no matter how worthwhile it might be. Therefore, except as it can be shown to promote America's national interest, the Foreign Aid program is unconstitutional."[56]

Goldwater's argument was the last attack on foreign aid by a major US politician based on the traditional libertarian objections that public assistance for improving the human condition abroad was an inappropriate use of national resources and not permitted by the Constitution. By the 1990s, even the Cato Institute in Washington—a think tank inspired by libertarian ideas—was arguing against aid on the pragmatic grounds that it was ineffective rather than on the philosophical grounds that it was inappropriate or even unconstitutional.

The argument that foreign aid for development was not a legitimate use of public resources was part of a broader political discourse involving the role of the state in society that dated back to the founding of the United States. Both the Declaration of Independence and the Constitution were inspired by the ideas of John Locke and other classical liberal philosophers of the Enlightenment, who argued that human beings were equal (at least, before the law) and that they should be free to pursue their individual aspirations in life with a minimum of government restrictions on their liberty. In Thomas Jefferson's words, "The government that governs least, governs best." And while there were differences among Americans on the extent of government's role in society in regard to specific issues, "the American political tradition," observed the historian Arthur Schlesinger, Jr., "is essentially based on a liberal consensus."[57]

Over time, libertarianism, or "classical liberalism," retreated in the face of changing conditions abroad and evolving norms at home. But criticisms of aid in the post–World War II period did not go away. The political right in the United States argued that aid was wasteful, ineffective, and even counterproductive in furthering economic and social progress in poor countries. Foreign aid, as a state-to-state transfer, was seen as strengthening the role of the government in the recipient country's economy, permitting it to avoid needed reforms and sapping initiative, self-reliance, and responsibility (an argument that has a whiff of classical liberalism about it). The following remark in the conservative journal *The National Review* articulates this view, framing foreign aid as an international welfare program:

> a strong case can be made that foreign aid has been the problem for many developing countries, rather than the solution. . . . The issue is very analogous to the debate on welfare. Welfare enabled people to make bad choices without paying the price. . . . The real tragedy is . . . the fact that foreign aid allowed poor countries to escape market discipline, resist changing their economies and their laws to encourage growth, and continue with failed policies year after year after year . . . negative policies were perpetuated in the same way that welfare perpetuated dependency.[58]

In short, many Americans held negative views on welfare programs, in part reflecting the liberal consensus, mentioned earlier—that is, that the other side of equality, liberty, and personal freedom was personal responsibility and self-reliance. Welfare was often seen as an unjustified "giveaway" to those unwilling to bear responsibility for their own well-being. However, when welfare (or foreign aid) was framed as a transfer to the vulnerable (e.g., the aged, children, mothers), suffering from afflictions not of their own making and struggling to survive, there tended to be widespread support for those transfers.

A second critique was that because of corruption and incompetence in developing countries, aid rarely got to those who needed it or could use it well. One commentator put it this way: "the World Bank and many foreign governments continue to provide large government-to-government loans, which are rarely used in cost-effective ways but often are stolen by the recipient countries' corrupt rulers, which saddle the citizens of those poor countries with massive debts they repay to the lenders."[59] These views resonated with many conservative politicians and with the public as well. According to a public opinion poll done in 2001, "When asked to give their best guess about 'what percentage of US aid money that goes to poor countries ends up helping the people who really need it,' respondents gave a median estimate of just 10 percent. That is, 90 percent of the money never reaches those it was meant to help."[60] And the absence in the United States of a sizable or sustained effort on the part of the government or NGOs to inform the public about the purposes and positive accomplishments of aid (in contrast to the "development education" efforts of other aid-giving governments) left much of the public uninformed about the amount, purposes, and impact of foreign assistance for development.

The prolonged debate on foreign aid for development appears to have dampened public support for aid, reinforcing the views of the skeptics and raising doubts about aid's efficacy among those without strong opinions. A variety of public opinion polls over several decades found just over half of the public favorable to foreign aid.[61] A study of public opinion toward foreign aid in DAC countries, published by the UN Development Program, showed that support in the United States was the lowest of all DAC member states, both in 1983 and 1995—at 50 percent and 45 percent, respectively—well below all other countries for which there were data and below the DAC averages of 78 percent and 80 percent for the same two years.[62] (It seems likely that the extent of public debate of aid in the United States also led the public to assume that foreign aid was much larger than in fact it was and thus further dampened public support for assistance.) The tepid public support for foreign aid for development in the United States made it imperative that there were other rationales for aid-giving if sizable amounts of aid were to be sustained over time.

The Role of the United States in the World

One other set of ideas played a major role in shaping US aid in the post–World War II world: the role of the United States as great power and leader of the Western alliance against the socialist bloc and its allies and associates. However, the active engagement and leadership by the United States in world affairs, in contrast to US policies in the interwar years, was by no means inevitable. There were still strong isolationist tendencies within the US Congress and among the public that could have led not to international leadership but to withdrawal from playing a major role in world affairs—as the United States in effect did during the interwar years while Nazi Germany grew in power and assertiveness. That this did not happen was in significant measure the work of an extraordinary group of men who guided US foreign policy in the early postwar years: Dean Acheson, Averell Harriman, John McCloy, and others, who were internationalists, tough minded, pragmatic, flexible, and far-sighted.[63] Their legacy was an engaged, internationalist diplomacy with foreign aid an important tool of that diplomacy. And their view that an expansion of Soviet influence was ultimately a threat to US security and that the United States must resist it, including with foreign aid, was also the key rationale—indeed, the only rationale—that could overcome resistance to aid in the late 1940s from libertarians, political conservatives, and isolationists.

But it soon became apparent that a sizable program of aid driven entirely by national security considerations would not survive long in the cauldron of Washington politics. To critics on the left (and at times on the right), it looked too much like "walking-around money"—a form of international payoff to gain political support from foreign governments for US policies. Tagged with this label, aid would have truly been the temporary expedient described by President Truman and others who first proposed it. And there was a particular problem with the effectiveness of aid purely for diplomatic purposes. It had been justified as a means of containing Soviet influence, but, as mentioned earlier, the continuation of the Cold War and its spread to less-developed countries in the 1950s undercut that argument. There needed to be an additional rationale that justified the prolongation of aid-giving that appealed to realists—many of whom were on the political right but not a few on the left as well—and to idealists on the left and among the general public. Promotion of development in poor countries as a means of Cold War containment as well as an end in itself blended the realist and idealist rationales (a common theme in US foreign policy generally). Both of these ideas—involving national interest and national values—were important for sustaining US foreign aid throughout the twentieth century and provided the intellectual and normative basis for the constituencies inside and outside government supporting it and the enduring dualism in its purposes.

Institutions

It is not only the ideas that have made US aid different from that of other major aid-giving countries but also US political institutions. The US system is a presidential one—the only fully presidential system of any major aid-giving government. That means that the major elements of government are politically autonomous from one another, with the president and members of Congress (both Senate and House of Representatives) standing for election independently—in contrast to the parliamentary systems, in which the prime minister is elected by the parliament. Further, elections are based on a winner-take-all system, discouraging the creation of third parties that could (as many do in the parliamentary systems of Europe) put niche issues like foreign aid on the national political agenda. Political candidates are chosen in local primary elections, making members of Congress more beholden to their constituents than to their parties, thus tending to weaken party discipline.

Finally, both the executive and legislative branches of government play a role in shaping policies and especially in determining federal expenditures. The executive proposes annual levels of expenditures that must then be appropriated by Congress, which can be cut, increased, amended, or ignored. As a result, the Congress (including members and their often powerful staffs) plays an active and pervasive role in deciding not only the amount but also the use of those expenditures and then oversees the programs they fund. Congress has a practice of directing federal government expenditures to specific activities favored by members and their constituents—often called "pork" (from "pork-barrel politics" intended primarily to provide benefits for members' constituents). This tendency has been particularly evident in foreign aid legislation, with the numerous earmarks and directives that are frequently regarded as the price for garnering votes from members who fear they will pay a political price with their constituents for voting for an unpopular program.

The role and influence of Congress effectively expands access to the political process not only for members of the House of Representatives and Senate but for many private groups and individuals who have ties to individual members. If the executive branch fails to accept a favored policy, those individuals and groups can seek support from members of Congress for earmarks and directives in legislation and legislative reports. This fragmentation in political power makes US aid both more rigid in what it can do and more diffuse in what it does do than aid programs of other countries. It also results in aid policy-makers spending an often significant portion of their time managing relationships with Congress and responding to demands for reports, briefings, and other policy concerns there.

These characteristics make the US political system the most adversarial of any considered here—arguably, of any in the developed world—and those characteristics have influenced US foreign aid. The separation of powers and the weak party discipline typical of US politics enables members of Congress to act relatively independently of their parties, from the executive, and from one another (but with an eye always on the preferences of their constituents). And, except in times of humanitarian crisis abroad, citizens supporting aid are typically less vocal than those opposing it. Thus, members of Congress are often confronted with aggressive criticisms of aid at public events in their constituencies that make them wary of supporting aid and create incentives for them to criticize it and vote against it. Indeed, many members of Congress have not hesitated to attack aid and support cutting it, even when their party controls the White House. For example, during the Reagan administration, Republican members of Congress actively worked to cut the administration's aid request and attack Democrats who supported it until Congressman David Obey, the Democratic chairman of the Foreign Operations Subcommittee of the House Appropriations Committee (who was an aid supporter) privately threatened White House chief of staff James Baker to work to defeat the aid bill himself if the White House did not restrain its anti-aid militants in Congress (which it subsequently did).[64]

Interests

It is often said in Washington that aid has no constituency—meaning no powerful interests to lobby for it with Congress and the executive branch—and without such a constituency, aid has been vulnerable to attack and to being cut in Congress. This contention is too simplistic. There is a constituency for foreign aid both inside and outside government—weak, perhaps, compared to the powerful organizations representing the elderly, the defense industry, the union movement, or elements of the agricultural sector. But those supporting foreign aid are not without a measure of influence of their own.

Inside government, the main constituents for foreign aid have been the White House, the Department of State, the Treasury, and USAID. Presidents have on occasion become engaged in efforts to increase and reorient US aid—typically for programs addressed to urgent diplomatic concerns or issues of domestic political importance. Aid for Greece and Turkey, the Marshall Plan, the Alliance for Progress, and aid to the Middle East and

Central America all had presidential backing and all were addressed to important diplomatic concerns. On rare occasions, presidents have intervened to further developmental goals, as with the support of President Bush for the Millennium Challenge Account. When presidents exert themselves for foreign aid, their preferences trump other priorities or opposition within the administration and, usually, with Congress. But direct presidential advocacy of foreign aid—especially its development purposes—is not common. Indeed, since the 1980s, presidents—both Democratic and Republican—have often avoided public identification with aid issues for fear of losing votes.[65]

The principal advocate within the administration for the diplomatic purposes of foreign aid is the Department of State, which must manage US relations with foreign governments and international organizations. Aid has proven a useful, even indispensable, tool in support of Cold War containment, peace-making, antiterrorism, and other policies associated with US national interests. And as a cabinet-level agency, the Department of State can wield considerable influence in Washington battles over the amount, allocation, and use of foreign aid.

The Department of the Treasury is responsible for aid to the international financial institutions and for debt relief. Not surprisingly, it has tended to emphasize fiscal responsibility in its approach to the use of aid and debt relief. However, it has had little to say about bilateral aid, and other agencies have had relatively little influence over its policies regarding US contributions to the international financial institutions. (There has been greater interagency engagement on issues of debt relief, including by the White House, since that issue became so prominent on the international agenda of development concerns, especially during the 1990s.)

USAID has been the principal advocate within the administration for the development use of aid. However, as a subcabinet-level, semiautonomous agency, USAID has been relatively weak in the overall bureaucratic pecking order of the US government, giving it a voice for development in policy circles but not always a significant one. I found while serving as deputy administrator of USAID between 1993 and 1996 that it was often difficult for USAID to get an invitation to high-level interagency policy discussions— even at times when development related issues were on the agenda. Cutting agencies out of senior meetings is a venerable bureaucratic tactic in Washington and elsewhere—one that is a lot easier to pull off where the agency in question is a subcabinet one. As a result, it has often sought allies for its positions (usually resisting pressures from the Department of State to direct funding for diplomatic purposes) elsewhere in the Executive Branch—including in the National Security Council, in the Office of Management and Budget, in the vice president's office, and even among first ladies and second ladies.[66] USAID has also sought allies outside the executive branch, including members of Congress and their staffs, development and relief-oriented NGOs, and even in the media, for support on development issues. It was often able to protect development interests relating to foreign aid in the programs it controlled (Development Assistance and food aid), has had less influence over programs controlled by the Department of State (ESF and aid to Eastern Europe and the newly independent states of the former Soviet Union), and has seldom been able to inject development considerations into other areas of US foreign policy, such as trade. USAID's relative weakness as a subcabinet agency is compounded by the fact that there are often strong private interests behind trade and other issues (e.g., small arms exports), and where they collide with development concerns, the latter tend to come out second best. This is one of the reasons why development policies in the United States have lacked "coherence" and have had limited influence over trade or investment programs.

Agencies within the administration favorable to allocating aid by country and using it directly for commercial purposes (as in "mixed-credit" project financing schemes)—the Department of Commerce, the Export-Import Bank, and the Department of Agriculture (for food aid)—have had limited influence on US foreign aid or access to decision-making on the allocation and use of aid. The Department of State has not been willing to allocate significant amounts of aid to further specific commercial goals (and is powerful enough to fend off attempts by other agencies to divert aid for that purpose), and USAID developed a tactic—evident in the 1990s—of simply not attending interagency meetings where aid for commercial purposes was likely to be discussed, thus limiting the interagency pressures that could be put on it. However, US aid does indirectly further commercial purposes abroad through the high percentage of that aid that is tied to the purchase of US goods and services—between 70 percent and 80 percent are the figures most often used.[67]

Turning to the constituencies for aid outside government, we find an "aid lobby" made up primarily of NGOs focused on relief, development, and associated issues such as the environment, population and family planning, women's rights, and HIV/AIDS. Some of these organizations are arms of major churches; some are universities; some are service delivery groups (implementing US aid programs as well as their own based on private contributions); some are purely advocacy groups. A few are think tanks that focus some or all of their work on foreign aid. (A few think tanks have also been major critics of aid, including the conservative Heritage Foundation and the libertarian Cato Institute.) This large and often fractious group of organizations collaborates in a loose network (often led by InterAction) and lobbies for high aid levels, aid for development broadly defined, and at times, aid for their own particular missions and activities. The expansion in the number and activism of development-oriented NGOs during the 1970s, described earlier, helps explain why the development purpose of aid enjoyed a sustained increase in priority beginning at that time. NGOs began to lobby Congress, engage the media, and organize public campaigns on issues of development, most notably, at least in the 1970s and 1980s, on world hunger. Similarly, in the 1990s, when aid to address global problems gained prominence, it also resonated with environmental NGOs. Later, when the Clinton and Bush administrations turned to problems of international disease and HIV/AIDS, a variety of groups were already active on these issues. Despite differences among them on development strategies during the 1980s and early 1990s (especially regarding the emphasis on structural adjustment versus direct action to reduce poverty), development-oriented NGOs, together with groups of business-oriented coalitions formed in the mid-1990s, were able to help block further cuts in foreign aid. In the context of the US political system, the aid lobby was relatively weak—but at times of crisis or with a compelling issue, it could increasingly act with political effect.

The power and influence of what I will call ethnic or religious affinity organizations in the pluralist, multicultural political system of the United States should never be forgotten. These groups promoted aid to their favored countries. Among such affinity organizations, the most powerful has undoubtedly been the American-Israel Public Affairs Committee (AIPAC), formed in the 1950s to lobby Congress for policies supportive of Israel. After the Yom Kippur War in 1973, the United States began to provide substantial amounts of aid to Israel to help it rearm and recover. Israel remained the largest single recipient of US aid for three decades after the 1973 war, in part because of the work of AIPAC—one of the most effective lobbyist organizations in the United States.[68] Its membership (numbering 65,000 by the turn of the century, located in communities throughout the United States), contributed to congressional campaigns and was active in lobbying Congress in support of aid to Israel and on foreign aid generally. AIPAC gave many members of Congress a reason to support foreign aid who might have been indifferent to aid or disinclined to vote for it. Indeed, by the 1990s (when the Cold War rationale for aid was gone and another, equally compelling national interest rationale had yet to be found) it was widely believed in Washington that without US aid to Israel and the support for foreign aid from AIPAC, foreign aid appropriations would have had a much more difficult time getting through Congress.[69] AIPAC was not alone in lobbying for aid to particular countries. Greek Americans, Polish Americans, Armenian Americans, Baltic Americans, African Americans, and many other groups and diasporas lobbied actively and often effectively (often gaining earmarks or directives from Congress) for aid to their favored countries or regions as well as supporting foreign aid generally.

Commercial interests outside of government involved in aid issues included three main sectors: manufacturers, agricultural interests, and labor. The US Chamber of Commerce and other major business groupings paid relatively little sustained attention to foreign aid during most of the second half of the twentieth century. The overall volume of US aid was relatively small compared to the size of turnover in large US companies, and business-oriented agencies within government had little influence on aid decisions in any case. However, one business sector did have a concrete interest in aid—agriculture. A variety of farm organizations and commodity producers' groups supported foreign aid, primarily food aid, because it was long regarded as helpful in reducing farm surpluses, keeping farm prices high, and expanding markets abroad. The support for food aid in Congress from members from farm states was so reliably strong that at times the administration would propose an amount of food aid in its annual budget request to Congress well below the previous year's level—for example, as part of an effort to cut government expenditures in times of deficit reduction—knowing that the Congress, because of farm support, would likely appropriate the same amount as the previous year. (This tactic is popularly known in the US government as the "Washington Monument Strategy"—the administration cuts drastically or eliminates a highly popular program in the budget to minimize expenditures, knowing that the Congress will put it back in. The name comes from an incident where the National Park Service proposed closing the popular Washington Monument to save money at a time of budget stringency—a proposal quickly reversed in Congress.)

The main labor federation, the AFL-CIO, was also highly supportive of foreign aid (except where that aid appeared to encourage US firms to invest abroad instead of in the United States). The driving force behind this support was not general solidarity with workers in poor countries (as was often the case in aid-giving governments in Europe) but a goal of limiting the influence of communist unions and strengthening noncommunist unions abroad. USAID provided the AFL-CIO an annual grant to work in developing countries for these purposes. After the end of the Cold War, the focus of the AFL-CIO aid-funded activities turned to strengthening unions in developing countries.

The key point in the evolving interests engaged with foreign aid is the rise of NGOs and their advocacy for development-oriented aid. As I noted above, these organizations grew in number and influence beginning in the 1970s and supported foreign aid for development *as an end of policy* independent of its use as a means to other, diplomatic purposes. Their emergence in the 1970s as a nascent political force coincided with the professionalization of USAID and its efforts within the administration to protect and advance its mission of furthering economic and social progress abroad. At times, these two groups collaborated—for example, USAID provided NGOs with capacity-building grants and NGOs supported USAID's general development mission. Over the years, USAID channeled a portion of its aid through NGOs.[70] NGO leaders on the Advisory Committee on Voluntary Foreign Aid (ACVFA) met periodically to discuss with USAID leadership and officials prominent issues and report back to the broader NGO community. At times, there were tensions between USAID and the NGO community. But in general, these two constituted the core of the constituency for development aid during much of the period of this study, and they explain in significant part why development became an end of aid-giving in itself—a widely shared and familiar, if continually contested, element in American foreign aid during the latter half of the twentieth century.

Organizational Architecture of US Foreign Aid

USAID was the main aid agency in what I have already remarked is a fragmented aid system and the key voice for development within the US government. That voice was muffled often by the bureaucratic location of USAID—as a subcabinet-level agency "taking foreign policy guidance" from the secretary of state. This organizational arrangement institutionalized the ideas of the Kennedy administration that development should be a separate purpose of aid but that aid should also serve diplomatic purposes—and it protected those separate but related purposes throughout the last four decades of the twentieth century. This arrangement proved to be extraordinarily resilient. Efforts to elevate the priority of the development mission of foreign aid and make it independent of US diplomacy in the Nixon and Carter administrations failed, just as efforts to eliminate a major development-oriented program (US contributions to IDA) or to merge bilateral aid into the Department of State were defeated. These failures were partly due to the influence of entrenched interests and partly a reflection of the essential political dualism that carried foreign aid in the United States for both diplomatic and developmental purposes.

The ambiguity in performance and accountability generated by the complexities of aid's organizational architecture created difficult problems for USAID, which gained a reputation in Washington of being poorly managed, difficult to deal with, often ineffective, and unresponsive to new challenges and opportunities, especially during the tumultuous decade of the 1990s.[71] There were undoubtedly problems of poor planning and implementation that can rightly be laid at USAID's doorstep. More fundamentally, however, USAID also suffered from a classic political problem—having more responsibility than power. Because USAID managed programs serving a mix of motives, it was at times held accountable for aid failures in programs that were driven by diplomatic purposes, often in countries where positive development outcomes were difficult to achieve because of the quality of the recipient government, political instabilities, or other local problems. No government agency with USAID's responsibilities combined with limitations on its authority could have avoided becoming the whipping boy for perceived failures of foreign aid.

Eventually the problems of USAID affected its standing within the executive branch. First, other government agencies began to establish their own "foreign aid" programs in the 1990s—a form of "globalization" of the US government, partly stimulated by their frustration with USAID when they sought assistance for their particular lines of activities abroad and USAID's understandable reluctance to allocate its monies to other government agencies. Thus, in the mid-1990s, the US Treasury established a program of technical assistance on tax and other financial policies for foreign countries, estimated to reach nearly $19 million by 2004. By 2003 the Department of Labor had programs to combat child labor in fifty-one countries worldwide.[72] The Centers for Disease Control in the Department of Health and Human Services financed research, surveillance, and response services in the area of international disease control in all developing regions. The US government does not publish data on the foreign aid expenditures of its domestic departments, but available data suggest that such expenditures may have amounted to at least $500 million per year by 2000, above aid funding from foreign affairs agencies.[73] This "globalization" of the US government was probably inevitable, given the increasing importance of transnational problems and the increasing ties among cabinet ministers across borders working on similar issues, but the way it proceeded—apart from and often excluding USAID (which had international experience in most of these areas)—was striking.

A second major organizational change involving US aid was the creation in 2004 of the new Millennium Challenge Corporation to manage the Millennium Challenge Account (MCA) monies. The administration chose to create an entirely new agency to manage these funds rather than to locate them in USAID. (This decision reportedly reflected a lack of confidence in USAID's capacity to manage the MCA monies as intended. I have been told by a number of sources that the decision memorandum presented to the president on where to locate the MCA funds included only two options: putting them in the Department of State and putting them into an entirely new agency. Putting them in USAID was not even an option.) MCA funding would be provided in the context of a multiyear agreement between the United States and the recipient government that included development objectives, the actions expected of each party, and indicators of performance. This approach was intended to put maximum responsibility for designing and implementing aid-funded activities in the hands of the governments and groups receiving the aid. It was also intended to show that aid was achieving the planned results. Selectivity in the choice of recipient governments would help ensure that aid would be effective—all these initiatives were intended not only to make aid more effective but to garner sustained support for increased aid from the political right in the United States.[74]

THE NEW CENTURY: HAS ANYTHING CHANGED?

This political analysis of US aid in the second half of the twentieth century describes an enduring dualism in aid's purposes, arising from conflicting ideas involving foreign aid that were amplified by American political institutions, strengthened by the interests engaged in aid, and embedded in the organization of US aid. This system accommodated the new purposes of the 1990s. But these new purposes (which had within them elements both of "national interest," or diplomacy, and of "national values," i.e., human betterment) were not enough to protect foreign aid—especially development aid—from being slashed during the efforts of the 1990s to cut the federal budget deficit and the size of government.

Why, then, the dramatic increase in the volume of aid at the beginning of the twenty-first century, much of it dedicated to development? Does it indicate a resurgence of the dualism of diplomacy and development of the past—a new version of the old "Cold War paradigm" in which aid for friends and allies in a global diplomatic cause (in this case, fighting terrorism) is balanced by aid for global good works, like development? Or has even something more basic changed in the politics of US aid—a change in the fundamental political forces supporting the development purposes of aid?

In 2006, it is still too soon to answer that question definitively. The War on Terror and the aftermath of the military interventions in Iraq and Afghanistan have certainly boosted the usefulness of aid to reward allies and stabilize supportive governments, much as in the early years of aid-giving. But it also appears that something important has begun to change in American politics that could affect US aid purposes in the future. That is the rise of the evangelical movement and the Christian right and its increasing engagement in national politics and public policy, described earlier. Their rising role and importance politically was acknowledged and encouraged by several US presidents, beginning with Ronald Reagan in the 1980s but most prominently by George W. Bush (himself a born-again Christian), who spoke at their functions and gave priority to "faith-based organizations initiatives" in US government programs in helping the poor at home and abroad. As they became more familiar with the terrible problems of poverty, disease, and suffering in the world and involved in aid-giving to address those problems, these groups also became advocates for foreign aid—voices for aid for the most part from the conservative side of American politics.[75] Should the evangelical movement's engagement in foreign aid continue to expand, it could circumscribe or even undercut the traditional resistance to aid—especially development aid—from the right of American politics, expand the political consensus supporting aid across the political spectrum, and reduce the dualism of purposes so long necessary to sustain political support for foreign aid within the United States. Indeed, the evangelical movement could conceivably become *the* essential constituency for aid, replacing AIPAC and other pro-Israel groups that have been so important in the past but are likely to find their interest in foreign assistance diminished as economic aid to Israel is eliminated.

Constituencies for government spending programs always bring their own agendas to those programs and the evangelicals are no exception. Their socially conservative values are already reflected in some aspects of US aid-giving: the opposition to using aid for anything or any group remotely associated with abortion. (The evangelicals are not alone in opposing abortion. It has long been a hot-button issue for social conservatives of all inspirations on the right of American politics, just as the importance of women's right to choose abortion has been an important issue for much of the women's movement and also much of the left of the political spectrum.) Other reflections of the Christian right's values have been the requirement that a portion of the new funding for the fight against HIV/AIDS be dedicated to emphasizing abstinence from sexual activity as a means of preventing the spread of the disease. But the most fundamental difference between the evangelicals and the traditional supporters of foreign aid may turn out to be the role of religion in the allocation and use of aid. To what extent should faith-based organizations managing foreign aid tie their hiring and other practices and their provision of aid to religious concerns? Officially, US government assistance cannot be delivered as a means of proselytizing for any particular belief or in a manner that discriminates according to the religious beliefs of those receiving the aid. The evangelicals recognize this essential separation of church and state. But there are the temptations on one side and the fears on the other that this separation may become blurred in practice. Should that happen or even be perceived to be happening, it could create serious dissension within the aid community, not to mention the problems it could create in foreign countries.

However, not all the policy orientations of the evangelicals involving foreign aid collide with those of the political left. Both oppose human trafficking, slavery, religious oppression, human rights abuses, corruption, and authoritarian governments. There are seemingly broad areas of potential agreement among aid's traditional supporters and the evangelicals. But the differences will have to be managed if this new force in American politics is to expand the constituency for aid rather than divide it.

In sum, the politics of US aid may be in the process of fundamental political change, with potentially enormous implications for the future amount and direction of that aid. These changes may take US aid in directions quite different from the past—a greater emphasis in aid-giving on development and related issues, a broader basis of domestic support for development aid, drawing together an unexpected coalition of the Christian right and the secular left and possibly leading to higher aid levels over time. If these changes come to pass, they could be the most important shift in the politics of US foreign aid since its creation in 1947.

CHAPTER 4

Japan: The Rise and Decline of an "Aid Superpower"

Japanese aid has long been viewed as driven by commercial motives—expanding exports and ensuring access to needed raw materials imports. Commerce certainly played a major role in the country allocation and use of Japan's economic assistance. But this purpose was always embedded in the government's fundamental goals of prosperity, autonomy, and international respect. And by the late 1970s, once Japan made significant progress on its economic goals (reflected in rapidly rising incomes and balance of payments surpluses), the orientation of its aid began to shift. External shocks in the 1970s and *gaiatsu*—that is, pressures on the government from abroad (primarily the United States)—helped bring about that reorientation. Diplomatic concerns (especially managing relations with the United States) became more prominent, playing a direct role in both the amount and country allocation of Japanese aid. By 1989, after doubling its aid several times over during the 1980s, Japan became the "aid superpower"—the largest single donor in the world—and remained so during much of the 1990s.

During the 1980s and especially the 1990s, as a world leader in aid-giving, the Japanese government sought to increase the development focus of its aid and to align it more with the approaches of other major aid-giving governments, which—unlike Japan—emphasized institution building rather than infrastructure construction. Japan proved unable to hold to its position as the largest aid donor in the face of domestic economic crises and several major scandals involving its assistance. Japanese aid was cut sharply at the end of the 1990s, and the government was never able fully to align its development aid policies with those of other governments. Japanese bilateral aid remained heavily focused on funding infrastructure, especially in East Asia, leaving Japan more a niche player in development aid rather than a world leader.

The political dynamics of Japanese aid help explain this story of the rise and decline of Japan as an aid superpower. Japanese political institutions are among the most opaque of any in major aid-giving countries, with many decisions made behind closed doors among government bureaucrats, leaders of the long-dominant Liberal Democratic Party (LDP), and business interests—sometimes called the "iron triangle."[1] From the start, Japanese aid was influenced by the same set of actors: the bureaucrats from various ministries made the decisions on the amount, distribution, and use of Japan's aid; the Japanese business community—especially construction, engineering, and consulting firms—implemented much of Japanese aid; LDP politicians supported Japanese assistance (without getting much involved in its details) and often relied on contributions from the business community for their election campaigns. In contrast to Europe and North America, there were—until the twentieth century was drawing to a close—few NGOs in Japan that functioned as either implementers or advocates of aid for development. The organization of Japan's aid reflected the original purposes of that aid, with key roles in decision-making played primarily by the Ministry of Foreign Affairs (MOFA), the Ministry of Finance (MOF), and the Ministry of Trade and Industry (MITI[2]). Two subcabinet-level agencies, the Overseas Economic Cooperation Fund (OECF, which later became part of the Japan Bank for International Cooperation, or JBIC) and the Japan International Cooperation Agency (JICA), implemented these aid decisions. This arrangement meant that, inside the Japanese government as well as outside it, the voice for the development purpose of aid was limited.

The powerful Japanese bureaucracy—sensitive to Japan's role in the world and to pressures from major allies—proved able and willing in the 1970s to shift the priorities of its aid from commerce to diplomacy. But aligning its aid with the development norms and practices of other major aid-giving governments proved much more difficult because of the weakness of the development constituency inside and outside government and its lack of broad expertise and experience in development work (other than infrastructure). Nor was the government able to make the fundamental organizational reforms that might have facilitated such an alignment.

However, changes in the domestic determinants of aid within Japan—the increasing number and importance of development and relief NGOs outside government and the beginnings of change in Japan's political institutions evident at the beginning of the twenty-first century—suggest that more fundamental shifts in Japan's aid-giving might be in the offing in coming years.

THE ORIGINS AND ESTABLISHMENT OF JAPANESE AID: THE 1950S AND 1960S

Japanese aid originated in war reparations the government was obligated to pay in the wake of its defeat in the Second World War. Some thirteen Asian countries were eligible for reparations payments at levels the Japanese government negotiated with each recipient. Japan began to make reparations and reparation-like payments (other financial transfers associated with war damage) in 1954 and finished in 1977. The total amount reached $2 billion.

The arrangements put in place by the Japanese government for managing those reparations shaped the way Japanese aid was administered later as well as the purposes that aid would serve. Reparations were used to finance projects requested by the recipient government—the beginnings of Japan's "request-based" approach to the selection of aid-funded projects. In theory, a government wishing to receive Japanese aid would identify a project for Japanese financing. It would make a formal request to the Japanese government for that financing, which the government would consider and, if the project was deemed worthwhile, approve. In reality, Japanese firms in developing countries would often identify projects and propose them to the governments of the developing country, which would then "request" that the Japanese government fund them. Those same Japanese firms would later implement the projects once they were approved by Tokyo.

This approach was intended to benefit Japan as well as the recipient country—the projects would help Japanese companies expand their production and exports, thereby reaping economies of scale at home and gaining new markets abroad for their goods and services. Some of the projects also involved the development of raw materials production, such as cotton and wood products, that Japan could then import for its industrial needs. Both expanding exports and gaining access to needed imports fit the requirements of the Japanese economy and, even more importantly, the broader diplomatic goals of ensuring the prosperity, security, and independence of Japan.

The reliance on Japanese enterprises in managing reparations payments had another advantage: it kept down the public costs of delivering the aid, because Japanese firms acted in effect as the field representatives of the Japanese government in identifying and implementing reparations-funded projects. (Indeed, it is said that Japanese business missions abroad did much of the negotiating for the government on project proposals.[3]) The Ministry of Foreign Affairs coordinated the requests from foreign governments, which had to be approved by the Ministry of Trade and Industry, the Ministry of Finance, and the Economic Planning Agency (EPA), as well as the relevant sectoral ministry—for example, Transportation for road projects,

Health and Welfare for hospitals, or Agriculture, Forestry and Fisheries for activities falling into those areas. This rather cumbersome decision-making process enabled the key agencies—in particular, MOFA, MITI, MOF, and (to a lesser extent) EPA—to bring to bear their expertise in project assessment and to ensure that their interests were adequately reflected in the yen loans provided.

By the middle of the 1950s, it was evident that reparations were not enough to achieve the diplomatic and commercial purposes of the Japanese government. Japan wanted to reestablish good relationships with countries in Asia and elsewhere not on the reparations list. Important sources of raw materials and potential export markets existed in countries, such as India, not receiving reparations. Providing aid was a useful element in what was often a package of policies for achieving these goals. In 1954 Japan joined the Colombo Plan and provided a small amount of technical assistance to its Asian member states—marking the official beginning of Japan's aid. Soon, the government decided that yen loans on concessional terms were the vehicle it needed to expand its relationships in Asia and elsewhere. The first of these was negotiated with India in 1958 to pay for Japanese goods and services associated with the development of iron ore in Goa.[4] A second credit for India soon followed the first, and in 1959 other loans were negotiated with Paraguay (one of a number of countries in South America with a Japanese immigrant community) and South Vietnam.

Organizing Japanese Aid

In 1960, under pressure from Keidanren (the Japan Federation of Economic Organizations—an influential association of Japanese enterprises) and from the ruling Liberal Democratic Party in the Diet (the Japanese parliament), the government created a new agency—the Overseas Economic Cooperation Fund—to manage the growing number of aid loans. OECF lending would be overseen by the four agencies—MOFA, MOF, MITI, and EPA—that had supervised reparations payments. Initially, OECF lending was managed by Japan's Export-Import Bank (JEXIM) exclusively through Japanese firms. Subsequently, the management of these loans was transferred to OECF but with projects still tied to implementation by Japanese enterprises.

In 1961 the Japanese government put into place the final piece of its aid machinery, the Overseas Technical Cooperation Agency (OTCA, later to become the Japan International Cooperation Agency, or JICA), which combined the technical training and assistance activities of several existing agencies, provided in the form of grants. After a bureaucratic tussle, MOFA was put in charge of the new agency, with an understanding that a signifi-

FIG. 4.1. THE ORGANIZATION OF JAPANESE AID, 2004

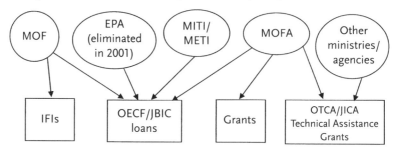

cant portion of its senior officers would be seconded from other government agencies to ensure those agencies' views and interests were taken into account. MOFA also managed the government's grant aid program. MOF was responsible for Japanese participation in the international financial institutions.

Figure 4.1 is a somewhat simplified diagram of the organization of Japanese aid, with the policy-making and allocation decision-making responsibilities located in the top ovals and the implementing agencies and programs in the bottom squares. "Other ministries and agencies," numbering some nineteen in total, were intermittently involved with aid. They included the Cabinet Office; the National Police Agency; the Financial Services Agency; the Ministry of Public Management, Home Affairs, Posts, and Telecommunications; the Ministry of Justice; the Ministry of Education, Culture, Sports, Science, and Technology; the Ministry of Health, Labor, and Welfare; the Ministry of Agriculture, Forestry, and Fisheries; the Ministry of Land, Infrastructure, and Transport; and the Ministry of Environment. The total aid budget of these ministries remained modest but significant—reaching approximately 100 billion yen out of an aid budget of 900 billion yen in 2003.[5]

The organization of Japanese aid, reflected in figure 4.1, did not change until 1999, when OECF was merged into the Japan Export-Import Bank to create the Japan Bank for International Cooperation (JBIC). This organizational change had a minimal effect on how Japanese aid functioned. The aid portion of JBIC's lending was kept separate from the export credit portion and, for the most part, the personnel remained separate as well.[6]

The Volume and Distribution of Japanese Aid: The 1960s

Japan started out as a relatively small aid donor—its aid during the 1960s averaged around 0.25 percent of GNP, compared to an average of 0.50 percent for all of the DAC. Its absolute amount of aid grew slowly during the first half of the decade and then increased rapidly at the end of the 1960s, having tripled by 1970. However, with the rapid growth in its economy, Japan still remained one of the smaller aid donors, both relative to the size of its economy and to the aid levels of other donors. The increase in aid at this time is often attributed to *gaiatsu*, in this case, from Asian countries for more development assistance and above all from the United States, to share the burden of the Western aid effort. Japan joined the OECD in mid-decade (it had already joined the DAC in 1960) and came to regard a sizable aid program, in Professor David Arase's words, as "membership dues . . . owed after joining the OECD and being received as an advanced country."[7] Figure 4.2 shows the amount of Japanese aid from 1960 to 2004.

A snapshot of Japanese aid in 1970 provides further insights into its purposes at that time. The aid amounted to $458 million.[8] As a percentage of GNP, it was 0.23, one of the lowest and below the DAC average of 0.34. The bulk of it was provided as bilateral aid, with only 15 percent multilateral. Bilateral aid was almost entirely directed to Asia, with two-thirds in the Far East, especially in Indonesia, Korea, the Philippines, and Thailand. Another quarter went to the countries of South Asia, primarily Pakistan and India. The aid itself was concentrated in commercially attractive sectors, especially energy, industry, mining, and transportation. A significant amount was provided as import support and food aid. Very little was allocated to social sectors like health or education. The grant element was the second lowest of any DAC member state, at 39 percent (with the DAC average at

FIG. 4.2. TOTAL JAPANESE AID (NET)

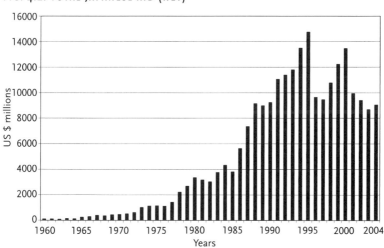

Source: DAC, "International Development Statistics (IDS) Online," http://www.oecd.org/dac/stats/idsonline/ (accessed October 2005).

63 percent). And the terms of Japanese aid were among the hardest of any among DAC members.[9]

The emphasis on bilateral aid, on Asian countries, and on the sectors attractive to Japanese exporters, and the relatively hard terms of Japanese aid were indicators of the primacy of commercial purposes, nested within broader diplomatic goals of the government: Tokyo wanted to reestablish good relations with the governments in Asia in particular, regain its position as a respected member of the international community, and, most immediately, gain export markets and access to raw materials in countries relatively familiar and close to home. Aid was seen at this time less as a gift directed at reducing poverty abroad than an investment (at below commercial rates) in growth, both for Japan and the recipient country. Like other aid-giving countries at the time, the government of Japan assumed that poverty reduction would eventually follow from sustained growth.

THE DRIVE TO AID PRIMACY: THE 1970S THROUGH THE 1990S

By the middle of the 1970s and especially in the 1980s, Japan's export drive had become successful and its balance of payments moved into surplus, lessening the urgency of expanding the economy's export markets. At the same time, the first half of the 1970s brought several shocks that had a significant effect on the amount and direction of Japanese aid. The first was the 1973 quadrupling in the price of petroleum, on which Japan was highly dependent. This sudden increase in the price of an essential import, plus uncertainties about reliable access to Middle East oil, caused consternation in Tokyo. The government quickly acted to strengthen its relations with Arab oil-producing countries, including initiating a number of aid-financed projects in those countries (the first major, direct use of Japanese aid for explicitly diplomatic purposes).[10] The uncertainties surrounding the price and availability of petroleum raised fears that other raw materials might become scarce or controlled by producer cartels, jeopardizing the flow of imports essential for the Japanese economy. Aid came to be thought of as a useful instrument for helping to ensure access to needed raw materials through creating good relations with a variety of countries producing those commodities in Asia and elsewhere.

A second shock was the visit to Southeast Asia by Prime Minister Kakuei Tanaka in 1974. Indonesian and Thai students rioted, attacking Japan as interested primarily in promoting its commercial advantages in the region. These criticisms led the government to reconsider how it did business—including aid-funded business—in Asia.

A third shock was the Nixon administration's opening to China. The

Japanese government was not briefed ahead of time on Nixon's visit but moved quickly to normalize relations with Beijing in the wake of the change in US policy. By the end of the 1970s, Japan had commenced an aid program in China, and, from 1982, it became Japan's largest single aid program.

Nixon had yet another surprise for Tokyo. In 1973, with a shortfall in the production of soybeans and consequent rises in prices, the administration imposed an embargo on soybean exports. Japan, reliant on soybeans from the United States, suddenly found itself with its own serious shortage. Japanese food security took on greater importance as a goal of foreign policy. Aid was directed toward countries like Brazil, where there was potential to expand the production (and export to Japan) of soybeans and other essential agricultural imports.

Finally, not so much a shock, but a growing source of concern in Tokyo, were the rising criticisms from the United States of Japan's expanding trade and foreign exchange surpluses. Its export success had created its own political problem for Japan—critiques, especially from Washington, that Japan was competing unfairly in international trade: its increasing balance of payments surpluses showed that the yen was undervalued and should be revalued, its home market was protected from foreign competition, and its export practices were unfair and possibly illegal (involving dumping, for example). These critiques, combined with continuing pressures from the United States to contribute to security in Asia and elsewhere (especially as the United States withdrew from Indochina in the 1970s) and Japan's inability, based on its constitution, to share directly in the military burdens associated with the Western alliance, were part of the political environment in which Japanese aid became a major tool of foreign policy and led to shifts in the priorities in Japanese aid in the second half of the 1970s.

One shift involved a dramatic increase in the volume of Japanese aid.[11] In 1977 the government announced its intent to double its "economic cooperation" programs in five years. The following year, Prime Minister Takeo Fukuda, at the Bonn G-7 Summit, was more specific: Japanese aid would double in dollar terms, now within three years rather than five. Raising aid volume would, it was hoped, ease US pressures for burden-sharing and for a reevaluation of the yen and eventually give Japan a lead role in world affairs—especially in international cooperation and development.

Other changes appeared in Japanese aid at this time. The government started to spread its aid beyond Asia, providing some assistance to all major developing regions of the world and sizable amounts to countries of economic and strategic importance—for example, in regions of conflict or countries of particular interest to the United States and the West. Aid increased to Pakistan (next door to Soviet-occupied Afghanistan), to Turkey (strategically situated in the Middle East), Egypt (key to Arab-Israeli peace), and to Sudan. In contrast to the 1960s and early 1970s, when Japan provided 90 percent of its aid to Asian countries, by 1980, Japan was providing Asian countries (including the Far East and South Asia) with 70 percent of its aid, with 10 percent each to Latin America, Africa, and the Middle East.

Finally, with the growing surpluses in Japan's trade with the United States and criticisms of the strongly commercial orientation of Japanese aid, in 1978 the government (in a joint communiqué with the United States) announced its intention to untie Japanese aid loans. US firms would now be able to compete for Japanese aid–funded contracts in developing countries, a move (according to some Japanese officials) specifically intended to benefit US firms and the US economy.

As the amount of Japanese aid increased, the government—or rather, different elements of the government—sought to articulate the role of Japanese aid in the country's foreign policy. One effort involved the theme "comprehensive national security," which was provoked by the oil crisis and, among other things, attempted to establish the links between traditional security concerns and Japan's "economic security."[12] Within this broad theme, during the late 1970s and early 1980s, both MITI and MOFA issued their own reports and white papers on foreign aid policy, each with a somewhat different emphasis.[13]

Reflecting its responsibilities for the Japanese economy and Japanese business, MITI proposed a policy of "Comprehensive Economic Security" in which aid (together with trade and investment) would continue to strengthen Japanese ties with developing countries in an interdependent world, expand and diversify the sources of needed food and raw materials imports (above all, petroleum), and help restructure Japanese industry by encouraging basic industries to move overseas and permit more investment in high-technology industries at home. There followed MITI's Asian Industries Development Plan and an ASEAN-Japan Development Fund, both of which had aid components. (ASEAN is the acronym for the Association of Southeast Asian Nations.)

MOFA also produced in 1980 a report on the rationales for foreign aid. For MOFA, aid's purpose related to its concepts of international security and development: to help create a stable, peaceful international society and to provide developing countries with a non-Western model of successful development (as well as to manage Japanese resource vulnerabilities).

The 1980s was a decade of continued and rapid expansion in Japanese aid. In 1981 the government announced its second five-year aid doubling. In 1985 it was announced that aid would be doubled yet again; and in 1988 there was a fourth doubling plan. In 1989 Japan claimed the role of the "aid superpower"—the largest aid donor in the world. Japan continued to expand its aid until the mid-1990s, remaining the largest single bilateral donor for most of the rest of the decade.

Part of being a lead aid donor involved sizable contributions to international financial institutions, such as the World Bank and the regional development banks. The Japanese government increased its aid to these institutions at this time to one-third of its total aid commitments by 1985.[14] Japan was by far the major contributor to the Asian Development Bank, which was traditionally headed by a Japanese official and came to be seen by many as a "Japanese bank." It also became a significant donor to the Inter-American Development Bank, the African Development Bank and Fund, and other international development organizations.

Despite its rapid increases, Japanese bilateral aid stood out among DAC member states as the least consistent with evolving DAC norms for development assistance. The mainstream emphasis in aid-giving in the DAC in the 1970s was on addressing "basic human needs"—working in the poorest countries and in agriculture, primary health care, and basic education, much of it in institution building. Japanese aid was still concentrated on financing infrastructure projects (the highest percentage of any donor). In 1981 Japan was the least concessional donor save Austria—the grant element in Japanese aid was 75 percent, while the average for all DAC members was 90 percent.[15] The administration of Japanese aid was centralized in Tokyo, with limited representation in the field on the part of Japanese aid agencies. And despite its doubling of aid after 1977, Japan still had one of the lowest percentages of its GNP dedicated to foreign assistance.

In 1981 the Japanese government announced a number of changes intended to make its aid more consistent with DAC norms. It proclaimed a basic human needs focus in its aid and moved gradually to ease the terms of its lending. In the early 1980s, both MOFA and OECF created evaluation services. (JICA had established one in 1975.) However, it proved difficult for the government of Japan fully to realize a number of these commitments. Aid from the OECF (half to two-thirds of Japanese aid at this time) was in the form of yen loans—difficult for the poorer, cash-strapped countries in Africa and Latin America to manage financially. And because the government had concentrated its aid on creating physical assets—infrastructure and the delivery of equipment—the technical and local expertise especially useful in basic human needs projects was scarce in government, in Japanese consulting firms, and in the few NGOs that existed in Japan. As a result, while the government increased its aid for social infrastructure and services in the late 1970s (moving closer to the basic human needs focus), these projects were concentrated in expanding clean water and sanitation and typically emphasized engineering and the construction of physical facilities.

Untying Japanese Aid

One of the most significant signs of a move away from the commercial orientation of Japanese aid had been the government's announcement that it was untying a portion of that aid. This commitment proved to be the one most disputed by foreign governments and observers of Japan's aid program. Only yen loans were to be untied. Grant aid (including technical assistance) remained tied to Japanese goods and services.[16] Even when Japanese yen loans were formally untied and a rising proportion of the aid was channeled through foreign-based firms, many foreign critics—especially in the United States—suspected that there was a considerable amount of informal collusion between Japanese bureaucrats and Japanese enterprises to ensure that the aid was spent on Japanese goods and services. It was also thought that many of the foreign-owned firms receiving contracts involving Japan's aid may have in fact been Japanese subsidiaries set up in developing countries.[17] (Japanese officials pointed out to me that after reforms in Japan's procurement process, which by 2004 was identical to that of the World Bank, such informal collusion was illegal.)

There is evidence that in the 1980s the Japanese government did, in fact, begin to untie its yen loans in reality as well as in rhetoric. Robert Orr provides data that show a declining percentage of the untied portion of yen credits won by Japanese firms—falling from 66 percent in 1984 to 27 percent in 1988. JBIC documents show that by 1998 aid credits were 90 percent untied and that only 20 percent of the contractors for those credits were Japanese. The percentage of Japanese contractors winning JBIC aid loans was the same in 2002. It is clear both from the increasing number of contracts and the volume of credits awarded to non-Japanese firms or consortia of firms with non-Japanese as well as Japanese enterprises that a great deal of aid has been untied, in contrast to the situation in the 1970s. Another indication of the untying of Japanese aid was the "firestorm of lobbying" in the 1980s by Japanese companies in the construction and engineering fields against untying aid, suggesting that the business community felt that the untying had gone too far.[18] The comment one frequently hears in Japan from those in the business community and outside observers is that Japanese enterprises have lost interest in aid because of the declining number of contracts they win. Finally, there were also the pressures from the business community in the late 1990s to tie the special $5 billion in government concessional credit for the Asian financial crisis to purchases in Japan. (If this aid had already been tied informally, the business community would not have needed to exert such obvious pressures, which they did with some success.)

The Rise of Japanese NGOs

Nongovernmental organizations working on relief and development—so common in North America and Europe—were few in Japan at the beginning of the aid era in the 1950s and 1960s. Japanese NGOs really got their start in the 1970s, when a few were created in the wake of the war in Indochina, primarily to provide services to Vietnamese and Cambodian refugees fleeing to Thailand.[19] As happened earlier in other parts of the world, these relief-oriented NGOs soon turned to development work. But their advocacy activities remained limited—government officials often disdained to meet with the NGO staff or take them seriously, while a number of NGOs were quite critical of government, gaining the image of "radicals," both in official circles and in the opinion of the public. Most NGOs struggled with severe funding constraints—small contributions from a public unused to private giving, few gifts from philanthropic foundations (which were, in any case, limited in number themselves), and little funding from the public sector. In some cases, Japanese NGOs working in areas of interest to foreign NGOs were able to obtain financial support from abroad. For example, Friends of the Earth, based in the United States, established a branch in Japan. But even from abroad, funding remained limited.

During the 1980s, NGOs began to become more involved in policy advocacy within Japan, commencing with environmental NGOs. The NGO movement got a further boost in the 1990s from pressures on the Japanese government from foreign governments and international NGOs to expand their access and financing.[20]

Additionally, the series of international conferences and summits that took place in the 1990s called public attention to conference topics (e.g., the environment, population issues, women's issues, food security) and created opportunities and incentives for consultations between NGOs and governments for each of these world events. By the Conference on Population in Cairo in 1994, Japanese NGOs were asked to serve on the official delegation to the conference.[21] Toward the end of the 1990s, a coalition of Japanese NGOs, part of the worldwide Jubilee 2000 campaign, sought to persuade the government to cancel debts owed it by poor countries. Since 1978, the government had reluctantly provided grant aid to fund debt repayments on the part of developing countries. Tokyo had resisted outright debt cancellation on several grounds: it would complicate funding arrangements for OECF (later JBIC), which had made the loans and had borrowed from other government accounts to help finance them. On the ideological side, Japanese officials were afraid of the moral hazard created by debt cancellation—it could provide incentives for borrowing governments to misuse aid funds in the future, believing that their debts would be canceled later. It was only in late 2002 that the Japanese government finally announced an outright cancellation of debts owed it by the poorest countries.

In the 1990s the government began to take NGOs more seriously as implementers of aid activities as well as potential supporters of foreign aid within the Japanese political system and with the public. Government had already begun to provide a small amount of financing to NGOs during the late 1980s. Subsidies and grants for NGO projects increased from around 400 million yen in 1989 (roughly $3.7 million) to 1.2 billion yen by 1998 (around $10 million) and then began to decline somewhat with the decrease in Japanese aid overall. In 1991 the government set up an innovative scheme in which Japanese citizens depositing their savings in postal savings accounts were given the option by the Ministry of Posts and Telecommunications to dedicate from 10 percent to 100 percent of the interest on those savings for use by qualified NGOs in development work abroad. The funds generated by this scheme (amounting to $125 million between 1991 and 1997) remained relatively limited in amount, but they did provide additional financing for NGOs and engaged the public directly in aid and development issues.

In an additional initiative in 1998, the government supported the passage of a law easing the conditions of incorporation for Japanese NGOs—these had been so restrictive that few could qualify and, therefore, could not act as legal entities, set up bank accounts, and accomplish the other tasks necessary for organizations to function in the modern world. Even with the new law, however, challenges remained for NGOs to establish themselves, including the lack of tax breaks for them and for their contributors. (In 2001 a law was enacted to provide tax relief to private contributors to qualified NGOs, but the standards for qualification remained difficult.[22]) By 2003 Japanese funding of NGOs (grants to NGOs as a percentage of ODA) reached the DAC average of 2 percent.[23]

In the 1990s the government created a number of consultative mechanisms with Japanese NGOs. By the end of the decade, these mechanisms proliferated and were institutionalized, with MOFA, MOF, JICA, and JBIC all meeting periodically with NGOs and seeking their advice on policy and programmatic issues. MOFA helped to establish four "platforms" (networks) of NGOs—one each involving emergency relief, education, agriculture, and health—through which it channeled funding to NGOs in these sectors. These efforts by government to engage NGOs were viewed by many NGO staff as both useful and well intentioned. In interviews in Tokyo in 2003 with a variety of NGO leaders, I found they regarded them as valuable openings for making their views known to government. Nevertheless, the

Japanese NGO movement, despite all these changes, remained one of the weakest of any DAC member state.

Challenges to Japanese Aid

As Japanese aid grew, so did criticisms of it. Three in particular emerged in the late 1980s: the lack of transparency and problems of corruption, the fragmented nature of Japan's aid organization, and the absence of an overall policy framework for Japan's assistance. The loudest criticism was stimulated by revelations of corruption in Japanese aid. Several scandals erupted in 1986—the major one involved extensive kickbacks of Japanese loans in the Philippines under President Ferdinand Marcos, which came to light after his overthrow when evidence of these practices, obtained from Marcos's own papers, was published by the US Congress. The scandal caused quite a stir in Japan, generating demands for greater transparency in Japanese aid decisions.[24] The government reacted by promising to publish aid procurement documents but later failed to carry through.

Other criticisms pointed at the fragmented nature of Japanese aid, especially in decision-making, making the aid process slow, cumbersome, and rigid. At one point in the 1980s, elements in the Japanese private sector called for a single, cabinet-level aid agency to improve efficiency and general performance. This idea had been raised by Prime Minister Tanaka in the mid-1970s but was resisted then by the powerful bureaucracies whose influence over aid decisions would inevitably be diminished by such a fundamental reorganization. As in the 1970s, the same resistance appeared and no radical reorganization was undertaken.

Toward the end of the 1980s, the large volume of aid and the number of new activities the government had announced for its aid, including democratization, women's rights, environmental protection, and other internationally popular initiatives, were raising questions about the fundamental purposes of Japanese aid. No single official statement or document laid out those purposes, so the government decided to create one. In 1992 the cabinet adopted the "Official Development Assistance Charter"—the first major document setting forth the main rationales and guidelines for Japanese aid. The charter declared that Japan provided aid because of its humanitarian concerns for the poor, to strengthen international interdependence, to protect the environment, and to further "self-help" on the part of less-developed countries.

The charter also offered four guidelines for allocating ODA:

1. Environmental conservation and development should be pursued in tandem.

2. Any use of ODA for military purposes or for aggravation of international conflicts should be avoided.

3. Full attention should be paid to trends in recipient countries' military expenditures, their development and production of mass destruction weapons and missiles, their export and import of arms, etc., so as to maintain and strengthen international peace and stability, and from the viewpoint that developing countries should place appropriate priorities in the allocation of their resources on their own economic and social development.

4. Full attention should be paid to efforts for promoting democratization and introduction of a market-oriented economy, and the situation regarding the securing of basic human rights and freedoms in the recipient country.[25]

The adoption of an ODA charter was one approach to providing a coherent rationale for Japan's aid. The government also undertook other initiatives consistent with its new role as the "aid superpower." Japan began to take a more proactive role in identifying projects in recipient countries, moving away from its "recipient-based" approach and started in 1993 to develop country studies—the beginnings of a country programming process. It committed itself to strengthen its evaluation service as well. Additionally, in the 1990s the government created several organizations to undertake research and training in development and to act as centers for public discussion of development issues, for example, the Foundation for the Advanced Study of Development (FASID). These functioned partly as sources of ideas and debate and partly as vehicles for involving the informed public in Japanese foreign aid.

To engage a wider public in supporting Japanese aid, recognized by the government as necessary to sustain its high annual aid levels, the government initiated a yearly International Cooperation Festival in Tokyo, beginning in 1992. Additionally, it began publishing annual reports on Japanese ODA; it created the International Development Plaza in Tokyo the same year; and it encouraged local engagement in development work—the hosting of trainees by local governments, "twinning" between Japanese and developing country cities, the sending of local technical experts (that is, from Japanese provinces and municipalities) to developing countries, and providing funding to local governments in Japan to become active in development work. Eventually, information on development was included in school curricula, informing many Japanese children of the problems of poverty and poor countries from an early age.

The government set out to claim the international leadership role in foreign aid that its status as the largest donor potentially accorded it. One of the government's goals was to gain greater visibility and international acceptability for its view of an approach to development somewhat different from the emphasis on free markets on the part of the World Bank, the United States, and others supporting the "Washington Consensus"—specifically, that governments had an important role in furthering development, including guiding industrialization and promoting exports. This view was based on Japan's own successful experience of development and that of a number of its neighbors, like Korea. In an effort to further this idea, the government funded a study by the World Bank entitled *The East Asian Miracle*,[26] exploring the causes of economic successes in Korea, Thailand, Indonesia, and elsewhere in its region. The report did highlight the key role of government in guiding these economies toward success but also underlined the importance of institutional capacity on the part of government to make efficient and effective policy choices and to terminate policies when they were no longer useful—a capacity shared by relatively few governments in poorer parts of the world. As a result, the report did not carry quite the endorsement of an alternative approach to development that the Japanese government had hoped for.

A further Japanese effort to take a leadership role in development was the series of TICAD (Tokyo International Conference on African Development) conferences. The first of these was held in 1993 and brought together the leaders of African countries, Japanese aid officials, and representatives of aid-giving governments and organizations to discuss development in Africa and the relevance of the Japanese development experience for Africans. The second of these conferences was held in 1998, followed by a third in 2003. TICAD conferences have produced a set of unobjectionable consensus statements about the importance of development in Africa, commitments on the part of Africans to further that development, and commitments on the part of the Japanese government to support African efforts. The apparently meager outcomes of these conferences puzzled a number of foreign observers. Many concluded that, in fact, the real reason for these conferences was to bolster support among the Africans for Japan's campaign to gain a seat on the UN Security Council, for which African votes would be essential. Japanese officials involved with these conferences affirm in private that gaining a seat on the Security Council was one goal.[27] Another was to use the large, well-reported meetings in Tokyo as a means of educating the Japanese public on development and the importance of Japanese aid. In 2002 Japan organized a conference on Initiatives for Development in East Asia with the ten countries from ASEAN plus China and South Korea, which sought to pull together the successful experience of development in the region for the benefit of Africans and others.

Effective Japanese leadership was more evident in a number of specific international development issues. In 1992 Japan chaired the International Committee on Reconstruction of Cambodia. In the mid-1990s one of its senior diplomats played the key role in launching the DAC report *Shaping the 21st Century: The Contribution of Development Cooperation*, which was one of the first documents to set out concrete future goals for development achievements, thus setting guidelines for applying aid and standards against which it can be assessed.[28] During the 1990s, it took a lead in promoting international assistance to Mongolia. In 1999 it hosted a consultative group on East Timor. In 2002 Tokyo did the same for Sri Lanka after the devastating conflict in that country, co-chairing the Tokyo Conference on Reconstruction and Development there. In the same year, Japan played a lead role in reconstruction in Afghanistan and in promoting the peace process in Aceh.

However, aligning its aid practices with those of the rest of the world proved more difficult, and this challenge likely dampened the effect of its increasingly active leadership in foreign aid issues. A number of statements and official documents produced by the Japanese government—for example, its ODA annual reports—endorsed many of the international development priorities of the day. In 1993 and 1994, for example, the government emphasized the use of its aid for basic human needs and for addressing global issues such as environmental problems, HIV/AIDS, population, and women in development, and stressed the importance of democracy and good governance among aid recipients.[29] In 1995 and 1996 the government highlighted its commitment to children's welfare (much like the US focus on "child survival" at that time) and "people-centered development"—a phrase picked up from the annual UN Human Development Report. Later in the 1990s, Japanese aid documents began to mention "human security," another phrase borrowed from the UNDP Human Development Report and elaborated by Sadako Ogata, the UN High Commissioner for Refugees in the 1990s. (Mrs. Ogata, as a Japanese citizen serving in a prominent international post, had considerable access and influence in Tokyo, and her promotion of the notion of "human security" gained a following there.[30]) Additionally, a focus on global issues (promoted by the United States through the Common Agenda meetings with the Japanese government during the 1990s) and problems and on "peace diplomacy" or "peace-building" also gained currency as new purposes of Japanese aid in the late 1990s—involving such activities as demining and postconflict reconstruction.

The extent to which these initiatives and multiple commitments were reflected in the way Japan actually used its aid was far less clear. Narrative materials, government budget documents, and Japanese aid data published by the DAC indicate that Japan allocated some funding for these new types of activities, both through its bilateral aid program and through its contributions for these purposes to multilateral aid agencies. For example, Japan spent just over $800 million on "government and civil society" activities between 1995 and 2000.[31] During the same period, the government also spent $2.3 billion on "general environmental protection" and just over $160 million on family planning programs. In some of these areas, the primary forms of activities financed were studies, technical assistance, and advice. In others, like the environment, much of the aid monies were spent on infrastructure and equipment. Thus, the Japanese government did put funding behind its various new aid initiatives—though this funding appears to have been concentrated on infrastructure and the export of equipment to fit the particular initiatives, for example, in the area of environmental activities.

Other changes in Japanese aid were implemented in the 1990s. Grants as a portion of overall Japanese aid (including multilateral aid, which is all grant) continued to rise, from 48 percent in 1993–94 to 66 percent by 2004, but still remained well below the averages for the DAC as a whole (90 percent grants in 2004). Japanese aid was still by far the least concessional aid from any DAC government.[32]

Between 1981–82 and 2001–2, Japan's bilateral aid for social and administrative infrastructure rose from 11 percent to 20 percent, while its aid for industry and other production fell from 17 percent to 3 percent. Its aid for economic infrastructure remained around one-third of its total bilateral aid. These shifts, too, were a sign of convergence with the practices of other donors, but Japan remained by far the largest funder of economic infrastructure in 2001–2 and among the smallest funders of social and administrative infrastructure during the same period. Also, much of the latter funding was still for infrastructure in these sectors, rather than the institution building that was more common in the aid programs of most aid-giving governments.

In short, while Japanese aid continued to converge with DAC norms, it continued to emphasize the "hardware" of development (infrastructure and equipment) rather than "software" (especially knowledge transfer) and focused on strengthening activities that tended to benefit higher income rather than poorer segments of recipient country populations.[33] In the words of a 1999 DAC report on Japanese aid:

> The health sector in 1996–7 took up 3 per cent of Japan's bilateral commitments . . . mainly concentrated in tertiary and curative health, such as support for hospitals and high technology equipment, medical research institutions, high level training, and posting of Japanese advisors. . . . In 1996–7, 6 per cent of bilateral ODA was allocated to education. Further breakdown suggests that only 1 per cent of Japan's bilateral ODA was committed to basic education. . . . The majority of support went to higher education such as

universities, research institutions, and vocational training, particularly in engineering and high technology. . . . Assistance towards water supply and sanitation has taken up half the share of social sector allocation, partially due to construction of large urban water supply and sewerage facilities.[34]

The DAC *Peer Review* five years later made much the same point: "Japan's allocation in the social sector tends to be directed to the tertiary levels such as universities, research institutions, urban water systems, hospitals and so on. Sustainable development would be impossible without access for the poor to adequate services for health, education, water and sanitation."[35]

Japan's heavy focus on the hardware—infrastructure (especially economic infrastructure)—rather than the software of development differentiated it from most other aid agencies and mainstream development thinking. The importance of infrastructure was not ignored by other aid agencies, but they gave more emphasis to institution and capacity building, even in infrastructure projects, to help ensure that aid-funded activities were both effective in achieving their immediate goals as well as sustainable. For example, roads needed to be maintained—an institutional as well as a financial challenge. Schools needed trained teachers and effective curricula if the expansion in education was to have a development impact.

Further distinguishing the Japanese from other aid-giving governments, Tokyo justified its approach to aid-giving as promoting growth that, it was assumed, would eventually lead to poverty reduction. Most other aid donors sought to provide a portion of their aid directly to benefit the poor, for example, by focusing on primary education (rather than tertiary education) or on providing primary health care. These characteristics of Japanese aid-giving left Tokyo rather isolated in the thrust of its aid funding. And clearly, despite declared intentions to align its aid with mainstream DAC practices, the government had found it difficult to do so.

Although Japan did take leadership, as I have described, in a number of specific and important activities, it was not able to come up with the compelling new ideas or to mobilize other donors to follow policies initiated by Japan. One Japanese scholar complained, "The global debate on development assistance is largely determined by others. . . . Japan's role is no more than that of a timid co-pilot at best."[36] Part of the problem of Japanese leadership may have been language—the limited facility with English that many senior officials and scholars had—and hence, the constraint on their ability to participate fully in international discussions of aid and development. (In contrast, midlevel and junior officials and scholars—many of whom have studied abroad—seem much more comfortable in functioning in foreign languages; thus, this problem is likely to abate over time.) Other limitations on Japanese engagement and leadership on international development issues reflected the unfamiliarity on the part of many MOFA officials (who usually represented Japan in official international meetings and events) with development issues and the nuances of development discourse. MOFA officials were diplomats, usually with only a limited background in development. They tended to rotate jobs every two years and therefore may have lacked the knowledge and development experience to propose innovative approaches to development. And because of the rapid turnover of Japanese officials seconded to international bodies, they often found it difficult to establish the personal relationships with colleagues from other countries that provided the basis for effective participation in international deliberations. They may also have felt uneasy with pushing their ideas to move them forward—it is not usually the Japanese diplomatic style to press ideas forcefully on others. Further, Japanese aid officials sought to avoid any appearance of aggressive public behavior toward other governments (especially in Asia) so as not to provoke a hostile backlash based on memories of the war. Whatever the reasons, the Japanese were not always able to claim the international leadership role that should have been theirs by virtue of their generous aid levels.[37]

TOWARD THE TWENTY-FIRST CENTURY: RETRENCHMENT AND REFORM

In 1996 Japanese aid fell by one-third from the previous year. The drop was part of a general decrease in public expenditures as the Japanese government attempted to deal with the economic recession and fiscal deficit facing the country. (The size of the decrease was magnified somewhat by a weakening yen, a drop in Japanese contributions to replenishing multilateral development institutions, and a high level of repayments to the Japanese government of past concessional loans, thus reducing net aid levels.) Japanese aid fell again in 1997 by a small amount. After a surge in 1998 and 1999 as Japan made a major contribution to Asian countries suffering from the financial crisis, its aid again fell off, declining by one-third between 2000 and 2003,[38] suggesting that the reductions that took place before the Asian financial crisis reflected an underlying trend in Japanese aid—the result of economic problems at home. (The easing of those problems toward mid-decade led to a modest uptick in Japanese aid in 2004.)

In other ways, Japanese aid appeared to be in crisis at the end of the 1990s and in the early years of the new century. Criticism at home of the high aid levels had risen in the midst of a prolonged recession. Then, another scandal erupted, this time involving a prominent Japanese politician—Muneo Suzuki—accused of pressuring MOFA to channel aid through enterprises in his constituency,[39] feeding public perceptions that aid was misused and that the Japanese aid system still lacked transparency. The collapse of the Suharto government in Indonesia and reports of widespread corruption there also provoked criticism of Japanese aid, which had flowed in large quantities to the Indonesian government over several decades. In the words of one observer, "For the first time in memory, Japan's official development assistance program is a controversial public issue. . . . Japan's foreign aid program, long insulated from public scrutiny, has come under fire because of its relationship to both administrative and fiscal reform."[40] Opinion polls, undertaken annually for the prime minister's office, showed that those supporting increases in ODA had declined from a high of 41 percent in 1991 to 19 percent in 2002, while those wanting to reduce ODA as much as possible rose from 8 percent in 1989 to 24 percent over the same period.[41] Japanese citizens, in town hall meetings with their representatives in the Diet, demanded to know why there was so much foreign aid when there were so many problems at home and were particularly critical of Japanese aid to China, which was beginning to compete with Japan in world markets and making formidable economic progress itself.[42] In 2003 eight thousand residents of Sumatra in Indonesia brought a class-action suit against the Japanese government (in a Tokyo court), claiming that they had been forcibly displaced and deprived of their jobs as a result of a Japanese aid–funded dam project. They demanded $400 million in compensation. The case received a considerable amount of attention in the media, where one commentator called it "the worst problem in the history of Japanese ODA."[43]

The Japanese government, sensing the need to bolster public support for aid, moved toward further aid reforms. In 2002 alone, it created a number of advisory groups and boards to examine Japanese ODA and make recommendations for reforms, including the Board on Comprehensive ODA Strategy, the Advisory Board on Organizational Reform for the Ministry of Foreign Affairs, the Task Force on Foreign Relations for the Prime Minister, the Second Consultative Committee on ODA Reform, and the Advisory Group on International Cooperation for Peace. The recommendations of these groups emphasized strengthening the transparency, accountability, and efficiency of Japanese aid. The Liberal Democratic Party's ODA Reform Working Group also produced recommendations for aid reform, as did Keidanren.

This multitude of studies and recommendations led the government to make a number of changes in the way it organized and managed its aid: to draft a new ODA charter; to strengthen the evaluation function in Japanese aid; to reshape its policies on debt relief, now providing debt cancellation rather than using grant aid to fund debt relief; and to enhance transparency and public participation. The Board on Comprehensive ODA Strategy, made up of government officials, journalists, and representatives of NGOs, business, and other interested groups, was asked to review periodically ODA policies and country assistance strategies. The new ODA Charter, issued in 2003, was a broad synthesis document, encompassing the views of various groups inside and outside the government on the appropriate purposes of ODA. It emphasized the importance of Japan's own security and prosperity in its ODA programs (advocated by business, the Ministry of Economics, Trade and Industry, or METI, and a number of prominent academics, but criticized by NGOs[44]) as well as highlighting the importance of promoting "human security" and poverty reduction (reflecting the views of MOFA, JICA, and the NGOs). It also embraced the new purposes of aid—for example, addressing global problems and conflict management.

As in the past, however, the charter left plenty of room for interpretation and a wide variety of activities involving Japanese ODA, so it was unclear what real changes in ODA policies there were. The charter also promised greater transparency in Japanese aid and increased engagement with NGOs and its public in a more systematic fashion. Finally, the new charter announced two organizational innovations. First, MOFA would "play a central role" in coordinating the various agencies involved in foreign aid. In fact, this appeared to represent little change from existing arrangements—MOFA had taken the lead in the past in coordinating Japanese aid, but its efforts at coordination had not in the past overcome the problems of fragmentation in the organization of that aid. Second, JICA would become an "independent administrative institution," still governed by MOFA but now implementing aid activities without MOFA's supervision. (MOFA officials had tended in the past to try to micromanage the implementation of aid projects.) JICA would also "assist" MOFA in the planning of aid activities, though it was left unclear what this would mean.

As with the enhanced role of MOFA, these various changes did not suggest a significant shift in the way Japanese aid was organized and managed. (One potentially more important decision involving JICA was the appointment of Mrs. Ogata to head it. She brought considerable stature to the position and, because of that, elevated the influence of JICA inside and outside government. For example, she, rather than MOFA officials, led Japanese delegations to international meetings of aid donors. Whether JICA would sustain its increased visibility and clout once she departed was questionable.) In short, the organizational reforms announced by the government in 2003 seemed quite limited and unlikely to bring about fundamental change in the way Japan managed its aid. Nor did they give much promise of furthering the government's efforts to align its aid policies and practices with those of other DAC member states. The actions taken fell far short of the recommendations from the LDP, the advisory panel to the foreign minister, and Keidanren that the government consider establishing a unified aid agency.[45]

Thus, in the early years of the new century, Japanese aid faced a set of challenges: it had gained the much desired "aid superpower" status for a time based on the volume of its aid but could not maintain that position as the largest aid donor in the face of domestic economic problems. And policy leadership among aid-giving governments still remained elusive. The stated purposes of its aid tended to echo those of other major aid-giving governments, as the government tried to align its aid-giving with that of major DAC member states. However, the allocation and use of its aid continued to focus on Asia, rely to a considerable extent on credits rather than grants, and emphasize the creation of physical assets in recipient countries. The 2004 assessment of Japanese aid by the DAC urged the Japanese government to "more fully mainstream poverty reduction and other cross-cutting issues throughout its development cooperation system. . . . Past emphasis on economic growth has not always taken full account of the poverty reduction dimension."[46] And it had proved difficult for the government, led by MOFA, even after extensive study and consultation, to make significant changes in the fragmented organization of its aid system. The reasons for this dilemma and other particularities of Japanese aid take us into the domestic politics of that aid.

POLITICS

I have tried to show how the purposes of Japanese aid have evolved over time, often in relation to external challenges and especially *gaiatsu*. Japan's need for raw materials imports and export markets to ensure its prosperity was a policy given, leading to the extensive use of aid for commercial purposes. Japan's relationship with the United States was critical to its security and economic success, making *gaiatsu* from the United States a powerful influence in government policy-making, including policies involving Japan's foreign aid.

But they were not the only forces driving Japanese aid policies. *Naiatsu*—internal pressures—also played a major role in the purposes and priorities in Japanese aid, along with widely shared ideas and norms in Japanese society, the nature of Japanese political institutions, and the organization of Japan's aid system. The domestic influences on Japan's aid are especially important for explaining the relatively low priority put on the development purpose of that aid and, later, the difficulties Japan has had in aligning its development aid with that of the rest of the DAC.

Ideas

There are three major categories of ideas that directly and indirectly influenced Japan's aid. First was the tradition of a "strong state, weak society." Second were attitudes involving obligations of the rich to help the poor. And third were values involving national prestige.

From its early encounters with the West, major elements in Japanese society had collaborated to create a strong and prosperous country, free of Western control. (The example of China in the nineteenth century, with its weak state, unable to resist European incursions and eventually partitioned and occupied by European powers, was a sobering illustration to Japan of the potential consequences of state fragility.) Well before World War II, a powerful bureaucracy guided and supported the development of a strong economy and military—not through taking over the ownership of productive assets or even regulating them closely, but by providing advice and incentives for private enterprises to develop in directions preferred by the state. After the war, the military no longer played an important role in Japanese politics and economics, but the old tradition of a strong state soon reappeared, embodied in a powerful bureaucracy, not very accessible or accountable to the public, guiding large financial, trading, and industrial conglomerates. A strong bureaucracy, working closely with business, was a natural framework for managing foreign aid—one quickly adopted for that purpose. Decisions on aid were made primarily within the Japanese bureaucracy, collaborating with business interests, with a minimum of external interference, participation, or public debate.

A corollary of the strong state was a weak civil society. In the words of one Japanese professor, looking back on the history of his country, "From the point of view of the Meiji state, the public good could be none other than that which conformed with the objectives of the state."[47] The public space in which civil society developed in other societies was usually occupied by the state in Japan. This tradition continued in postwar Japan: "the subordination of society to the state, a prominent feature of modern Japan, has not only remained intact, but has been taken for granted by the government and bureaucracy, as well as the politicians and people."[48] Thus, the pattern evident in many European countries and in the United States of private individuals forming NGOs to further their goals, whether they involved service delivery or political advocacy, did not exist in Japan during much of the period of this study, limiting the political voice and activism of those concerned with issues of development, global problems, human rights, and other concerns so often giving rise to civil society organizations and influencing the direction of aid in other countries.

However, ideas can change, and, in the case of civil society organizations involved in foreign aid issues, this appeared to be occurring during the 1990s, as the number of such organizations expanded and their access to government grew. What contributed to this change? A combination of internal shocks and external pressures—the failure of government to respond adequately to the Kobe earthquake, the scandals in various government agencies during the 1990s that discredited the public sector (especially MOFA), and the long recession in the Japanese economy all contributed to dissatisfaction with the government, opening the way for the public to consider alternatives to government agencies to address their problems. Additionally, there was the model of active civil societies in other developed countries and encouragement on the part of foreign NGOs for Japanese citizens to form their own NGOs and pressure on government to provide them access and funding. The government began engaging with NGOs and providing them with support. By the end of the century, civil society organizations in Japan had become much more common and accepted in the eyes of the public, even if the social movements they represented still remained small. This represented a significant change in ideas, with a potentially large eventual impact on the purposes and operation of Japanese aid.

A second set of norms, involving obligations of the rich to the poor and the role of public charity, distinguishes Japan from Europe and North America vis-à-vis the fundamental rationale for foreign aid. Private philanthropy was not the tradition in Japan that it was in other parts of the world. Nor were there the appeals to "Christian duty" or "working-class solidarity" with the poor to justify such obligations, as there were in a number of Western countries. Traditionally in Japan, families were responsible for looking out for the elderly and other relatives requiring assistance.[49] Enterprises, especially the large ones, provided health and other family benefits for their employees. The state provided for education. Even as late as the devastating earthquake in Kobe in the mid-1990s, the Japanese government initially considered that it was primarily the responsibility of individuals affected by the quake to deal with their own needs. This does not mean that Japanese people had no sympathy for the needy at home or abroad. Many voluntarily agreed that a portion of the interest on their postal savings accounts should be used to help the poor in developing countries. Japanese volunteers had organized themselves to help Indo-Chinese refugees in Thailand at the end of the 1970s. And the private response by Japanese to the Kobe earthquake in 1996—in the form of donations and volunteer workers—was extraordinary. But a custom of private philanthropy or the tradition of the welfare state evident in much of Europe was weak in Japan—and thus, that intellectual bridge that led easily from collecting private and public monies to help the needy at home to using public resources to assist the poor abroad did not exist. As a result, there was relatively little pressure on government officials to justify Japanese aid in moral or ethical terms. About as far as the government would go in making the ethical case for aid was the following statement in the 1992 ODA Charter: "Many people are still suffering from famine and poverty in the developing countries, which constitute a great majority among countries in the world. From a humanitarian viewpoint, the international community can ill afford to ignore this fact."[50]

The common justifications for Japanese aid—and therefore, the implied purposes of that aid—were focused primarily on Japanese national interests, both commercial and diplomatic, and on maintaining a significant role and respect for Japan in the world. And this was the way most of the Japanese public regarded the aid. In one 1987 poll that asked about the perceived reasons for Japanese ODA, only one-third responded that "humanitarian obligations" were among the rationales.[51] Another poll, done in 2005, found that in terms of Japan's role in the world (which could be taken as a proxy for the rationales for Japanese aid, because it was an instrument for pursuing the purposes listed), 49 percent of the public thought the country should help maintain international peace; 43 percent wanted their country to address global problems (reflecting Japan's own experience with environmental degradation as it developed rapidly and, later, as Chinese development led to greater pollution in Japan); and only 14 percent expressed a concern for supporting development abroad.[52] These views on aid and foreign policy on the part of the public help explain the lower priority accorded to the development purpose of aid, especially during the early decades of Japanese aid-giving.

Finally, there was the value placed on national honor and prestige. In this, Japan was little different from most other countries, which usually sought to project an image abroad that brought them international respect and admiration. However, in Japan's case, there was an additional factor: that country's defeat in World War II. Regaining and maintaining a respected role in the international community was important to Japan, as it was to Germany. This goal, embedded in the Japanese constitution, was cited in Japan's 1997 annual report on ODA: "If, as the Japanese Constitution says, 'We desire to occupy an honored place in international society' and to bring its ideals to life, and if we desire to ensure our own stability and prosperity in this world of interdependence, we must indeed assume some of the attendant costs on behalf of the international community as a whole."[53] Undertaking a sizable aid program became a means of regaining that "honored place" in the world. Furthermore, calling on this personal value was a way of framing and justifying the government's foreign policies and aid policies for maximum public support. For example, one of the arguments used by MOFA officials against too deep a cut in Japanese ODA was that Japan would lose its position as one of the major aid donors in the world—a position that had brought it international esteem.

An additional consequence of Japan's wartime experience was its postwar pacifism. Written into the Japanese constitution was the statement that "Aspiring sincerely to an international peace based on justice and order, the Japanese people forever renounce war as a sovereign right of the nation and the threat or use of force as means of settling international disputes. . . . In order to accomplish the aim of the preceding paragraph, land, sea, and air forces, as well as other war potential, will never be maintained."[54] This provision, which was reflected in widely accepted pacifist values in postwar Japan, limited that country's ability to share the military burden of the Cold War resistance to the expansion of communist influence. Foreign aid was eventually embraced as the substitute for Cold War burden-sharing.

Another carryover from the Second World War affected the way Japan implemented its aid. Tokyo was especially eager to reestablish good relations with neighboring countries in Asia, and aid proved important in this goal—part of the reason why so much aid was concentrated in that region. As I have noted, to avoid provoking resentments in Asia toward Japan resulting from World War II, the Japanese government took a low-key approach to how it managed its relations with governments receiving its aid, long emphasizing a "recipient preference" approach and a disinclination to link its aid overtly to policy reforms.

Institutions

T. J. Pempel, a scholar of Japanese politics, observed that "the definition and implementation of foreign economic policy in Japan rests essentially on the domestic political structures of the country, particularly the strength of the state and its network of conservative support."[55] These words were written in 1978, but political realities—*gaiatsu* notwithstanding—changed little during the remainder of the century to alter this observation, which applied to foreign aid policy as well as foreign economic policies.

The basic outline of the Japanese government is the following: it is a constitutional monarchy with a bicameral parliament, called the Diet. Elections are based on a mixed single-member constituency and proportional representation.[56] There are several political parties of the right and left, the largest being the Liberal Democratic Party (LDP), which has ruled singly or in coalition for nearly all of the period since 1955, making Japan a "dominant-party state."[57] The LDP itself is divided into political factions, based on history and prominent individuals (but without, for the most part, ideological differences), which create intraparty alliances and coalitions to select prime ministers and cabinet members. This arrangement produces powerful ministers and weak prime ministers. In order to become prime minister, "the candidate of one faction usually must establish an alliance with other factions. After this selection is made, the formation of the cabinet is based more upon political balancing among the factions than on merit. As a result, factional leaders or influential politicians who are immediate subordinates or heirs to factional leaders usually preside over important ministries. . . . Therefore, the prime minister's cabinet is composed of formidable colleagues including political opponents who either lead their own factions or are senior members within those factions."[58]

The weakness of prime ministers led to a fragmentation and devolution of power within the Japanese bureaucracy. Prime ministers were reluctant to take strong positions in pushing favored policies on reluctant ministries (often headed by key factional leaders) or in resolving disputes among ministries. As a result, differences among ministries had to be coordinated, negotiated out, or simply ignored, making it difficult to impart strong policy directions or to bring about substantial policy and, above all, organizational changes in programs like foreign aid that adversely affect the interests of those ministries involved in it. (The election of 2005, in which Prime Minister Junichiro Koizumi won a decisive vote for reform in the face of opposition from the conservative elements within the LDP, was seen by many as weakening the LDP factions, while strengthening the prime minister as well as the LDP party in the Diet. At the time of this writing, it was too soon to say whether Koizumi's landslide was the beginning of significant change in the nature of Japanese legislative politics.)

The Diet played a limited role in policy debates and decision-making on aid (except in cases of scandal or major crises). Because of the predominance of the LDP, to the extent that such debates took place, they occurred privately within the LDP itself and not in the Diet—thus in effect excluding the public. In any case, opposition parties in the Diet have generally supported Japan's aid. As a result, for most of the period of this study, the existence of a sizable foreign aid program was not controversial. Thus, few politicians, including those of the LDP, followed foreign aid policies or became expert on their government's aid activities. Additionally, there was little regular oversight of foreign aid on the part of the Diet or challenges to the government's policies or purposes.[59] Much of the real decision-making in Japan took place within the powerful bureaucracy—reinforcing the historical tendencies within Japanese politics toward a lack of transparency on decision-making.

Changes in Japan's political institutions toward the end of the 1990s and early years of the twenty-first century suggest that foreign aid could be in for some real reforms in the future. Parliamentarians began to take a more active interest in Japanese aid and in Japanese foreign policy in general. The LDP established its own Special Committee on External Economic Assistance to follow aid issues. Parliamentarians examined the ODA reforms being considered by the government in the late 1990s. According to one member of the Diet, the government was forced to make several changes in its new ODA charter as a result of the intervention by Diet members. The government was also put on notice that members of the Diet would be watching the implementation of ODA reforms and, should they be regarded as ineffective, the Diet would consider more fundamental aid reforms, including unifying JICA and the aid account in JBIC and locating them in MOFA. (At the time of this writing, the government had decided on—but had not yet implemented—a unification of JICA and the ODA lending function of JBIC. But this decision was part of a broader reorganization of the Japanese government, not an effort to strengthen the development voice and function within the government. If the reorganization is implemented, however, that could be the result.)

Several factors contributed to the apparent awakening interest of parliamentarians in aid issues. One was public criticism of foreign aid. An increasingly engaged public was reinforced by a gradual increase in NGO activism on aid issues. And a younger generation of Japanese politicians was more willing to challenge the government on policy issues than many of the older, established members of the Diet. Finally, the scandals of the late 1990s and an especially public one in 2002 intensified public criticism of aid and, consequently, the concerns of parliamentarians over the way Japanese aid was being managed.[60]

Interests

Initially, the principal interests competing for influence over foreign aid were commercial and diplomatic. Development interests inside and outside government remained relatively weak. Commercial interests within government were represented by METI, one of the most powerful ministries. Outside government, Japanese business organizations, such as Keidanren, supported the use of tied aid to help expand Japanese business activities abroad. Individual enterprises, especially in the construction and engineering fields, were heavily involved in implementing Japanese aid projects and could make their own specific concerns known in direct contacts with members of the Diet and bureaucracy. However, Japanese business interests did not control Japanese aid. Clearly, decision-making on aid rested with the bureaucracy, and when it was no longer deemed necessary to apply aid to expanding Japan's export markets, the government turned its aid to serve its diplomatic purposes more directly—above all, managing its relations with the United States.

The engagement of business interests in Japanese aid diminished after the government began to untie its aid in the 1980s—businesses felt they had fewer opportunities to win aid contracts. According to Japanese officials, the influence of METI on aid within the government (specifically, involving the allocation of aid from JBIC) also diminished. Business interests in aid, however, reemerged during the 1990s. With the long recession in Japan, organizations like Keidanren began to press for a greater Japanese "national interest" component in Japanese aid—meaning a greater focus on implementing aid projects through Japanese firms. Japanese business had some success in this effort, as a portion of the aid provided to Asian governments during the Asian financial crisis was tied to Japanese exports. But even this success was a temporary one, tied only to the special aid fund set up to address the crisis. The long-term prospects for business influence over the allocation of Japanese aid appeared limited by the beginning of the twenty-first century.

The Ministry of Finance—described by one observer as "at the apex of the Japanese bureaucracy"[61]—played a role in aid decisions, primarily on the overall amount of Japanese aid. It had responsibility for Japan's participation in international financial institutions and managed the government budget; and it was one of the ministries governing aid from JBIC. It focused most on the volume of expenditures and the terms of Japanese aid. Its hard-headed goals (like almost all ministries of finance) were to limit overall spending, to favor loans rather than grants in foreign transfers, and to resist debt relief. It drove the decrease in Japanese aid at the beginning of the twenty-first century (in the face of resistance from MOFA) as part of the government's program of economic reform.

Diplomatic interests were promoted by the Ministry of Foreign Affairs. As with all such ministries, one of MOFA's main responsibilities was managing Japanese relations with other governments and international organizations. Foreign aid was a useful tool in these relationships, both indirectly through managing its relationships with the United States and directly with countries of strategic and economic importance to Japan, especially in East Asia. And because Japan's aid agencies had little role in policy-making, MOFA became the principal external representative of Japan's aid programs and the main conduit within the Japanese government for the views and pressures from other governments and from international organizations on aid issues. With the untying of Japan's aid and the subsequent decrease in METI's active role in aid decisions, together with the reforms of 2003,

MOFA appeared to have become the most important ministry shaping Japan's aid. But this role had its complications. MOFA officials typically had little expertise in the development business and were, therefore, ill-positioned to drive a fundamental shift in the way Japan managed and used its aid away from infrastructure and toward institution building. And MOFA's influence weakened—especially with regard to decisions on the overall amount of Japan's aid—with several scandals associated with it and ensuing public criticism.

Within the Japanese government, the voices for development interests other than MOFA were relatively weak. The two agencies responsible for implementing Japanese aid—OECF/JBIC and JICA—which might have been advocates of development, had little say in the internal politics of Japanese aid because of their status as subcabinet, implementing agencies governed by ministries. Further, in the case of JICA, its leadership was often borrowed from MOFA, thus preventing inside professionals from rising to the highest leadership levels of the agency. The weakness of the internal voice for development within the Japanese government was paralleled by the weak external constituency for development—the group of NGOs working on relief and development. Toward the end of the 1990s, this external voice grew stronger as NGOs began to develop other points of access to the Japanese political system, working with the media to get their ideas out and beginning to work with members of the Diet. Their public image had become positive enough that members of the Diet had begun to seek their support as part of their electoral campaigns.

One NGO leader told me that, of course, they could not endorse any candidate for parliament. But what they did do was send a questionnaire to all candidates on issues of importance to NGOs and then compile and publish the answers they received—a form of reverse pressure on aspiring politicians. NGOs had also begun to lobby Diet members on issues of importance to them—a fact that was confirmed in my interview with a senior Diet member.

Undoubtedly the most important achievement of the NGOs during the 1990s and early years of the new century was gaining a measure of access to government agencies involved with Japanese aid. This change could well lead to a greater voice for development and related purposes in Japanese aid in the twenty-first century, especially as NGOs learn to combine their tactics with the media and Diet with their access to the bureaucracy and the public. The one concern regarding the future influence of NGOs in Japan related to me by a number of NGO leaders was financing. They were highly reliant on government funding, which, if that did not change, could limit their ability to use their voices in Japanese aid politics, especially where they disagreed with government policies. They required a new tax law to ease their ability to seek private contributions and then a strategy for generating such contributions. This would be a challenge in a society where private giving was still novel.

Organization

A major impediment to fundamental change in Japanese aid was the way it was organized. Japanese aid was fragmented in several important ways. Policy was divided from implementation. For JICA, MOFA determined policy (with, according to officials, informal consultations between the two agencies). MOFA, MOF, and METI—all with rather different institutional interests—participated in policy and lending decisions that JBIC then carried out. This divorce between policy and implementation posed challenges to the government in its efforts to align and professionalize its aid operations. Those making key decisions on aid policies and allocations lacked development knowledge and experience, and those with such knowledge did not make key decisions. This arrangement also separated responsibility from accountability—a poor recipe for coherent, effective aid. Further, implementation was divided too, with JBIC managing loans, JICA managing grant-based technical assistance, and MOFA taking care of another set of grants. Numerous other government agencies had their own small aid programs. Not surprisingly, the challenges of coordination between these agencies were substantial, and it is not yet clear that the reforms of the twenty-first century—involving the creation of a variety of intragovernmental coordinating mechanisms—can resolve them.

Exacerbating those challenges, the two aid agencies differed in their approach to development. JBIC focused on economic growth as the central goal of Japanese ODA, with an emphasis on funding infrastructure as a means of achieving that end, while JICA had a greater focus on poverty reduction and aid's newer purposes, including conflict management and global issues. (An outside observer can even sense something of a cultural difference between these two organizations, both in the way their officials discuss development and the way they talk about one another.) In short, the organization of Japanese aid, within the broader context of Japan's political institutions, has acted as an impediment to fundamental change in that aid. The reforms of the early years of the new century—giving JICA greater institutional independence from MOFA, giving MOFA the lead inside government in coordinating Japanese aid, revising the ODA charter, increasing the transparency of Japanese aid-giving—are all laudable, but none appears sufficient to bring about major change in the way Japan manages its aid or its ability to align with DAC practices. If JICA and parts of JBIC are combined, however, this change—together with others seemingly underway involving NGOs, the breakup of LDP factions, and the expanding role of the LDP generally in aid issues—could produce a major shift in the purposes and development uses of Japan's aid and an increased alignment of that aid with the rest of the DAC.

CHAPTER 5

France: Rank *et Rayonnement*

French aid has been among the most diplomatically motivated aid from any major aid-giving government. Its allocation by country, often its use, and its organization all reflect the role aid has played in France's postcolonial foreign policy, especially in sub-Saharan Africa. But the deepening economic and political crises of that region and the apparent failure of French policies there (including its aid policies) provoked a rising critique of that aid from within France, above all from the younger generation of France's political class. In 1998 the French government implemented a major reorganization of its fragmented and opaque aid system to reorient its use from an instrument of France's postcolonial policies of maintaining a sphere of influence and cultural presence in its former territories in Africa and elsewhere to a more development-oriented aid program, with greater transparency and coherence and better alignment with DAC norms and practices. While ambitious in intent, the reforms appeared in many ways to be only partial steps in the intended direction of change and may prove inadequate to achieve the government's stated goals. Whether France's aid in the twenty-first century would look substantially different from its aid in the twentieth century was at the time of this writing still uncertain.

A HISTORICAL PROFILE OF FRENCH AID

The four periods in the evolution of French aid over the second half of the twentieth century include its origins from 1950 to the mid-1960s, when French aid emerged from previous colonial transfers; its consolidation from the mid-1960s to 1990, during which time French aid increased dramatically; a period of criticism and reform, from the beginning of the 1990s to the end of the decade, when French aid first continued to rise and then dropped dramatically; and at the beginning of the new millennium, an era

FIG. 5.1. TOTAL FRENCH AID (NET)

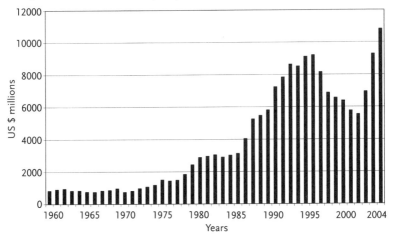

Source: DAC, "International Development Statistics (IDS) Online," http://www.oecd.org/dac/stats/idsonline/ (accessed October 2005).

of reform and increase in French aid-giving. Figure 5.1 shows the changes in the overall level of French aid during the period of this study.

The Origins and Establishment of French Aid

French aid grew out of that country's colonial experience, especially in sub-Saharan Africa. As with other European colonial powers, France's early policies toward its colonies were based on the assumption that they would finance their economic advancement through revenues from their exports of raw materials, through taxation, and through private investment. This policy of "self-sufficiency" started to change in the 1920s, as various colonial administrators began to finance basic services. But the Depression and Second World War intervened and few such expenditures were undertaken.[1]

An important change in French thinking took place after World War II, with the creation of the Fourth Republic in 1947. This republic encompassed the "French Union," which included colonies in Indochina, the Caribbean, and Africa. Echoing assimilationist sentiments evident in French colonial policies in the nineteenth century, the inhabitants of these colonies were made citizens of France, with the right to vote in French elections (though suffrage was restricted to educated elites in the colonial territories) and to send representatives to the French parliament. The logical implication of political equality was to move toward economic equality, including, eventually, equal access to public services and comparable levels of development in all parts of the Union. Thus, with the extension of the political boundaries of the French state to include its overseas territories, government ministries began to undertake activities in those territories in their respective fields of responsibility—for example, education, health, and agriculture. Additionally, a number of semiautonomous government agencies were established to provide technical assistance and undertake research on pressing problems of health and agricultural production in the tropics, where most of France's colonies were located. The government also set up several funds aimed specifically at financing development plans in its territories: one, FIDES (Fonds d'Investissements pour le Développement Economique et Social) would finance development plans in "Overseas Territories"—most of France's colonies. A parallel fund—Fonds d'Investissements des Departments d'Outre-mer, or FIDOM, was set up to provide financing to France's overseas departments (Martinique, Guadeloupe, French Guiana, and Reunion). The Ministry for Overseas France oversaw the management of these two funds. The Caisse Centrale de la France d'Outre-mer implemented the programs and delivered the checks. Thus, a whole complex of economic ties, involving a wide variety of government agencies, ministries, and semi-independent institutions grew up in the postwar period to sustain the development of "overseas France," with relatively little central direction in what was, ironically, a highly centralized state. These organizations were the precursors of France's foreign aid bureaucracy.

Neither the Fourth Republic nor the French Union proved durable. In the 1950s France's territories in Indochina opted for independence (after defeating the French at Dien Bien Phu in 1954) as did Morocco and Tunisia. Algerians also demanded independence, but the large number of French settlers there created a powerful lobby against separating Algeria from France. A prolonged and bloody war broke out in 1954 that threatened to bring France itself to the brink of political chaos. In 1958, after several years of retirement, former Prime Minister Charles de Gaulle was called back to government to deal with the crisis, rewrite the constitution for a Fifth Republic, and become France's president. The new constitution created a "hybrid" government—a combination of a presidential system (with the president elected by the entire country and having responsibility for broad national policy directions as well as for foreign affairs and defense) and a parliamentary system with the prime minister and cabinet drawn from the legislature, responsible for managing day-to-day operations of the government.

The new constitution also discarded the idea of a French Union and instead created a French Community in which France's remaining colonies— mainly in Africa—would be "departments" of France with a degree of individual autonomy (but with foreign and defense affairs still being handled by

Paris). The reason for this change was captured well by Teresa Hayter: "The contradictions in assimilation became increasingly clear; if France really did treat Africans as equal members of one great community, and gave them the weight in French politics which their numbers deserved, France would become, as Herroit had warned, 'a colony of its colonies.'"[2] And that, it did not want.

In 1958 eligible Africans in France's colonies were asked to vote on the new constitution. A "no" would mean that they would be opting for independence and a complete separation from France. And independence would include no further assistance from Paris, as President de Gaulle made clear: "one cannot conceive of an independent territory and a France continuing to help it."[3] Only one territory voted no—Guinea. Guinea became independent, but the French promptly cut all assistance and left the country—taking even the light bulbs, according to some reports.

But within two years, France's fourteen other African territories demanded and received their independence. And in their cases, French aid, along with numerous other ties, continued and increased. The French government really had no choice if it wished to ensure a smooth transition to independence and political stability in these poor and underdeveloped countries and to maintain its influence there, given the readiness of other governments, above all the United States, to provide aid (and, potentially, to replace French influence—at least, this is what some French officials feared). And so, French aid to its former African territories rose rapidly, as France quickly became an important aid-giving country. It also undertook sizable aid programs in its other former protectorates and colonies in North Africa, the Caribbean, Asia, and Oceania.

The fourteen newly independent francophone countries of sub-Saharan Africa[4] carried a surprising importance for Paris. Many of them were quite small and impoverished, but they served as the essential core of a sphere of influence for France, which aspired to a place in the front rank of world powers that would have been difficult to claim solely on the basis of its own size, affluence, and military strength.[5] French politicians are often quoted as having worried that "Without Africa, France would become a power of the third rank."[6] Additionally, the French aspiration to "shine" (*besoin de rayonnement*) through the spread of its language, its values, and its culture was deeply felt, and its fourteen former African colonies—where French continued to be the national language—were symbols of a realization of this aspiration.

These diplomatic and cultural purposes of France in Africa were supplemented by commercial interests. The French government was concerned to obtain reliable access to oil and later to uranium for its nuclear weapons and energy needs. Both of these resources were found in its former African territories. French construction companies and manufacturers were interested in benefiting from aid expenditures on infrastructure and exports. French entrepreneurs had invested in the production of raw materials in Africa—cacao, coffee, cotton, minerals—to sell to France, and others exported French processed goods and manufactures back to these former colonies. French commercial interests in Africa became a domestic constituency for continuing French involvement in West and Central Africa, for concessional commercial arrangements, and for aid to these regions. Promoting development in the countries receiving its aid was a further purpose of French aid and the motivation of many of France's experts, advisors, and officials managing their government's assistance. These experts and officials tended to think of development in terms of economic growth, planned and led by the state, much as it had been in France. However, at the senior levels of the French government, development tended to be a secondary purpose for France's aid and a means to the diplomatic end of promoting political stability and maintaining France's influence in its former territories.

This set of priorities—diplomatic, cultural, commercial, and developmental—was reflected in the allocation and use of French aid. In 1966, for example, nearly all of France's bilateral aid went to its former territories. (Of $588 million in bilateral aid allocated to specific countries, only $18 million was shown to be provided to countries not associated with France's former colonial empire or to the francophone countries Rwanda and Burundi. These other recipients were two Latin American countries and Turkey.[7]) The largest single recipient of French aid that year was Algeria. Other better-off countries, like oil-rich Gabon or the relatively prosperous Côte d'Ivoire, received sizable amounts of aid along with desperately poor countries like Chad, Burkina Faso, and Niger. French aid in its former territories in sub-Saharan Africa at that time typically amounted to anywhere from 80 percent to 90 percent of those countries' total aid inflows, ensuring that France remained their predominant external partner. The importance of aid as an instrument of postcolonial diplomacy led France to become the second largest aid donor in the mid-1960s, after the United States.

The uses of French aid reflected the importance ascribed to consolidating the use of the French language. A substantial portion of the aid was used to finance cooperants—French citizens who taught in the schools (in French) and provided advice to the government. There were nearly forty thousand cooperants in 1965.[8] In 1971 (when detailed data on the sectoral allocation of aid is available) just over half of France's bilateral aid went to education. Program assistance (primarily budgetary support and calculated separately from sectoral aid) was the next largest expenditure after education. Assistance to agriculture (emphasizing the development of exports like cotton and fish), communications infrastructure, and food also bulked large in France's bilateral aid—all suggesting a mix of purposes.

In 1965 French aid had an 80 percent grant element—quite concessional by DAC standards at that time. Over half of France's bilateral aid was used to fund technical assistance—primarily the *cooperants* mentioned. (At this time, the DAC average for technical assistance was only 20 percent.) Finally, France provided a relatively small amount of its total aid—only 7 percent—to multilateral institutions, reflecting the strong diplomatic impulse behind its aid, which was best realized through bilateral rather than multilateral channels. (In any case, the World Bank and other international development organizations were, in the eyes of French officialdom, too much under the thumb of "*les anglo-saxones*" and, therefore, not organizations France was eager to support.)

French aid to its former African territories was part of a dense network of relationships set up in the wake of independence—monetary unions among most of France's former territories in West and Central Africa, with the *Communauté financière africaine*, or CFA, franc as their common currency, backed by the French franc; preferential and protected trade relations (with higher than world market prices for many African exports); defense agreements and military cooperation; and a set of close personal and political relationships between French and African political elites—all emerging out of the colonial period and important for France to maintain its sphere of influence in what came to be called *les pays du champ* (often translated as "ambit" or "concentration" countries).

Organizing French Aid

France's aid organization, emerging from the colonial period with the added gloss of the government's postcolonial diplomacy, was the most complex, fragmented, and opaque of any aid donor. I will begin at the top of the French government. Diplomatic relations with the fourteen African states were sufficiently important to France that in 1959 President de Gaulle created a General Secretariat for the African and Malagasy States in the office of the presidency (often called the "*cellule*," or cell) to manage those relations and named Jacques Foccart to head it. Foccart had long been associated with the president, especially in the area of intelligence gathering and covert action (including in Algeria during the bloody war there). His task was to protect political stability and France's influence in France's former African territories. To do so, he created networks of information sources in Africa and personal relationships with the heads of state and other prominent elites in the region: "For them [African leaders], Foccart is not only the only access sure and direct to the General [de Gaulle], but also the only person capable of solving all their problems, whether political or personal or family. . . . With him, they feel at home in France and treated as friends."[9]

Foreign aid was one of the lubricants of this network. The source of a portion of that aid was the Ministry of Cooperation which was established in 1961 (replacing the old Ministry of Colonies). It was responsible for technical assistance and grant aid (including budget subsidies) only to the *pays du champ*, giving the Africans in effect their own aid ministry.[10] The ministry's funds were channeled through the Fonds d'aide et de cooperation (FAC) (replacing the old Fonds d'Investissements pour le Développement Economique et Social, or FIDES, of the colonial period) to be paid out by the *Caisse Centrale de Coopération Economique* (CCCE).

The CCCE was a semiautonomous agency, reporting to the Ministry of Economy, Finance and Industry, the Ministry of External Affairs, the Ministry of Cooperation, and the Ministry of State for Overseas Departments and Territories (known as DOM/TOM). The CCCE implemented aid expenditures and activities for these ministries in addition to disbursing some aid loans of its own to countries not among the *pays du champ* (which were called *pays hors champ*—or outside the "ambit" countries). The CCCE grew out of the *Caisse Centrale de la France d'Outre-mer* which had evolved from *Caisse Centrale de la France Libre*, set up in London in 1941 to manage funds (many from the colonies) for the Free French movement.

The Ministry of External Affairs had its own aid program. This program provided technical assistance to the *pays hors champ*, assistance for cultural exchanges, and French contributions to UN development agencies. The Ministry of Economy, Finance and Industry provided loans to governments outside of the purview of the Ministry of Cooperation as well as transfers to members of the CFA franc zone in deficit. It managed French contributions to the international financial institutions and food aid. The Ministry of State for Overseas Departments and Territories provided aid to France's overseas departments and territories that were not independent countries. (Some of this assistance was counted as official development assistance by DAC and some was not.) The Ministry of Research provided aid to a variety of research endeavors relevant to developing countries, for example, in agriculture and health. The Ministry of Education provided its own aid to education.

In total, there were twenty-five ministries and forty institutes and semipublic agencies active in providing advice, research, and aid funding in developing countries. The organization chart in figure 5.2 attempts to capture the complexity and fragmentation of this system.

This system was divided by type of recipient, by type of aid (grant versus loan), by policy and implementation, by sectoral focus, and by function (policy, implementation, expenditure). Within this aid system, there was

FIG. 5.2. THE ORGANIZATION OF FRENCH AID, 1965

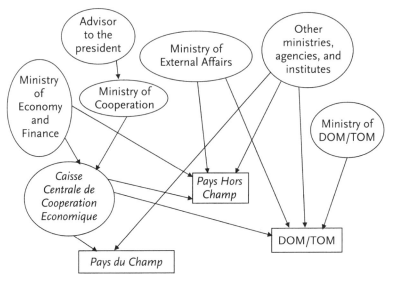

no central focal point for aid policy-making, leadership, and coordination. There were no white papers or major policy statements setting out the main goals and strategies guiding France's aid. There was no process for coordinating the aid within the government to ensure coherence. Nor was there a country programming process, increasingly adopted by other aid-giving governments—French aid was (in theory at least) "request based," with ideas for projects coming from the recipients themselves and discussed periodically with the French government in joint commissions. There was little in the way of evaluation of aid's effectiveness. No sane person would have designed such a system. Rather, it grew out of France's colonial and organizational arrangements, which were not revised once the colonies had gained their independence.

Consolidation

The period from the mid-1960s to the beginning of the 1990s showed considerable continuity in the purposes of French aid. Diplomatic purposes remained paramount in country allocations, with one-third of bilateral aid concentrated in sub-Saharan Africa—over half in its former colonies there, where France remained by far the predominant donor, providing between one-half and two-thirds of total aid to most of these countries. Nearly all of the largest recipients of France's aid outside of Africa were also former colonies, the exceptions being Egypt, Indonesia, and Thailand. During the

1980s, the proportion of French aid to multilateral organizations had averaged around 25 percent, with over half of that aid going to the European Union aid program.

Technical assistance continued to play an important role in French aid, representing 40 percent of bilateral aid expenditures in 1990, making France the largest donor of technical assistance among DAC governments. The aid was used to fund 12,600 *cooperants*—fewer than in 1965 but still a very large number. French assistance continued to be concentrated in education—in 1990, nearly 25 percent of its bilateral aid funded activities in that sector (primarily in secondary and tertiary education), the highest of any aid donor. One thing new to French aid in 1990 was a rising proportion devoted to debt relief—5 percent in 1990—making France the second most generous donor of debt relief after the United States. This was the consequence of the fact that a large portion of French aid in the past, especially that managed by the *Caisse Centrale*, had been provided in the form of concessional loans that governments, especially in Africa, found it difficult to repay.[11]

At the beginning of the 1990s, a relatively high proportion of France's bilateral aid (over 50 percent) remained tied or partially tied to the purchase of French goods and services—and this percentage had also increased during the previous ten years as the French government sought to "associate as many partners as possible (especially from the private sector) with the implementation of the aid programme."[12] Finally, France channeled the smallest portion of its aid of any donor (0.4 percent of ODA in 2003, compared to an average for all DAC members of 2 percent) through NGOs. These organizations were active in France, but the government did not use them for implementing its aid activities, which continued to involve government-to-government relationships primarily. French NGOs enjoyed little systematic access to the government on aid issues, and while a number criticized French aid, they had little apparent impact on its operation.

Perhaps the most interesting aspect of French aid during the years from the early 1960s to the mid-1990s was the ongoing discussion within France on the organization of its aid and, by implication, on the purposes of that aid. This discussion reflected the recommendations from most experts and critics of France's aid that it be "normalized." By "normalized," critics usually meant two things: that the diplomatic focus of French aid be diminished in favor of a greater development focus (meaning less use of aid to support political and personal relationships with African heads of state); and that the aid be provided to other regions and countries with greater international political weight, commercial importance to France, and developmental potential.

This discussion really commenced back in 1963, when most French colonies and territories had gained their independence and the Algerian war was over. It was an opportune moment to reflect on what French aid should look like in a postcolonial world. Some questions had already been raised by critics of French aid about its high cost and the need for increased government expenditures to address domestic problems. Thus, the government decided to commission a report on the future purposes and organization of French aid. The resulting "Jeanneney Report" (after Jean-Marcel Jeanneney, the chair of the commission preparing it) began by justifying French aid on ethical grounds: "The first reason, sufficient in itself, for a French policy of cooperation with the Third World is the feeling which France has of her duties towards humanity."[13] The second reason underlying French aid was that "France has always experienced the need to act beyond her own frontiers. . . . France desires more than any other nation to disseminate her language and culture."[14] The report, which, it should be remembered, was not an official statement of government policy but rather the views of a commission, went on to mention diplomatic and commercial advantages for France of its aid.

The recommendations of the report were interesting, as they implied a radical break with policies at that time. They urged that French aid no longer be so heavily concentrated in Africa (though that region should remain a priority) but that, as the amount of aid increased, it should be distributed elsewhere in the developing world; that France should not remain so predominant a source of aid for African countries; that a greater share of French aid be channeled to multilateral institutions; that French technical advisors be replaced more rapidly by nationals in its former colonies and territories; that less financing be directed to infrastructure and more to productive activities; and (in a part of the report not published but eventually leaked) that aid functions should be combined and merged into the Ministry of External Affairs.

The report provoked a discussion of the purposes of French aid in the public domain, but its recommendations were largely ignored by the government. In 1966 President de Gaulle merged the Ministry of Cooperation into the Ministry of External Affairs, but this move involved more political packaging than substantive change, because the old ministry retained its own independent budget, its staff, its responsibilities for the same states, and much of its autonomy despite its new bureaucratic location. Thus, this apparent organizational change, made for reasons involving politics and personnel, did not really mark a break with the policies or orientations of the past.

In 1971 the French government commissioned another major report on its aid program and organization. This report by the *Comite d'Etude de la Politique de Coopération de la France avec les Pays en Voie de Développement*, called the "Gorse Report," made many of the same criticisms of French aid as the Jeanneney Report, including its excessive concentration in francophone Africa, its emphasis on education, and its lack of a coherent organization within the French government that led to *ad hoc* activities abroad with too little effectiveness.[15] As with the Jeanneney Report, the Gorse Report produced no significant changes in the allocation, use, or organization of France's aid programs.

After becoming president in 1974, Giscard d'Estaing detached the Secretariat of State for Cooperation from the Ministry of External Affairs to recreate a Ministry of Cooperation, underlining the importance he gave to relations with France's former colonies in Africa. In 1981, when François Mitterand became president, he appointed Jean-Pierre Cot as minister of cooperation. Cot attempted to move in a new direction—to "internationalize" the Ministry of Cooperation, dropping its exclusive focus on *pays du champ* and putting greater emphasis on human rights and development in the activities of the Ministry. His ideas provoked considerable criticism and resistance on the part of African heads of state who stood to lose their special access and treatment with regard to French aid and other attentions with Cot's reforms. Their influence in Paris was significant when they exerted themselves. As a result of their pressures and other tensions within the French government, Cot was eventually dismissed as minister. His reforms regarding the geographical scope of the ministry were reversed in 1986 with the focus of the ministry again on *pays du champ*.[16] Cot's efforts to reorient French aid failed, just as earlier suggestions to reorient that aid failed—the diplomatic purposes and political forces shaping aid were strong and well entrenched in the organization and orientation of the French government.

History repeated itself yet again in 1990, with another government-commissioned report—the "Hessel Report" on French cooperation.[17] Like its predecessors, this report recommended that France drop the special focus on francophone African countries, that it channel more of its aid through multilateral institutions, and that it create within the government a "high council for cooperation," made up of representatives of civil society and parliament to advise the government on foreign aid. This report was also buried and its recommendations set aside. Indeed, one expert on French aid lists forty "more or less official" reports between 1960 and 2003 that criticized the allocation, use, organization, and effectiveness of French aid—most with similar messages and with similar results.[18]

Why did repeated French governments ignore the recommendations of these many reports, even though the organizational disarray in French aid was clear for all to see, along with the deepening economic crises and authoritarian (and often corrupt) rule in many of France's favored aid recipients? The answer is that a portion of the French political class had developed vested interests in the existing purposes and organization of French aid. In addition to maintaining a sphere of influence and of cultural *rayonnement* with the aid, some of them had developed more concrete and less savory stakes in the close relationships and generous aid transfers to African governments.

There were frequent stories of sweetheart deals for French businesses in Africa (e.g., overdesigned and overpriced, aid-financed infrastructure, or monopoly control of certain imports and manufacturing in particular countries). And there were the special political ties: the heads of state of a number of African countries often contributed to French presidential electoral campaigns. Senior French political party officials would make a swing through these countries before an election to collect such support. Downgrading France's special relationships with African leaders could endanger a French politician's future political and financial support. Further, exposés by French journalists and writers suggested that *argent noir* ("black money," or corrupt payments) was transferred from certain French companies, like the giant oil company ELF, or even from the French government itself to African leaders and that these payments appear to have in part financed the contributions of African leaders back to French politicians. Other corrupt practices also became well known. For example, Jean-Christophe Mitterand, the son of President Mitterand (whom the president appointed as his African advisor), came to be known as Papamadi (from "*Papa m'a dit*," or "Father told me") as a result of his influence peddling and reputed deals in Africa involving arms sales, secret financing, and a variety of shady activities.[19] The close relationships and informal network of influence between French elites of both major political parties and African politicians and their clients (which came to be called *Françafrique*) provided a powerful constituency for continuity both in the purposes and organization of France's aid.[20]

Transition

The decade of the 1990s was a period of significant change in French aid. The beginning of the 1990s marked a period of rising public criticism of that aid. For example, an article in the influential journal *Le Monde* in 1990, by one "Victor Chesnault" (believed to be a pseudonym of a senior government official), argued that French aid to Africa had been "recycled, privatized, even transferred outside the country by its (African) elites, whose personal fortunes are greater than the debt of their countries. . . . But we (France) are largely responsible for this disaster. We have financed the worst caprices of our African presidents for short-term goals of having them in our pocket. . . . our aid has arrived at an ultimate point of perversion: it maintains in place crumbling powers and parasitical structures whose continuance is the greatest obstacle to development."[21]

Several widely read books on French aid published in the early 1990s made many of the same arguments. One, by Serge Michailof, a mission director for the *Caisse Française de Développement* (CFD—this was the old CCCE renamed), urged that French aid "drop the logic of entitlements; limit the value of 'political gifts'; avoid projects involving public administration; stop supporting ineffective state-owned enterprises; systematize audits; redeploy aid geographically; and be more selective in terms of aid recipients."[22] Such criticisms continued in the press and in books and articles published on French aid during much of the rest of the decade, reflecting a growing view among an element of France's political elites and by the public that a good part of their government's aid had been wasted in Africa over many years and that fundamental reforms were needed. Indeed, the criticisms of French aid began to overshadow the positive contributions of that aid to development in Africa and elsewhere—the young people educated, the infrastructure built, the research undertaken.[23] Nevertheless, in the early 1990s, the government showed no sign of making policy or organizational changes.[24]

Events abroad, however, began to move the government toward reform. The end of the Cold War diminished the importance of Africa in world affairs and, eventually, in French foreign policy as well. Problems in the CFA franc zone created additional pressure for change. Over the years, the CFA franc became increasingly overvalued. The French treasury had to spend more and more money to sustain its value internationally, in effect, financing the balance of payments gaps of African countries. Some speculation put the cost of this subsidy (which was not revealed by the government) at $1 billion per year at the beginning of the decade. African leaders and a number of France's political elites resisted devaluing the CFA franc, arguing that it would disrupt African economies and be seen as a signal of a lessening commitment on the part of France to the region. The overvalued CFA franc also benefited African elites, making the costs of their visits abroad and imports relatively cheap, and these benefits likely strengthened their opposition to a devaluation.

As a first step to address the cost of the CFA franc to its treasury, the French government in 1993 announced that, henceforth, balance of payments support from Paris would be conditioned on an IMF-approved economic reform program. This was an effort to encourage their African aid recipients to implement reforms to reduce the gaps in their external payments. But it was not enough to stop the drain on French resources from the overvalued CFA franc.

It was only after the death in 1993 of Félix Houphouët-Boigny of the Ivory Coast—the African president with the greatest personal influence in Paris— that the French government overrode the objections of the Africans and French politicians who opposed changing the value of the CFA franc and in 1994 implemented a 50 percent devaluation. This change was driven by Prime Minister Edouard Balladur, whose right-wing party, the Rassamblement pour le Republique, together with the Union for France and several other conservative parties, had won the legislative elections. Balladur was known to be a technocrat and not part of the old *Françafrique* network. The devaluation permitted the French government to reduce its aid transfers to Africa, some of which had been associated with supporting the CFA franc's value. It also signaled the limits on French generosity to the region and the beginnings of a "normalization" of its relationships with francophone African countries.

Yet another signal of the beginnings of change in France's African policies was the statement by President Mitterand at the French-African Summit in 1990 at La Baule, France, that his government would henceforth take into account in its aid the commitment of recipient governments to democracy. This was a response to the demands sweeping African countries for multiparty elections after decades of single-party or military-led authoritarian regimes. The first major breakthrough toward multiparty elections occurred in Benin in 1990, with its "national conference," made up of representatives of a variety interests in Beninese society, which claimed sovereignty, rewrote the constitution, and demanded elections. The president of Benin, Mathieu Kerekou, reluctantly agreed to these demands, and, before long, other francophone African governments were calling for their own "national conferences." Mitterand's statement at La Baule represented an effort on the part of the French government to support the aspirations of the Africans for democracy and improved human rights. However, French policies did not immediately shift to reflect the statement at La Baule. Indeed, France continued to support dictators with its aid and French politicians continued to collect contributions to their political campaigns from those same dictators. But even if Mitterand's statement did not signal an immediate and significant change in France's aid policies, it did open the space for the government later to incorporate concerns about democracy into its aid-giving policies. There were signs by the end of the decade that France was beginning to do so by substantially reducing its aid to some of the worst autocrats and human rights offenders, such as President Gnanssingbé Eyadèma of Togo.[25]

Another change was quietly taking place in French aid, not much noted in the literature—the falling portion of aid managed by the Ministry of Cooperation. This Ministry handled approximately half of France's bilateral aid in 1986.[26] By 1992 that portion dropped to 17 percent. The Ministry of Economy, Finance and Industry had always played an important role in French bilateral aid, but during the late 1980s and 1990s that role increased greatly. The Ministry of Economy, Finance and Industry's share of bilateral aid rose from approximately 6 percent to 38 percent during the same period. Part of what was driving the rise in the Ministry of Economy's aid was the increasing transfers associated with the severe balance of payments problems of African countries, but this shift continued even after the devaluation of the CFA franc reduced those transfers. It was also the result of the increase in aid to the European Union and increased debt relief—both managed by the Ministry of Economy, Finance and Industry. These changes combined with a decrease in the number of *cooperants* (whose services were less needed as African countries produced their own teachers and trained professionals) and a decrease in aid for structural adjustment, both funded by the Ministry of Cooperation.

The end of the Cold War coincided with a dramatic decline in the overall volume of France's aid. That aid had reached a high point in 1995 of $9.2 billion. Beginning in 1996, French aid began to drop rapidly, falling by nearly half to $5.5 billion in 2001.[27] Factors contributing to this decline included the need for the government to cut its overall budget to accommodate its deficit to the 3 percent of GNP ceiling associated with the Maastricht Accord, in preparation for monetary union within the European Union. And the end of the Cold War eroded the value of a sphere of influence in Africa and the willingness of French politicians to exert themselves to protect aid levels in the face of pressures to cut the overall government budget.

Reform and Revival in French Aid

With all these changes and with mounting criticisms of French aid at home, the government began in the mid-1990s to consider ways of making its aid more effective, more transparent, more coherent, and more legitimate in the eyes of its citizens—in short, to make it a more professionalized instrument of development. One idea, long pressed by ministers of external affairs, was to fold the Ministry of Cooperation into the Ministry of External Affairs. The Ministry of Cooperation—primarily serving France's former African territories—had become a symbol of all that was wrong with aid. Rightly or wrongly, it had come to be regarded as highly political, nontransparent, and influenced by *Françafrique*. For example, Michel Roussin, who had been minister of cooperation during the 1990s, lamented that "The Ministry of Cooperation passes as a hideout for secret police, a pump for hidden financing, a substratum of colonialism."[28] Nevertheless, responding to pressures from African leaders to keep the ministry intact, President Jacques Chirac, at the 1995 Francophone Summit in Cotonou, Benin, announced that the Ministry of Cooperation would remain independent as long as he was president.

Despite the resistance to reform by the older Gaullists like Chirac and the Africans, several modest reforms in French aid were announced in 1996: the Ministry of Cooperation would be linked "more closely" with the Ministry of External Affairs (though it was not clear that this move had any real content); the scope of the Ministry of Cooperation's geographic responsibilities would be enlarged to include the thirty-seven countries in Africa, Latin America, and the Caribbean that were associated with the European Union; and an interministerial committee would be created to provide better coordination of the fragmented French aid programs. Not surprisingly, these rather limited changes produced little that was new or different.

However, after the Socialist Party won the parliamentary election in 1998, Lionel Jospin became prime minister, "cohabiting" with President Chirac. Jospin, who, unlike Chirac, had never been part of *Françafrique*, proceeded to implement a much more fundamental set of reforms in France's aid: the Ministry of Cooperation was fully merged into the Ministry of External Affairs; an interministerial taskforce on international cooperation and development (CICID) chaired by the prime minister would meet periodically to discuss, decide on, and coordinate broad guidelines for France's aid; the *Caisse Française de Développement* was renamed the *Agence Française de Développement* (AFD) and ("under the tutelage" of the Ministry of External Affairs and the Ministry of Economy, Finance and Industry) was the "pivotal operator" in managing the country's aid; and a new High Council for International Cooperation (HCCI) was created, with sixty members from civil society (NGOs, business organizations, unions, universities, research institutes, parliament, and local governments), to consider salient issues involving French aid and express their views to the government. (The HCCI was advisory; it had no authority over French aid or aid policies.) Finally, it was decided to create a Zone de Solidarité Prioritaire (ZSP), to include some sixty countries eligible for significant amounts of French aid. These countries included all those formerly in the *pays du champ* of the Ministry of Cooperation plus a number of other poor countries. The prime minister described these reforms as "an effort at coherence, clarity, and transparency."[29] In short, France was trying to raise the development purpose of its aid, increase its coherence and effectiveness, and align it more with DAC norms and practices.

Four years later, on the occasion of the UN Conference on Financing Development in Monterrey, Mexico, President Chirac made an additional change in French aid by committing France to increase its official development assistance significantly over coming years—from 0.38 percent of gross national income in 2002 to 0.5 percent by 2007 and to 0.7 percent by 2012. Half of this aid would be provided to African countries to support their efforts to realize the Millennium Development Goals. Later, the president also emphasized France's support for doubling aid for water projects and increasing its contributions to combat HIV/AIDS and to fight world hunger. Did these initiatives and reforms indicate a fundamental reorientation of French aid in the twenty-first century?

The reforms of 1998 represented a measure of real change in France's aid system. But it was questionable from the beginning whether they were sufficient to achieve the goals the prime minister and others set for them. They extinguished the old Ministry of Cooperation but located the ministry's funding and personnel in the Ministry of External Affairs, where the aid would likely still be used for strongly diplomatic purposes—not necessarily different from those of the past. Indeed, in 1999 the minister of cooperation (now a minister within the Ministry of External Affairs) summed up the new priorities for international cooperation: "to build up our capacities for influence abroad; to identify and anchor elites in our partner countries; to confirm our position in development cooperation; and to associate civil society with our ambition."[30]

The DAC, in a peer review of French aid published in 2004, pointed to the potential conflict between diplomatic and development objectives: "the two essential requirements that are development and the continuation or strengthening of France's influence in the world do maintain a degree of ambiguity. The twinning of 'solidarity and influence' expresses the difficulty of combining these two imperatives. . . . Because there is no single institutional agency for development assistance, it may be that trade-offs do not always work in its favour, the priority attaching to it sometimes coming up against the 'arguments with more influence.'"[31] The Ministry of Economy, Finance and Industry, which played a more prominent role in foreign aid management than ministries of finance in any other aid-giving government, managing one-third of France's bilateral aid and two-thirds of its multilateral aid in 2002,[32] had its own institutional orientation—toward lending rather than grants, toward expanding France's exports, promoting French investment abroad, managing international monetary relations, and managing the debts owed France. Its orientation and instruments were not for the most part focused directly on reducing poverty in poor countries, nor did its staff have extensive experience in that area.

The AFD, intended as the pivotal aid agency, managed development loans for other agencies that funded projects that directly or indirectly were expected to produce revenues to permit the borrower (in theory) to repay the loans—for example, infrastructure and financial institutions. The AFD also provided grant-funded development activities but was constrained by the limited amount of grant resources under its control (only about 170 million euros per year). These grants were essential for aiding the already indebted poor countries in sub-Saharan Africa and elsewhere and were necessary to finance non-revenue-producing activities such as postconflict relief and recovery, providing antiretroviral drugs to HIV/AIDS victims, strengthening civil society organizations, financing elections and political party training, or funding poverty-oriented interventions. The AFD was, in short, forced to operate more a like a bank than an aid agency because of the terms of the assistance it managed. And hence, its ability to function as a "pivotal operator" in French aid-giving remained in doubt. In the words of DAC in 2004, "France's stated intention of entrusting the principal role in ODA implementation to the AFD has not been fully translated into action."[33]

Another question related to the role of the AFD was the degree of freedom of action that the agency had within the French government. The AFD was "under the tutelage" of the Ministry of Economy, Finance and Industry and the Ministry of External Affairs in its decisions on the country allocation and use of aid, and its officers in the field reported to the French ambassadors there.[34] In fact, the relationship between the AFD and the Ministry of External Affairs (and its new Direction Générale de la Coopération Internationale et du Développement, or DGCID, which managed the ministry's aid) was never clearly defined; DGCID both oversaw and competed with the AFD for aid and leadership in development. The organizational ambiguity left the two agencies to maneuver for position as leaders in France's development work abroad, with neither fully equipped to do so.[35] It was a recipe for bureaucratic conflict (which, according to observers in Paris, is exactly what developed).

Apart from the elimination of the Ministry of Cooperation, the fragmented nature of the French aid system continued after the reforms. The CICID, created to improve interagency coordination on aid, met only once or twice a year and considered a few broad topics (like which countries should be in the Zone de Solidarité Prioritaire). While it has encouraged greater interministerial coordination, the CICID appears to have had little significant effect on rationalizing the aid operations of the many ministries and agencies involved in aid-giving abroad. As of 2003, for example, it had been unsuccessful in encouraging the government to come up with an overall strategy for French aid. There was still no white paper on government aid policy and no single budget document for that aid, although the Senat and Assemblee Nationale passed a law requiring the government to produce a budget for its foreign aid in 2006. In any case, it is never easy for an inter-agency entity like the CICID, even one chaired by a prime minister, to co-ordinate diverse, autonomous, and powerful government agencies.

The HCCI, while creating better access to government for civil society organizations interested in development aid, was an advisory body with little authority and with a large and diverse membership. It was not well sit-uated to have an appreciable impact on government and, in the view of a number of officials and individual experts on French aid, had not by 2003 had such an impact.[36] Other elements of the government—the AFD, the Ministry of Economy, Finance and Industry, and the Ministry of External Affairs—also established consultation bodies with NGOs. Meanwhile, the percentage of French ODA channeled through NGOs remained the same in 2003 as in 1998—one of the lowest of any DAC donor.

Additionally, the reforms did not touch the office of the African advisor to the president. This "cell," which had had a major impact on the allocation of aid in the past, especially from the Ministry of Cooperation, had weak-ened over time with the government's lessening interest in Africa. But it continued to exist and could still exert influence in the future, given its lo-cation in the Presidency (and especially when the same party controlled the presidency and the parliament and government). Apparently, the mainte-nance of the African advisor's post was a condition of getting French Presi-dent Chirac not to oppose the reforms as he tried to manage harmonious relationships with African leaders.[37]

Finally, while French aid grew rapidly in 2002 and 2003 and seemed set to rise further in the future, much of that aid was in the form of debt relief—one-third of ODA in 2003. (Debt relief was financed by the debtor countries paying their debts and the French government offsetting those repayments with grants.) This arrangement may have eased the pressures on the French budget of funding an increase in aid, but once debt relief commitments had been fulfilled, the government would face a challenge of coming up with funding for sizable new outlays (if commitments to increase aid were to be realized) to meet the Monterrey commitments.

In short, the French government had made significant reforms in the structure of its aid for the first time since it began providing foreign as-sistance and had made major commitments to increase its aid and reorient it toward poverty reduction and associated activities. However, the re-forms in French aid may not have gone far enough for the government to reorient the purposes of that aid and align it more closely with DAC norms and practices. At best, by 2005 the reforms appeared to have made only a limited improvement in the coherence, transparency, and effectiveness of France's aid.

POLITICS

The profile of French aid over the second half of the twentieth century raises three questions: Why did the diplomatic purposes of French aid predominate for such an extended period of time? Why did the French government attempt to reform its aid system, implicitly seeking to shift its purposes in the late 1990s? And why were the reforms limited—possibly too limited to achieve their goals? This section will address these questions using this book's common framework of political analysis.

Ideas

Two clusters of ideas have influenced France's foreign aid: obligations toward the poor and the role of the state in fulfilling those obligations, and broadly shared ideas regarding the identity of France and its role in the world. Throughout the second half of the twentieth century, there was little disagreement, even on the part of the critics of France's aid, that France as a relatively well off country had an obligation to help the poor abroad. Various reports on French aid and statements by French politicians often cited "France's duty toward humanity." The critics of French aid focused on its lack of effectiveness or the urgent needs for funds at home but did not challenge the basic idea that France should aid the poor and that public resources were appropriately used for that purpose. The public appeared to share this view, with support for aid to help people in poor countries varying between 70 percent and 78 percent during the 1990s.[38] The widespread acceptance of the idea that France should help the poor abroad likely came from two main sources: Christian duty and sentiments of social solidarity, much as in other European countries; and France's colonial experience, which eventually brought with it the sense of special obligation to help those in "overseas France" and, later, in France's former colonies to better their lives.

The second cluster of ideas influencing French aid is related to France's identity and its desired role in the world. Those ideas include universal values inspired by the French revolution: liberty, equality and fraternity, and human rights. Additionally, as I have noted already, there is also a widely shared sense that the French language and the civilization it conveys is worthy of universal appreciation and use. Tied to the notion that French language and culture had a special role in the world has also been the idea, articulated and pursued in the post–World War II period by French presidents beginning with de Gaulle, that France deserved to be considered among the great powers and to play an important role in world affairs. This emphasis on global role and rank was not inevitable. French leaders could have taken a less assertive, more regionally focused approach to France's foreign policy after World War II.

Part of the explanation for the emphasis on rank is history—rank had been a concern for French politicians before the Second World War, as France maneuvered for influence in Europe and beyond in the face of a powerful neighbor across the English Channel and of rising German power. But much of the postwar support of this idea could be attributed to the influence of one proud and powerful man, Charles de Gaulle, who as the first postwar president of France set the course and tone of French foreign policy. De Gaulle's insistence on France's role as a major power, despite its humiliating defeat and occupation by the Germans during the war, was intended to appeal to French pride and nationalism (and undoubtedly reflected his own pride and national sentiments)[39] and to provide a unifying theme for the French people, whose past politics had been fractious nearly to the point of ungovernability. (De Gaulle was said to have complained, "How can you govern a country that has 246 varieties of cheese?") De Gaulle's successors—even the socialists—continued his emphasis on France's international standing. Thus, it is not surprising that the notion of rank and role influenced France's use of its aid as a vehicle for creating and sustaining a sphere of influence, primarily in Africa, that would give content to its claim to a seat at the high table of world politics.

However, there was a contradiction at the core of the ideas shaping France's aid. On the one hand was the norm of helping the poor abroad to gain better lives—widely supported by the public. On the other hand, there was the political goal of maintaining France's standing as a great power—embraced by much of the political class—which was translated into creating stability and good relationships with key leaders in Africa, even where they were repressive, corrupt, and a hindrance to any economic or social progress in their countries. The latter idea governed much of France's aid during the second half of the twentieth century. However, the contradictions in these ideas became increasingly apparent in the 1990s, as criticisms of French aid by journalists and even government officials began to reframe the way French aid was regarded by the public—not as a means to human betterment but as a wasteful and ineffective expenditure of public resources. During the 1990s, public support for aid fell from 78 percent in 1996 to 70 percent just two years later—possibly a reflection of this gradual reframing of French aid. The evident failure of much of that aid and the scandals associated with it sharpened the inherent contradictions between these ideas and created pressures for reform.

Institutions

The fifth French republic, established in 1958, was a hybrid. It was a presidential/parliamentary system centered on a strong executive. Decision-making, drawing on a long French tradition of administrative centralization and unitary government, was located in the executive, with relatively little active input from parliament. On foreign aid issues, the legislature played almost no role: there was not even a standing committee, either in the Senat or Assemblee Nationale, responsible for those issues, little comprehensive information from the executive on foreign aid, and few parliamentarians knowledgeable about it. Further, as I have shown, there was little formal, systematized access to executive decision-making for nongovernmental organizations, either through advisory structures with a measure of authority or through parliament. As noted above, informal networks (*reseaux*) of individuals (including African politicians) and groups with connections to senior French policy-makers did have access to decision-making and appear at times to have wielded considerable influence over the allocation and use of the aid. The lack of transparency in government on France's complex and fragmented aid program permitted, and perhaps encouraged, the establishment and operation of informal networks of influence.

Two elements of France's political institutions that eventually challenged the lack of transparency in the way foreign aid was handled were the media and the courts. The French media was often critical of the government. Perhaps the world's most famous weekly for ridiculing government is *Le Canard Enchané*, whose criticisms have often been both witty and insightful. One of the world's most respected dailies is *Le Monde*, which has not hesitated to attack the government on a variety of issues, including its handling of foreign aid. The print media (together with books published by French journalists) became the major vehicle, especially during the 1990s, for exposing scandals and failures of France's aid in Africa. It became the channel for those best informed on the problems of aid—officials of the French government itself—to criticize the government's handling of its aid programs. It could be said that an informal alliance between a handful of journalists and key members of the French government forced a degree of transparency in an otherwise opaque system and that this unusual arrangement was really the source of eventual efforts to reform the French aid system.

Further, the criticisms of French aid were part of a broader set of criticisms of corruption and shady deals in France's political life during the 1990s, issues that French judges began to prosecute at the end of the decade, leading to the jailing of Jean-Christophe Mitterand and others associated with *Françafrique* and even threatening President Jacques Chirac with prosecution once he stepped down from the presidency.[40]

There is one other peculiar aspect of the French political system that played a role in efforts at reform. This is the phenomenon of "cohabitation," mentioned earlier. In periods of "cohabitation," when the presidency has been controlled by one party and the parliament (which elects the prime minister) by another, a degree of competition and political maneuvering between the president and prime minister has occurred on aid issues. In the two major cases of changes in France's aid policies—one involving the devaluation of the CFA franc and the other the 1998 organizational reforms—the political initiative was taken by a prime minister from a party different from that of the president, suggesting that cohabitation can result in new initiatives being undertaken that might otherwise not have occurred. Why should this be? In these two cases, the prime ministers driving the reforms were not part of the old network of political elites associated with Africa. Further, the office of the prime minister does not have primary responsibility for dealing with France's long-term African partners and does not have an African advisor to promote those traditional relationships. (When he was prime minister, Jacques Chirac appointed his own African advisor, but this post was not continued after he left the prime ministership.) This lack of responsibility and bureaucratic baggage may have made it easier for prime ministers, especially those not associated with *Françafrique* or the party of the president, to implement needed changes that were not welcomed by powerful forces, including some of the old political guard and certain business interests. Presidents, on the other hand, inherited a set of relationships with Africans, and even if they began with the intention of reforming those relationships—as socialist François Mitterand did before he was elected president—the weight of those ties (that is, the benefits of maintaining them versus the costs of reform) have more than once discouraged significant reform.

Interests

I have touched already on the various interests involved in French aid. For most of the life of French aid, diplomatic interests, lodged primarily in the presidency, remained predominant. And because the African advisor to the president was also a key point of access for Africans to French decision-making, the Africans themselves represented a significant interest group in support of French aid for diplomatic purposes (i.e., benefiting them). However, the end of the Cold War and the various crises in Africa reduced France's diplomatic stakes in this region and opened the way for a reduction in aid and eventual reform of the aid system that privileged *pays du champ.*

The Ministry of External Affairs was responsible, among other things, for promoting France's cultural interests abroad—especially in francophone countries—and in effect provided a constituency within the government for that interest. Commercial interests influenced the use of French aid, especially in Africa. But the business community was not homogeneous in their views on the country allocation and use of aid. Those supporting its concentration in *pays du champ* were a relatively small but influential portion of the French business establishment, including companies like Bouygues, Dassault, Thomson, and Alcatel.[41] The bulk of French commercial interests supported a geographical allocation of aid more in tune with the concentration of French business in developing countries—that is, in those countries where markets were large, prosperous, and full of potential. With the deteriorating economic situation and spreading political instabilities in Africa in the 1990s, the support from segments of the business community for aid to Africa and for its use for commercial purposes there diminished.

The influence of development interests on France's aid remained limited. As in other countries, the main constituency for that purpose outside of government was NGOs. NGOs working on relief and development were numerous in France. In the 1990s they were estimated to number several hundred and were organized in several collectives, some of which were financed by the government. Further, the government had created a Development Cooperation Board, with representatives from the Ministry of Cooperation, Ministry of External Affairs, and other ministries, together with NGOs for periodic discussions. The Ministry of Cooperation also created a set of sectoral networks of NGOs, working in such areas as education, health, and agriculture, to discuss programs funded by the ministry in those areas. These boards and advisory groups appeared to suggest that NGOs played a role in influencing the purpose of France's aid. However, this was not the case. Their influence proved to be limited, and the boards and networks did not become "solidarity organizations"—that is, a constituency of political advocates—in support of aid, as perhaps the government had hoped. They were more implementing mechanisms for the Ministry of Cooperation's limited funding of activities through NGOs.[42] In fact, despite their numbers, French development NGOs—with the exception of one or two (including the Nobel prize–winning Médecins Sans Frontières)—were for the most part relatively small and poorly financed. For example, no French NGO appeared in the list of the five largest NGOs in development in Europe.[43] Many of them relied on the European Union, United Nations organizations, other aid-giving governments, or the public for their funding. French NGOs did little in the way of "development education" with the French public (nor did the government fund such activity). One of the reasons French NGOs remained small in size and poorly financed relative to similar organizations in other parts of Europe was the limited support they received from their government. And, completing the circle, their small size lessened their influence with government and their ability and willingness to mobilize support for development aid on the part of the French public.

Scholars and members of the academic community working on aid and development policies also had relatively little influence with government on aid issues. The separation between scholars and practitioners in France has been relatively strict—few from either camp spend time in the other. Further, scholarly access to government has remained sporadic and limited. There is no single major research institute in France that focuses on French aid and development policies (like the Overseas Development Institute in London, the Center for Global Development in Washington, or the German Development Institute in Bonn) that could provoke reflection, offer critical analysis, and develop new ideas for French policy-makers.[44]

The interests it is most difficult to describe and, above all, to measure are the various informal networks, subsumed under the term *Françafrique,* that clearly influenced the purpose, allocation, and use of French aid but whose influence was seldom transparent. This amorphous and shadowy group was originally established by Jacques Foccart and developed, extended, and changed by the African advisors to the president who followed him. It began to erode in the 1990s, however, as the generation of French and African political elites that populated it retired or died off, as the successor generation of elites and the public lost interest in Africa and maintaining French influence there, and as public attention was called to the nefarious influence of these networks on France's aid policies. This change, in turn, opened the way for French officials and functionaries not part of the old networks to drive forward their ideas for reform during the second half of the 1990s. Working inside the French government and even criticizing French aid in books and newspaper articles, they contributed to the pressures that fueled Prime Minister Jospin's aid reform initiatives in 1998.

Organization

The organization of French aid long privileged the diplomatic purposes of that aid. Three characteristics of that organization were important in this regard. First was the location of an African advisor in the president's office itself, whose job it was to "transmit messages to the president from African heads of state, French enterprises, development activists and those who take an interest in Africa; to take the initiative in the presidency regarding Africa; and to coordinate the rest of the government on Africa policies."[45] This post engaged the presidency directly in day-to-day decisions on the allocation and use of French bilateral aid and ensured that the concerns of the president—which put a high priority on the stability of African governments and their support for French policies worldwide—played a major role in the allocation and use of French aid. However, the African advisor to the president lost much of his access and influence in the late 1990s and early years of the new century as the interests of French elites in Africa declined.

A second important characteristic of French aid has been its organizational fragmentation and lack of a central agency with overall responsibility for aid policies and implementation. This arrangement, long lamented in the many reports on French aid, meant that no one ministry or agency could challenge the presidency in terms of the purposes of French aid.

A third characteristic of the organization of French aid, the absence of an influential agency dedicated to the development uses of French aid, left the field of decision and action within government to the diplomatic and political purposes of aid. The Ministry of Cooperation could not play the role of a voice for development inside the government, given the influence of the African advisor to the president over it during much of the period of this study. The AFD and its predecessors were not able to play that role, because of their own small size and resource limitations.

Thus, the politics of French aid produced a system of aid-giving that put the highest priority on the diplomatic uses of that aid and, for most of the period of this study, kept it there. In the 1990s a number of changes undercut that system: the concentration of aid in Africa and the failures there, the scandals associated with the aid and exposed in the press, the end of the Cold War, the erosion of *Françafrique* and commercial interests supporting the allocation and use of that aid, and, finally, the political opening in 1998 created by cohabitation. Together, these changes produced the reform effort of Prime Minister Lionel Jospin.

However, Jospin's reforms, while significant, failed to produce the intended changes in the purposes and operation of French aid. There are two strong ministries—External Affairs and Economy and Finance—with their own aid programs and many other ministries that also run aid programs. All of these ministries have their own missions, among which development was not the most compelling. And the AFD—the pivotal aid agency—was limited in the amount of resources it controlled, in the terms of its lending, by its "tutelage" by the Ministry of Economy, Finance and Industry and the Ministry of External Affairs, and by its ambiguous relationship with the Direction Générale de la Coopération Internationale et du Développement (the old Ministry of Cooperation, now part of the Ministry of External Affairs). The organizational voice for development within the French government is still muted.

Why were Jospin's reforms so limited, given his apparent goal to align France's aid with that of other DAC member states, thus increasing the importance of development within France's aid programs? In an interview at the time of the reforms, Jospin was asked why he did not create a ministry of cooperation similar to the Department for International Development in the United Kingdom. His answer was evasive.[46] Clearly, he could not touch the African advisor to the president. On the other hand, because the Ministry of Cooperation had become such a symbol of the past failures of French aid, because the interests that had supported privileged access of *pays du champ* to the government and France's bilateral aid had weakened, and because the Ministry of External Affairs was eager to absorb the Ministry of Cooperation (and had been for decades), merging it was relatively easy, while elevating it to a full, independent ministry would have been difficult politically. Such a move would have challenged the prerogatives and the aid resources controlled by the powerful Ministries of Economy and Finance and of External Affairs. Creating an external advisory board with real influence and authority over French aid would have likely provoked the same reaction. Thus, the political costs of a more sweeping and fundamental reform would have been high—higher than the prime minister was willing to pay, even assuming he could have carried through with such reforms against the opposition of powerful ministries. As I have already discussed in relation to the United States and Japan, organization matters and it is often difficult to change fundamentally, even though such a change may be necessary to reorient the purposes of an aid program.

However, real changes in aid-giving do occur over time, especially when the fundamental factors shaping aid's purposes alter. There were several indications that French aid could move further toward elevating its development purpose in the future. First was the requirement that the government produce in 2006 a comprehensive budget on France's aid—for the first time—to be submitted to parliament. This budget could encourage greater collaboration among government agencies on the purposes and policies of aid-giving, and, more importantly, it will provide much better information on French aid and open the door to greater parliamentary and public involvement in aid debates. Polls indicate that the French public supports aid for reducing hunger in the world, continuing development in poor countries, and fighting HIV/AIDS.[47] With more knowledge of how France's aid is actually used, the public may insist on a greater orientation toward poverty reduction, forcing further organizational and operational changes.

Second, a generation of French and African elites is passing—elites that often had personal ties and networks of mutual help in Africa and elsewhere in which French aid had long played a role.[48] A younger generation of French professionals is less tolerant of the repressive practices and corruption of African elites, less patient with the history of economic and political failure in these countries, and less committed to the old Gaullist goals of doing whatever it took to raise and protect France's rank in global politics. This change is evident, for example, in the efforts of the AFD to professionalize its activities in the manner of many other aid agencies and, indeed, on the part of the government to appoint development professionals to head the agency. If these underlying trends continue and gain in influence, they should create possibilities for real changes in the policies and even organization of France's aid and eventually lead to the end of the postcolonial hangover and its obsession with rank and *rayonnement* that has shaped France's aid during the last half of the twentieth century. *On vera.*

CHAPTER 6

Germany: A "Middle of the Roader"

The profile of German aid over the second half of the twentieth century reflects its three main purposes: development, diplomacy, and commerce. Development emerged over time as the predominant purpose, but the others by no means disappeared. To understand the evolution of German aid it is critical to understand the nature of German political institutions, for they have had a significant indirect effect on the purposes of that country's aid.

A PROFILE OF GERMAN AID

There are three stages in the evolution of German foreign aid: its *origin and establishment* between 1952 and 1972; the *consolidation* of the aid program in general and of the development purpose in particular between 1973 and 1990; and a period of *reorientation, retrenchment, and revival* in German aid between 1990 and 2003.

Origin and Establishment

German aid originated in several different places in the German government. In 1952 the Ministry of Finance made Germany's first contribution to a multilateral aid organization—the UN Expanded Program of Technical Assistance. By the latter part of the 1950s, Germany had become the largest source of multilateral aid (even larger than the United States),[1] reflecting a diplomacy, similar to that of Japan, of rehabilitating itself as an accepted, responsible member of the international community.

In 1953 the Ministry of Economy, responsible for trade, established a small technical assistance program to encourage the purchase of German exports by developing countries, reflecting the early commercial purpose of German aid. Then, in 1956, the Bundestag (on the initiative of the Social

Democratic Party) voted to put 50 million deutschmarks (DM) in the budget of the Foreign Office, for "supporting economically underdeveloped countries"—in effect, putting forth a development purpose for German aid within the Foreign Ministry.[2] Thus, by 1961 the three major purposes of aid, evident in other case studies examined in this book, were also present in German foreign assistance.

In 1961 Chancellor Konrad Adenauer decided to expand the volume of German aid—especially bilateral aid—and create a Ministry of Development. These decisions resulted from two major sources of pressure—one external and one internal. On the external side, first the Eisenhower and then the Kennedy administrations had as one of their foreign policy priorities to persuade other well-off countries (now that they had recovered from the Second World War) to assume a greater proportion of the burden of Western security. This included encouraging those countries to expand their aid programs in poor countries, as the Cold War in Asia, Latin America, and Africa intensified. By 1961 Germany—well on its way to creating the "German economic miracle"—was a special object of Washington's attention. President Kennedy and his officials put direct pressures (including persuasion and threats) on Chancellor Adenauer and others to do more in foreign aid. According to one student of German aid, "If the Germans had not agreed to provide substantial development assistance to LDCs, the Americans would have demanded reimbursements for a larger share of its stationing costs [of US troops in Germany]."[3] Chancellor Adenauer agreed to step up Germany's aid effort. Figure 6.1 shows the history of German aid.

FIG. 6.1. TOTAL GERMAN AID (NET)

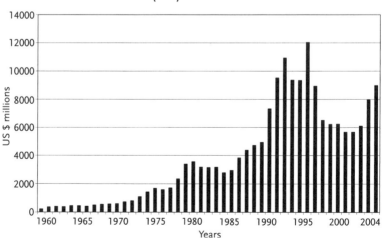

Source: DAC, "International Development Statistics (IDS) Online," http://www.oecd.org/dac/stats/idsonline/ (accessed October 2005).

Adenauer made another important decision on German aid at this time. He created a new Ministry of Development. He could have simply decided to expand German aid and place the additional aid in the Foreign Office or the Ministry of Economy—both of these ministries opposed the creation of a new ministry of development, seeing it as a threat to their influence over foreign aid. But the chancellor decided otherwise. This decision was less a manifestation of Adenauer's commitment to the development purposes of aid than a result of domestic coalition politics. When Adenauer, leader of the Christian Democratic Party (CDU), formed a government after the election in 1961, he negotiated a coalition government with the Liberal Party (FDP). The head of that party, Walter Scheel, wanted a foreign affairs portfolio and was specifically interested in development. Establishing a development ministry was the perfect solution; it created a second ministerial-level portfolio in foreign affairs, making it possible for each major party in a governing coalition to have such a portfolio, and it met Scheel's particular demand as a coalition partner.

The new development ministry (the Bundesministerium für Wirtschaftliche Zuzamenarbeit und Entwicklung, or BMZ) was initially a shell—it had responsibility only for coordinating aid policy. The policy and budgetary responsibilities for technical assistance and financial assistance programs were still located in the Ministry of Economy and the Foreign Office, respectively. And the implementation of German aid was handled by the Kreditanstalt für Wiederaufbau (KfW) and the German Corporation for Technical Assistance to Developing Countries (GAWI) together with the Federal Agency for Economic Cooperation (BfE). (These latter two were merged in 1975 to create the German Corporation for Technical Cooperation, or GTZ.) In 1964 control over technical assistance policies was shifted to the BMZ from the Foreign Office.

The organizational landscape of German aid had several other elements. There were three small, specialized agencies—the German Development Service (DED), which is a personnel service for German development volunteers; the German Investment and Development Corporation (DEG), which provided financing for German companies investing in developing countries (it was merged with the KfW in 2001); and the German Foundation for International Development (DSE, now the Internationale Weiterbildung und Entwicklung, or InWEnt), which provided a venue for dialog and training for development professionals from poor countries as well as from Germany. Finally, emergency aid was managed by the Foreign Ministry. As was the case in the United States in the 1990s, other ministries also began to undertake their own small aid programs abroad.[4] (See fig. 6.2 for a chart showing the organization of foreign aid responsibilities within the German government.)

FIG. 6.2. THE ORGANIZATION OF GERMAN AID, 1965

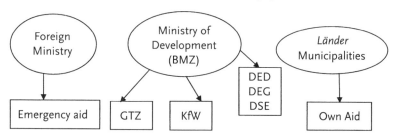

During these early years of the BMZ, the diplomatic and commercial purposes of German aid were prominent. Country aid allocation decisions were influenced by the diplomatic competition with the German Democratic Republic (GDR, or East Germany). The Federal Republic of Germany (FRG, or West Germany) claimed to be the rightful representative of all the German people, but East Germany, of course, rejected this claim. Under the Hallstein Doctrine, Bonn would not provide aid to any government that had diplomatic relations with East Germany.

Other diplomatic concerns also influenced the allocation of German aid. That aid was concentrated in two countries of particular diplomatic importance to Bonn: Israel, as compensation for Germany's treatment of the Jews during World War II, and Turkey, which occupied a strategic position in the Middle East and had a long association with Germany and many of whose citizens were "guest workers" in Germany. Other major recipients of German aid tended to be the larger developing countries—for example, India, Pakistan, and Indonesia. These countries had potentially attractive markets for German goods and services, were poor, and were influential regionally and globally (making them attractive diplomatic partners as well as promising markets for German goods)—in effect, furthering all three of the major purposes of German aid. At the same time, small amounts of German aid were spread widely throughout the developing world, the better to create a broad German diplomatic presence and support for West Germany's claim to be the legitimate representative of the German people. It also facilitated the entry of German enterprises in unfamiliar markets. The wide distribution of German aid was dubbed by the Germans as the "watering can approach"—a little aid for every poor country in the global garden. In 1970 Germany provided aid to over ninety countries worldwide.[5]

The uses of German aid also suggested an orientation toward commercial purposes—especially the export of goods and services by German firms. The types of aid of most interest to German firms involved engineering and construction projects, the export of heavy equipment, telecommunications, transportation, and similar elements of "economic infrastructure," in the terminology of the DAC. In 1974, for example, Germany allocated nearly half of its bilateral aid to economic infrastructure (e.g., public utilities and transportation) and to production sectors, including industry, construction, mining, trade, and banking.[6] (As a comparison, the average for the DAC as a whole was one-third.) Although data are not available, it is quite likely that this percentage was even higher in the previous decade, when the Ministry of Economy had control over the budget for financial assistance abroad and could direct aid to commercial purposes.

Consolidation

The second period in German aid began in the early 1970s, when the development purpose of German aid gained prominence. In 1968 there was the "youth revolution" in much of Europe, including Germany, involving a generation of progressive—even radicalized—students and young people, who were energized by opposition to the war in Indochina and active in pressing (and sometimes attacking) their governments on issues of war and peace and development. They were also supporters of a more developmental focus of aid in Germany. (Many of this generation—called the "*acht und sechsigers*" or "68ers" in Germany, later became development professionals, especially in the GTZ.)

Also in 1968, a new coalition government headed by the Social Democratic Party (SDP) named Erhard Eppler as minister for development. Eppler, even at the end of the century still widely regarded as having been one of the most active and effective ministers of development, pressed the new chancellor, Willy Brandt, to shift responsibility for financial cooperation from the Ministry of Economy to the BMZ and, after the election in 1972, the shift was finally made. According to Eppler, with greater control over financial cooperation, he was able to reduce the tying of German financial aid to German exports and to begin shifting that aid away from purposes that were more interesting to German businesses toward activities more consistent with development thinking at that time, such as health and education.[7] In fact, the proportion of German aid for economic infrastructure declined gradually, dropping to 37 percent in 1979–80, to 30 percent in 1985–86, and further to 26 percent in 1991. Even if the influence of commercial interests on German aid began to diminish with the shift of policy control over that aid to the BMZ, there was still a lot of momentum in the aid program toward financing projects of interest to German industry.

Under Eppler, the BMZ became more active and professional in its management of German aid policies. It produced the first official development policy statement in 1971.[8] This statement proposed that "Short-term foreign policy considerations were to be suppressed in allocation decisions and the growth objective of the development policy brought into line with other, equity-oriented objectives."[9] At this time also, the BMZ—along with aid agencies in other donor countries—began to professionalize its work, adopting country programming processes. (The use of country programming, by placing aid-giving in an overall country development strategy, put limits on the use of that aid for opportunities related to commercial or diplomatic purposes—apparently this was part of the intent behind setting up this system.[10]) Facilitating the rise in prominence of development as a purpose of German aid were also changes in German diplomacy. Chancellor Brandt adopted a policy of easing relations with East Germany, setting aside the Hallstein Doctrine (which in any case became moot once both Germanys had joined the United Nations in 1973).[11]

Finally, as figure 6.1 shows, during the first half of the 1970s, the overall amount of German aid rose rapidly, nearly tripling between 1970 and 1975 (rising from $600 million to $1.7 billion). The largest percentage increase was for multilateral aid, which rose from 22 percent of that country's total aid in 1970 to just over 30 percent in 1975. This change partly reflected a general view at the time among development specialists that multilateral aid—especially for IDA, the soft loan window of the World Bank—was more "developmental" than government-to-government aid and partly the escalation in German contributions of aid to the European Union aid programs.

German aid continued to rise during the latter part of the 1970s, responding to the deepening economic crises in developing countries. However, as figure 6.1 also shows, German aid fell at the beginning of the 1980s and stagnated for much of the first half of that decade. Inflation, recession, and unemployment at home, in part provoked by the oil price increases in the 1970s, explain this stall in German aid. During this period, the government also eased the constraints of the country programming processes and allocated more aid to "mixed-credit" financing schemes of interest to hard-pressed German businesses.[12] This was reflected in an increase in the proportion of German bilateral aid allocated to public utilities, industry, mining, and banking purposes, surging temporarily to 60 percent in 1984. These changes, plus the growing emphasis in aid policies during the 1980s on structural adjustment and economic reforms (in line with mainstream development thinking at that time), provoked increasing criticism—especially by NGOs—as a "change of direction" in West Germany's aid program.

It is worth noting that NGOs played an important role in German aid from the beginning. The churches, in particular, were early advocates of aid for development and active in their own right in collecting contributions and helping the poor abroad. The German political foundations (of which, more below) also became advocates of aid for development and democracy during the early decades of German foreign assistance. In the 1980s, as their numbers grew, NGOs began to organize and increase their advocacy for aid for development.[13] Most tended to support poverty-oriented development aid and criticized the use of aid for commercial or diplomatic purposes. They typically made their views known in the media, through their contacts with the Development Committee on the Bundestag (a group of parliamentarians of all parties with an interest in German aid and development), through access to a staff committee (created in 1983) in the BMZ charged with focusing on poverty, through participation on advisory groups attached to the Ministry, and through informal contacts with political parties (particularly through the political party foundations) and political elites.

The criticisms of the government's aid policies led the government to issue in 1986 a new development policy statement entitled *Basic Principles of Development Policy of the Federal Government*, which reaffirmed that "The aim of the German development policy is to improve the economic and social situation of the people in developing countries and to provide scope for their creative growth. It therefore helps meet the basic needs of the people and enable them to help themselves."[14] This document emphasized the importance of a supportive policy environment for growth and the role of policy dialogue on economic policies but did not otherwise deviate significantly from past policy statements on aid and development.[15]

German aid at the end of the 1980s showed both change and continuity compared with earlier decades. It was much larger, having resumed its growth during the second half of the 1980s in response to, among other things, the deepening economic crisis in Africa. Its uses were gradually shifting toward support for social and administrative infrastructure.[16] Three out of five major recipients of that aid were the same as in earlier decades—India, Indonesia, and Turkey (see table 6.1). The addition of Egypt and China in 1988–89 suggests that diplomatic and commercial considerations continued to play a role in the country allocation of German aid. Egypt is a poor country (though not one of the poorest) but also important to a diplomacy of peace-making in the Middle East. It is probable that German aid to that country was motivated in part by this fact (perhaps at the urging of the United States, which took the lead in trying to bring about peace in the region). Jumping ahead, aid to Yugoslavia in the 1990s was also clearly motivated by a diplomacy of peace-making in the Balkans.

The addition of China—a poor country (though not one of the poorest), but one with a poor human rights record—suggests that commercial motives continued to play a role in German aid. (The German government emphasized human rights as a criterion for the allocation of its aid. Strict enforcement of this criterion would have excluded China as a major recipi-

TABLE 6.1. TOP FIVE RECIPIENTS OF GERMAN AID

1970–71	1980–81	1988–89	1999–2000
India	Turkey	Turkey	China
Pakistan	Bangladesh	India	India
Israel	India	Egypt	Indonesia
Indonesia	Sudan	Indonesia	Turkey
Turkey	Indonesia	China	Yugoslavia

Note: Recipients listed by amount of aid, in descending order.

Source: DAC, *Development Co-operation* (Chairman's reports) (OECD, Paris, 1990), 236; and (OECD, Paris, 2000), 267.

ent. In fact, some German aid was used to finance the construction by German companies of the Shanghai subway—a use of aid for clearly commercial purposes and one that provoked criticisms from NGOs.) German aid continued to be provided, often in small amounts, to a large number of poor countries throughout the world.

Reorientation, Retrenchment, Revival

The third stage of German aid commenced in the 1990s. It was marked by three major changes: the addition of new purposes, such as addressing global problems, much like other aid donors; an initial sharp rise in total aid, above all, aid for countries in transition; and then a dramatic decline in overall aid levels together with a decision to reduce the number of aid recipients.

The drop in German aid in the mid-1990s raised questions about the future amount and purposes of German aid. Even the continuing existence of the BMZ was questioned. Some politicians urged that it be merged into the Foreign Office.[17] However, the German government, along with other European Union governments, committed itself to increase its aid at the Monterrey Conference on Financing Development in 2002. By then, it was clear that the emphasis on development and poverty would continue and that the BMZ would remain as an independent aid agency.

This third stage in German aid resulted from several major changes abroad and at home. First were the end of the Cold War and the collapse of socialist regimes in Eastern Europe and the USSR. With its geographical proximity to these countries, Germany had a considerable stake in their success and soon became their largest single bilateral donor. German aid for

FIG. 6.3. GERMAN AID TO COUNTRIES IN TRANSITION

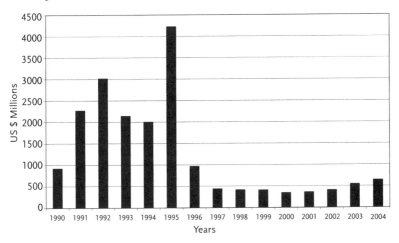

Source: DAC, "International Development Statistics (IDS) Online," http://www.oecd.org/dataoecd/50/17/5037721.htm.

economic and political transitions rose from less than $1 billion in 1990 to over $4 billion in 1995. Thereafter, German aid for transitions, along with German aid worldwide, dropped dramatically (see fig. 6.3).

A second change affecting German aid was the increasing prominence of what I have called here global problems and what the Germans have called global structural policies—meaning issues involving global public goods such as international health or environmental problems. Germany, with its Greens Party, has been especially concerned with the environmental issues in developing countries and elsewhere in the world. Also, by the middle of the 1990s, the German government was beginning to focus on another new purpose of aid: crisis prevention and peace-building. A new budget line was created to fund activities in this category. However, the German government, like other aid-giving governments, continued to grapple with the conceptual challenges of understanding the causes of conflict and aid's role in helping to prevent it.[18]

With regard to the purpose of democratization, which was new for many aid-giving countries at this time, Germany was the original aid donor working in the area of democracy promotion. One of the unique aspects of German aid is that each of the six major political parties has a foundation, most of which have worked for decades inside Germany and abroad on civic education, other aspects of democratic governance, and even more broadly on development related activities. They are funded by the German government through the BMZ.

Major German Political Parties and Their Foundations

Social Democratic Party (SDP)	Friederich Ebert Foundation
Christian Democratic Party (CDU)	Konrad Adenauer Foundation
Free Democrats	Friedrich Naumann Foundation
Christian Social Union (CSU)	Hanns Seidel Foundation
Greens	Heinrich Boll Foundation
Socialists (PDS)	Rosa Luxemburg Foundation

The third factor affecting German aid in the 1990s was domestic—the enormous cost of absorbing East Germany, which put a major claim on the government's budget, estimated to be $100 billion per year. Combined with that expense was the commitment on the part of the government as part of the 1992 Maastricht Treaty to bring the budget deficit down below 3 percent of GNP by 1999 (which the cost of unification made impossible). These budgetary pressures led the government to reduce German aid in the mid-1990s. In carrying out this aid reduction, Germany cut back on the number of countries receiving aid from 156 in 1996 to 70 "priority" and "partner" countries by the end of the 1990s and limited their aid-funded sectoral activities to three or fewer.

A new government took power in 1998—a "Red-Green Coalition" made up of the Social Democratic Party (SDP) and the Greens Party—and began a period of renewal in German aid. This left-wing coalition put a higher priority than its predecessor (a conservative coalition led by the Christian Democratic Party) on furthering development abroad. The agreement underpinning the new government stated that "Development policy today is global structural policy, aiming at the improvement of the economic, social, ecological and political conditions in developing countries. . . . The new federal government will reform, develop, and improve development policy along these principles, ensuring the coherence of this policy among the different ministries. . . . Authority will be concentrated in the BMZ. The BMZ will from now on be the leading actor in questions concerning EU-development policy. The BMZ is to become a member of the Federal Security Council."[19]

As in earlier instances, the creation of a governing coalition opened up an opportunity for niche issues of importance to one of the coalition partners to be put on the policy agenda and be addressed. In this case, the SDP was keen on the development purpose of German aid. As is evident in the Coalition Paper, the Greens wanted to increase the importance of environmental issues. Both the SDP and the Greens wanted to expand the role of the BMZ in policy-making involving poor countries—in the language of development discourse in Europe in the 1990s, to ensure greater "policy coherence" between development and German international economic purposes generally. Greater coherence was to be achieved by enlarging the scope of the BMZ's authority to review all policies affecting development, for example, the use of export credits, trade policies, or arms exports. As part of its effort to increase the coherence of development policies, the new government also shifted responsibility for aid to former socialist bloc countries and for the policy responsibilities involving German aid to the EU from the Ministry of Economy to the BMZ. The responsibilities of the BMZ were thus significantly enhanced by the results of the 1998 election and the coalition politics that followed it.

The new government appointed SDP Vice President Heidimarie Wieczoreck-Zeul as minister of development. She set about strengthening the poverty orientation of German aid and increasing its amount after the years of decline. A new statement of development policy, called the *Program of Action 2015*—based on achieving the Millennium Development Goals, including halving poverty by 2015—was drafted by the BMZ and used as a basis of broad consultations with NGOs and others outside government. It was then debated and approved by the cabinet in 2001, making it an official German government policy. While emphasizing the goal of poverty reduction, the *Program of Action 2015* contained a wide variety of other priorities, including affirming the right to food, supporting agrarian reform, supporting fair trade for poor countries, supporting debt reduction, furthering human rights, fostering gender equality, protecting the environment, resolving conflict, and others. The document is more of a catchall of development purposes than a real guide to action. Its function was clearly to raise the prominence of these issues within the German government and ultimately to provide the basis for increasing German aid.

In 1998 the government had stated its intention of reversing the decline in aid. In 1999 German aid began to increase once again, rising from 10.9 billion deutschmarks in 1998 to 12.4 billion in 2001. (The strengthening dollar during the late 1990s made it look like German aid was declining when expressed in dollars—when, in fact, it was rising.) The Monterrey Conference on Financing Development in 2002 gave a further boost to Germany's overall aid levels. The future amount of German aid was decided in the context of a common EU position for Monterrey that committed each member of the European Union to raise its aid to 0.33 percent of GNI by 2006 as a first step to realizing the common commitment to provide 0.7 percent of GNI as development aid. For Germany, providing 0.33 percent of GNI as development assistance by 2006 implied a significant increase in its assistance, on the order at least of several billion dollars.[20] In the years following Monterrey, German aid did begin to increase substantially—rising by nearly $2 billion between 2002 and 2003 alone, but this increase lifted the percentage of German aid only to 0.28 percent of its GNI. (German aid continued to rise in subsequent years, but it seemed unlikely that the government would reach the 0.33 percent target by 2006.)

The title of this chapter proclaims Germany as a "Middle of the Roader." This is a name used by the Germans themselves to describe their aid effort. They have been neither the largest nor the smallest of aid donors in percentage terms. They have moved with other donor governments to emphasize the development purpose of their aid but have not rejected other purposes. And, unlike the countries featured in other case studies in this volume, they have not felt compelled to attempt major organizational changes in their aid system. What are the political forces shaping this trajectory in German aid? It is to this question I now turn.

THE POLITICS OF GERMAN AID

Some of the factors explaining the evolution in the purposes of German aid are external to that country—above all, the Cold War and its termination. But these factors tell us only a limited amount about the evolution of German aid. As with our other cases, we must also look within Germany to understand the fundamental factors shaping aid—in particular, the ideas that influenced the way political elites and the public perceived German assistance, the political institutions in which diplomatic, commercial and developmental interests competed for influence and control over the aid and the impact of the organization of the German government on the management of aid.

Ideas

Two main sets of ideas shaped the way Germans thought about foreign aid: ideas about their country's role in the world and ideas about the appropriate relationships between rich and poor and between state and society.

Germany was a defeated power and a divided and occupied country in the wake of World War II. The occupation only ended formally in 1955, when sovereignty was restored to the Federal Republic of Germany. One of the goals of West Germany was to rehabilitate the country's reputation and reestablish itself as a responsible member of the international community. This idea predisposed the government to moving quickly on opportunities that would advance this goal, including undertaking a foreign aid program. It also predisposed the government to support strongly the creation of the European Community and, later, the European Union and to allocate a rising proportion of its aid to the EU (increasing from 13 percent of total German aid in 1974–76 to 25 percent in 2000, making Germany the most generous contributor relative to the size of its economy of all the major member states of the EU).

A second element in German ideas about their country's role in the world involved the Cold War. Germany could hardly avoid being involved in the Cold War competition (including deploying its aid in that competition), because East-West tensions were, in effect, in its front yard, with the division of the country between the Federal Republic of Germany and the German Democratic Republic and the division of Berlin between East and West. Next door to East Germany were the communist countries of Eastern Europe, backed by the Soviet Union. It is hardly surprising that West Germany used its aid as an instrument in its competition with East Germany. What is surprising is that West Germany did not use its aid more aggressively in this way and over a longer period of time. The bond between the divided German peoples may have lessened the temptation toward a more forceful diplomatic use of aid. West Germany may also have wished to avoid appearing assertive internationally for fear of raising remembered images of the aggressive Germany of the prewar period.

Fundamental to the evolution of German aid were also widely shared ideas about the obligation of the rich to help the poor, including with public assistance. The German public broadly supported the obligation to assist the poor abroad as reflected in the large annual private contributions to churches and NGOs working on relief and development in poor countries, amounting to 0.4 percent of GNI.[21] Both the public and the major political parties accepted the role of the state in providing aid abroad as well. The left wing of German politics—for example, the Social Democrats—had long had an international orientation and placed a priority on solidarity with the disadvantaged at home and abroad. Foreign aid for development, provided by the German government, was readily supported—indeed, it was the Social Democratic Party that provoked one of the first debates in the Bundestag, in 1956, on the need for Germany to aid the poor abroad.

For the conservative side of German politics—represented by the Christian Democrats—aid for the poor abroad was accepted as a Christian duty. And for many Germans after the war, having been aided themselves under the Marshall Plan, there was a widespread feeling that, as they recovered, they had an obligation to aid others less fortunate. In short, there was a considerable measure of consensus among Germans from a variety of political persuasions on the appropriateness of foreign aid.

One widely shared idea conditioned this consensus. This was the emphasis put by many Germans on "self-help" and the related importance of private initiative and, by extension, the importance of the private sector in development. "Self-help" is usually taken to mean that aid recipients, as individuals and governments, should take primary responsibility for their own betterment. The state was not to be the sole source of their betterment—least of all, West Germany. The emphasis on the private sector reflected the experience of Germany at home in its recovery and, indeed, in its development before the war. It was probably even more prominent in postwar thinking, as the Germans of the West compared themselves to the Germans under communist rule in the East. This value helped create a predisposition toward emphasizing the role of the private sector in furthering development abroad, particularly among those on the right of the German political spectrum.

Institutions

Interesting and important, but little noted in the literature on German aid, is the impact of German political institutions on the purposes of that aid. Germany is a parliamentary democracy with a form of proportional representation.[22] As is often the case in such systems, governments tend to be based on coalitions of minority parties. (Only once in postwar Germany—between 1957 and 1961—was the government not based on such a coalition.) The bargaining that takes place in forming a coalition has had a significant impact on the purposes of German aid and their evolution. As is also the case with Denmark, that process has often put "niche issues" favored by minority parties, such as foreign aid for development abroad, on the national political agenda. The "development wings" of the major political parties, together with minority parties (like the Greens) or prominent politicians with an interest in aid issues, can use the creation of a coalition to further their particular policy agendas. This has been the case at several important junctures in Germany, where coalition politics has repeatedly raised the prominence of development as a purpose of German aid. The first instance—and probably the most important one—was the creation in 1961 of the BMZ to accommodate the demands of the minority party for a foreign affairs portfolio. The very creation of a cabinet-level development agency, even one with few responsibilities initially, gave considerable prominence and legitimacy to development in German aid and gave successive ministers the status, access, and incentives to lobby at the highest levels of government for increasing responsibilities for their ministry (which many did). Indeed, nearly all the major increases in BMZ responsibilities—taking over financial aid from the Ministry of Economics, absorbing aid to former socialist countries from the same ministry, gaining greater responsibility for "coherence" in all German politics affecting developing countries—came as the result of coalition politics.

There is one other aspect of German political institutions that may have indirectly helped to strengthen the development purpose of German aid. Germany is a federal republic with sixteen states, or *Länder*. These states (and even municipalities within the states) have their own aid programs, funded from their own taxes. These programs are heavily oriented toward educating foreign nationals in Germany, but they often involve small projects abroad as well. The involvement of state and municipal governments in development abroad has helped inform and engage the German population in development issues and likely fortified their support for development aid at the federal level as well—a form of "development education" not evident to such an extent in other countries. Public opinion polls have shown the German public generally supportive of aid, with 75 percent in favor of German aid-giving in 1987 and the same proportion of West Germans in 1994.[23] (Public support for aid declined somewhat during the 1990s, undoubtedly reflecting the economic stresses associated with reunification. Support improved again during the first half of the first decade of the new century.[24])

Interests

The interests inside and outside government competing for influence over German aid are not different from those evident in other case studies. The diplomatic interests in aid are centered in the Foreign Office. Even though the Ministry of Development has the lead responsibility in aid policies and allocations, the Foreign Office has an informal role in aid decisions, for example, on the broad framework guiding German aid, on activities in sectors of particular diplomatic importance and sensitivity (such as democratization and conflict prevention and management), and, at times, on aid-giving for particularly important countries, such as Turkey. The Foreign Office country desks claim the right of review on aid activities planned in their countries, and the Foreign Office can block proposals it disagrees with, though that is reputedly an unusual occurrence. Over time, the influence of the BMZ over the allocation and use of German aid has grown. That of the Foreign Office has diminished somewhat but not vanished. The coalition agreement negotiated between the SDP and its partners in 2002 stated that "development policy is an independent part of a common German foreign policy," leaving room for both the BMZ and the Foreign Office to continue their involvement in German aid.[25]

A second important set of interests involved with German aid are those organizations inside and outside government whose goals and missions are to further development, broadly construed. Inside government, there are principally the BMZ, the GTZ, and the KfW. Within this trio, the BMZ plays a major role in aid policy-making, while the GTZ and KfW have much less prominent voices. Further, these latter two organizations tend to view development differently: the KfW takes more of a banker's perspective—concerned about growth and revenue-producing aid (the assistance they handle consists of credits rather than grants), while the GTZ has more of a hands-on, poverty-oriented perspective.

Outside government, there is a large, active group of NGOs engaged in development issues, many of which act as advocates with government for the development purposes of German aid. I have mentioned the central role played by both Protestant and Catholic churches in Germany, but many other NGOs have become involved in development and relief. The government itself funds around five hundred of them. German development NGOs are organized into several umbrella associations, the most prominent being VENRO, which includes more than one hundred of the larger ones (some of which include groups of NGOs themselves). The German government does not give an advisory board of individuals from NGOs authority over its aid programs, as the Danes do. But as I have noted, there are a number of points of access that NGOs have used to make their views known to the German government.

In considering the organized groups that play a role in German aid, it is important to recall that one unique aspect of the German aid system, the political party foundations. Germany has long funded political party foundations to promote democracy and fund some development activities abroad. These foundations have a natural interest in the development purpose of German aid, and they have extraordinary access to their political parties—to the extent that some in Germany call them "submarines," reflecting their often unseen but influential presence within their parties. They have been informal and, by most accounts, effective lobbies within their parties (both in government and in the Bundestag) in favor of the development purposes of aid (especially democracy promotion). They have been less effective on promoting increases in overall aid levels, especially during the fiscal retrenchment of the 1990s, but have been a major voice in the interparty consensus on the importance of aid for development abroad. No other aid-giving country has dedicated lobbies *within* its political parties for assistance for development.

Additionally, an informal network of constituents for development has emerged over time in Germany—the development professionals within the government, the "development wings" of the political parties, the political party foundations, the churches and NGOs involved in development, and the policy and academic community engaged in development issues. To some extent, development ministers in the EU and in the DAC are also part of this network, because what happens in these organizations can be used by development advocates within Germany to push their agendas. (For example, criticisms by the DAC of German aid are often taken up by the NGOs in their critiques of government policies—often with some effectiveness. This was clearly the case on the issue of "coherence," mentioned earlier.[26]) Not all of these constituents for the development purpose of German aid always agree on specific issues, but where these organizations are in agreement, they can be influential. For example, in 1994, during an election campaign, the SDP candidate for chancellor announced his intention of merging the BMZ into the Foreign Office if his party won the election, setting off a storm of criticism from NGOs, development specialists, and advocates who "unanimously rejected the idea for fear of development co-operation being subordinated to other interests and losing its societal support."[27] The "development network" in Germany does not enjoy quite the access its counterpart has in the United States, where political institutions are much more fragmented, but the German network has proven itself to be a factor to be reckoned with, especially on issues involving the use of aid for non-developmental goals.

Finally, there are German commercial interests. German firms wanting to expand their exports looked to foreign aid as a vehicle for accelerating their entry into foreign markets in the early years of the aid program, especially when the Ministry of Economy had responsibility for a part of the aid budget. By all accounts, their influence, like that of the Foreign Office, has diminished over the decades of German aid but not vanished. On occasion, when a particular enterprise has a strong interest in an aid project abroad, it may use its informal channels of access to German officials and seek support. The Shanghai subway system was one example of this phenomenon often mentioned in Germany as an example of the periodic influence of German business on aid allocations. Major German firms are reported to have lobbied government during the mid-1990s against further reductions in project aid (provided primarily by KfW), from which they benefited as implementing agents.[28] The access of German business interests to aid decision-making also occurs in the annual budget process. The BMZ proposes a yearly budget for aid, but that budget must be reviewed and approved by the Foreign Office and the Ministry of Economy, giving both ministries an opportunity to ensure that their interests are preserved in what finally goes to the Ministry of Finance for final approval and transmission to the Bundestag.

Organization of German Aid

Germany is the only major aid-giving government with a permanent ministerial level development agency. (Britain has on several occasions set up a development ministry under Labour governments, only to fold it into the Foreign Office under Conservative governments. Perhaps the current

Department for International Development will prove an exception and outlast a shift from Labour to Conservative governments.) The existence of such a ministry goes a long way toward explaining the gradually increasing priority of the development purpose in German aid, when both diplomatic and commercial purposes were prominent at the beginning of Germany's aid program. A ministerial level aid agency did not *guarantee* that that agency would have control over Germany's aid policies and programs; rather, its existence created that possibility. It took a succession of determined ministers of development, negotiating with their prime ministers, gradually to extend the control of the ministry over German aid and the influence of the ministry over development-related programs. That process continues today, helped by the existence of an active development lobby of NGOs and others outside of government—the major part of German emergency humanitarian aid remains in the Foreign Office.

If the existence of a ministry of development has strengthened the voice for development aid within the German government, the division between a policy ministry and two major implementing agencies appears to have injected an element of rigidity and weak integration of aid activities into German aid. The GTZ, focusing on technical assistance (in the form of grants) and the KfW, providing capital assistance, half in the form of concessional loans, have developed quite different organizational structures and cultures and have faced some challenges in collaborating, especially in the field.[29] The division between policy and implementation in German aid has also made it more difficult for the German government to engage in policy dialogue and sector-based investment programs, because development policy expertise is in the BMZ (which has few officials in the field) and field experience and responsibilities for the technical aspects of implementation reside with the KfW and GTZ. It has proven difficult for the German government to move rapidly toward greater grant-based aid, because much of what the KfW provides is in credit form. The German government, like the Japanese government and others with a division between development policy and implementation and between two different implementing agencies (one of which relies heavily on loan-based aid), may find it difficult to function effectively in the rapidly changing world of the twenty-first century, where better-off developing countries that can handle credit-based aid need it less and where poorer countries, which often need aid, find it difficult to repay aid loans.

Summing Up

The story of the evolving purposes of German aid is an institutional and organizational one. German aid began with a strong diplomatic and commercial orientation. The influence of coalition politics led the government to set up a Ministry of Development, which gradually increased its control over German aid and the development focus of that aid. The personalities of several ministers of development played a role in this evolution, as did the expanding number and activism of development-oriented NGOs. This process was also furthered by the easing of the diplomatic competition between East and West Germany resulting from Chancellor Willy Brandt's *Ostpolitik* in the late 1960s and early 1970s. This shift in priorities among the purposes of German aid does not mean that the diplomatic and commercial purposes have disappeared. The Foreign Office still has, in effect, a veto over aid allocations and can also make its own priorities known. The Ministry of Economy has an influence over the aid budget, and private firms can use their access to senior levels of government to lobby for aid for important projects abroad. But development and related purposes have priority—in large measure as a result of the decision made in 1961 to establish the BMZ.

The story of German aid has two more messages. One is that severe economic and budgetary stresses will usually lead to cuts in foreign aid. The message is that where there is a wide acceptance of the obligation of rich countries to help poor ones, combined with strong support for development aid inside and outside government, aid is likely to rise again once budgetary pressures ease. In the case of Germany, the election of 1998 and then the Monterrey Conference on Financing Development in 2002, combined with an energetic and politically well-placed minister of development, provided the triggers for a renewed increase in German aid for development.

What might this analysis imply for the future of German aid? First, discussions about merging the BMZ into the Foreign Office appear politically unrealistic. There are too many interests outside government (the development wings of the political parties, backed by the political party foundations, and, above all, the NGOs) and a strong voice within government that would oppose such a move and likely make it politically costly to a chancellor who attempted it. For this reason alone, the development purpose in German aid is likely to remain prominent. The challenge confronting the German government in its aid-giving is not the amount or direction of its aid but the management of aid and the government's ability to adapt a rigid and fragmented aid system to the challenges and opportunities of the twenty-first century.

CHAPTER 7

Denmark: The Humane Internationalist

Denmark is one of the smallest aid-giving countries, with a population of only 5 million in the year 2000. But for several years in the 1990s, it became the most generous source of aid relative to the size of its economy, with aid equal to 1.0 percent or more of gross national income during much of that decade. At the same time, it gained a reputation as a leader in development assistance, emphasizing poverty reduction in its aid projects and programs. As a result, Denmark has been termed both a "humane internationalist" (along with other Scandinavian countries) and a "front-runner" in aid-giving.[1]

However, generosity and a focus on development and reducing poverty are not the only characteristics of Danish assistance. Often overlooked has been the strong commercial purpose evident in that aid—it was long the case that roughly half of Denmark's bilateral aid was dedicated to promoting Danish exports and investment abroad. Further, at the end of the century, several new purposes were added in the provision of Danish aid. Finally, in an apparent rupture with past policies, a Liberal-Conservative government with a center-right orientation, elected in 2002, promptly slashed the level of Danish aid by 10 percent and Danish aid as a percentage of GNI fell to 0.85 percent—third place in the index of aid generosity. What explains the mix of purposes in Danish aid, its generosity in aid-giving during the latter part of the twentieth century, and then its apparent reversal of policy at the beginning of the twenty-first?

PROFILE

Danish aid has evolved through four stages: *origin and establishment,* from the early post–World War II period to 1970; *consolidation,* between 1971 and

1990; *transition*, during the 1990s; and a *reorientation* in the volume of aid and tone of aid-giving beginning in 2002.

Origin and Establishment

Denmark commenced its aid in 1949 when it first contributed to the United Nations Technical Assistance program. Considering that Denmark was still receiving aid from the Marshall Plan, this was a largely symbolic gesture, intended to demonstrate Denmark's commitment to the United Nations. In the early 1950s, the Danes provided aid to a Korean hospital and to several other activities in developing countries. But it was not until the early 1960s that the Danish government, along with most other European countries, decided it was time to create its own foreign assistance program.

As a first step in setting up an aid program, the government initiated a national campaign to raise private funds for poor countries, promising to match them with public funds. This campaign was an early mobilization effort to inform and engage the Danish population on development and aid issues and gather support for a governmental program of assistance abroad. The campaign clearly touched a sympathetic nerve among the Danes. In the words of a study of Danish aid, "Rarely has a cause received stronger and broader support in Denmark. In early 1962 all the political parties, radio and television, most newspapers, labor unions, industrial organizations, the cooperative movement, churches and a string of prominent people inundated the public with pro-aid arguments."[2] The campaign was a major success and quickly culminated in a unanimous vote in the Folketing (the Danish parliament) in support of the Bill on Technical Cooperation with the Developing Countries, establishing Denmark's aid program. In addition to initiating a program of aid, this bill set up a secretariat in the Ministry of Foreign Affairs (which eventually came to be called DANIDA, from the Danish International Development Agency) to manage the aid.

Aid planners from the beginning made an effort to create a strong coalition of interests—commercial as well as development-oriented—as well as public support for Danish assistance. Danish aid was divided into three parts. Half of total aid was allocated to multilateral organizations, above all UN agencies involved in development, such as the UN Development Program, where states typically had one vote each regardless of their size or wealth. This was in part a reflection of Denmark's diplomatic interests in aid as well as its development interests. UN organizations were especially valued by small states like Denmark as arenas where they could play a role and exert influence irrespective of their size and where internationally agreed upon rules and norms could be developed and used (in theory at least) to constrain larger powers.

The bilateral half of Danish aid was divided into roughly equal parts, between grants for low-income countries—linked to development purposes, which were supported by Danish NGOs—and loans to middle-income countries tied to Danish exports, intended to further Danish business interests abroad. In contrast to many other aid donors, the division of bilateral aid between promoting development and commercial interests was initially not so much a means of accommodating pressures from Danish manufacturers and farmers—such interests were quite passive at the time the aid program was established—as an effort to encourage Danish business to become engaged in the aid program in order to create a broad domestic constituency—or "resource base," as the Danes term it—for that aid.

Although responsibility for both policy formulation and implementation of Danish aid programs and projects was located in the Ministry of Foreign Affairs, several external advisory councils were created to guide the aid program. One was the Board on International Development Cooperation, which consisted of nine individuals drawn from major domestic groups with an interest in aid (e.g., development-oriented NGOs, the Agricultural Council of Denmark, the Danish Federation of Trade Unions, the Federation of Danish Industries, the scholarly and research community, youth groups, and prominent individuals) who were appointed by the minister of foreign affairs. The DANIDA Board, as it came to be known, met monthly to review aid projects, policies, and country allocations before they were approved by the ministers or the Folketing. While this board was advisory, its views were taken seriously by the parliament (which came to expect the imprimatur of the DANIDA Board before government aid projects were sent to it for approval) and by the government, giving it quite a lot of de facto power. The government also established the much larger Council on International Development Cooperation, made up of seventy-five members from the same groups represented on the DANIDA Board plus others, which met twice yearly to review the annual report of the DANIDA Board and the five-year, rolling aid budget. This council's influence over Danish aid was limited.

During the 1960s, Denmark was one of the *least* generous aid donors relative to the size of its economy, in stunning contrast to its position by the end of the century as the *most* generous aid donor in relative terms. In 1965, for example, Denmark's aid was 0.13 percent of its GNP—only three countries (Switzerland, Italy, and Finland) gave less proportionately, and the DAC average at that time was 0.48 percent.[3] However, after being roundly criticized by the DAC in mid-decade for its stinginess, the Danish government began to increase its aid rapidly during the latter part of the decade,

FIG. 7.1. TOTAL DANISH AID (NET)

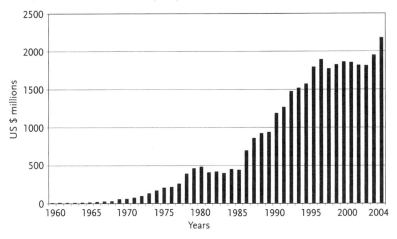

Source: DAC, "International Development Statistics (IDS) Online," http://www.oecd.org/dataoecd/50/17/5037721.htm.

more than tripling it between 1964–66 and 1970 (see fig. 7.1).[4] (The overall average increase for DAC members was just under 100 percent during the same period.)

As a small aid-giver, the government wanted to concentrate its bilateral aid for development in a few countries for maximum impact. It identified several "concentration countries" on which it would focus its aid efforts, including Tanzania, India, and Kenya. Tanzania was popular in Denmark because its president, Julius Nyerere, was seen as holding values and pursuing policies very much in line with the values shared by many Danes and especially by the Social Democrats and other left-wing parties in power there. India was the world's largest poor country (apart from China, which was inhospitable to Western aid at this time). Kenya held a special interest for Danes because one of their most famous writers, Karen Blixen (a.k.a. Isak Dinesen), settled there and had, in the words of one observer, established through her books on life in Kenya a "sentimental bond" between Danes and Kenya.[5] These countries remained those most aided by Denmark through the end of the 1980s (see table 7.1). (Kenya was finally dropped from the main aid recipients at the end of the 1990s because of its poor human rights record. India was dropped in 1998 because of its nuclear weapons program and testing in that year.)

In 1970–71 roughly 40 percent of Danish bilateral aid (mainly, its grant aid for development purposes) went to the four recipients listed in table 7.1. At the same time, Denmark provided small amounts of aid to numerous other developing countries, much of it in the form of tied loans aimed at ex-

TABLE 7.1. MAJOR RECIPIENTS OF DANISH AID

1970–71	1980–81	1989–90	1999–2000
Tanzania	Tanzania	Tanzania	Tanzania
India	Bangladesh	Bangladesh	Uganda
Egypt	India	India	Mozambique
Kenya	Kenya	Kenya	Egypt

Note: Recipients listed by amount of aid, in descending order, from the same source as table 6.1.

panding Denmark's export markets. Some sixty countries received this form of assistance between 1963 and 1998.

Consolidation

The 1970s through the 1980s marked a new phase in Danish aid, involving the consolidation of aid programs. The period saw periodic debates in parliament and among the interested public on aid issues—often generated by domestic concerns and the political process but also provoked by major international reports on aid and activities of the DAC. Compared to the United States or France, Denmark was unusually responsive to international debate and criticisms of its aid, in part because foreign aid became such a prominent element in Danish foreign policy and in part because of the degree of domestic interest in development issues.

In 1970, prompted by the publication of the Pearson Report, *Partners in Development*,[6] the government commissioned a review of Danish aid. This review led to the passage of the Act on International Development Cooperation in 1971, which for the first time formulated the objectives of Danish aid: "The objective of Denmark's public assistance to the developing countries is through cooperation with the governments and authorities of these countries to support their efforts to attain economic growth in order through that to contribute towards securing their social progress and political independence."[7] Also at this time, an effort to establish an aid agency independent of the Ministry of Foreign Affairs (reflecting fears on the part of those most attentive to the development purposes of Danish aid) was turned back by the government. DANIDA was upgraded to a full department within the ministry.

The rather broad formulation of the purposes of Danish aid and the issue of where DANIDA was located organizationally reflected the various interests maneuvering for influence over the aid. The quarter of Danish aid that was tied to Danish exports had now actively engaged Danish commercial interests in the program. These aid transfers were associated with the "modern" sector of the better-off countries receiving the aid—thus, the language in the statement of purposes about "economic growth." The developmental uses of aid, strongly supported by DANIDA and the many NGOs engaged in development advocacy, focused increasingly on "social progress" (which would soon be interpreted as "poverty reduction").

Continuing to locate DANIDA in the Ministry of Foreign Affairs reaffirmed the view that Danish aid was part of Danish foreign policy, and upgrading its status to a department underlined its importance in Danish diplomacy. Tensions between diplomatic and development purposes of Danish aid were mild, because Denmark did not have a foreign policy driven by geostrategic concerns. However, Denmark, as a small country on the periphery of Western Europe, did not want to be limited in the scope of its diplomatic presence only to its region. Aid was a vehicle for expanding that presence into distant lands. The choice of which countries to aid—and concomitantly, where to establish Danish embassies in Africa, Asia, and Latin America—was especially influenced by Denmark's choice of development concentration countries, especially those with a commitment to poverty reduction, such as Tanzania. Generous amounts of aid were also means of projecting an image of the country at home and abroad as a humane internationalist—an image that fit the role that Nordic countries had begun to envision for themselves as the "social conscience of the world."[8]

But I get ahead of my story. During the 1970s, periodic debates in the Folketing and elsewhere gradually forged a measure of consensus on the implementation of Danish aid: that aid should not carry political conditions and that it should respond to "recipient preferences." This meant that recipient governments were to play the major role in deciding on the use of the aid, not the government of Denmark. Further, Danish bilateral aid for development purposes would concentrate on the poorest countries—echoing mainstream development thinking of the period that emphasized using aid to meet the "basic human needs" of the poor. With regard to bilateral assistance for commercial purposes, during the 1970s DANIDA began to exercise a greater influence over this aid, now making sure it was not just opportunistic expenditures but also associated with development projects in recipient countries.

In 1980 the Independent Commission for International Development Issues (popularly known as the North-South Commission) issued its report *To Ensure Survival—Common Interests of the Industrial and Developing Countries* (also known as the "Brandt Report," from the chair of the commission). Like the Pearson Report of a decade earlier, this study, which contained a number of recommendations involving actions by rich countries to help further development in poor ones, led the Danish government to set up an internal commission to review its own development policies. The result of this review, which was called the "Ole Bang Report," urged that the poverty focus of Danish aid be made more explicit. In its debate on this report, the Folketing chose *not* to accept this recommendation, to avoid giving the impression that Danish business (which had limited opportunities to sell its exports in the poorest parts of the poorest countries) would be squeezed out of the aid program.

Perhaps the most dramatic debate on Danish aid took place in the parliament in 1985. At that time, the Social-Liberals proposed that Danish aid be increased to 1 percent of GDP by 1992.[9] The government was against this idea, but the Social-Liberals, Social Democrats, and other left-wing parties outvoted the government, and the government accepted the policy. This initiative reversed a stagnation in Danish aid over several years between 1981 and 1985, causing it to increase rapidly until it reached 1.0 percent of GNP in 1992 as planned, where it remained for most of the 1990s.

Following the parliamentary vote in 1985, the government produced an Action Plan for Danish aid in 1987 that confirmed the 1 percent goal, reaffirmed the poverty orientation of Danish aid, and also reaffirmed that 25 percent of that aid would continue to be tied to Danish exports. Additionally, the report stated that economic liberalization was needed in much of Africa—reflecting the prevailing development thinking at the time. This represented a shift away from Denmark's traditional position of "recipient preference," mostly reflecting Denmark's discouraging experience in aiding Tanzania, where a relatively large amount of Danish aid over an extended period of time had little apparent impact on Tanzania's economic progress or the quality of its economic management, both of which had proven disappointing. Furthermore, it was decided that Denmark would adopt a country programming process—something it had avoided in the past because of its previous orientation toward recipient preferences. Thus, Copenhagen would now take a more proactive posture in planning its aid. Finally, the Action Plan sounded several other cross-cutting themes that would influence Danish aid in the 1990s: environmental concerns, gender equality, and human rights. These issues were gaining increasing prominence in a number of aid-giving countries, especially among the NGOs.

In 1988 the parliament decided to change the tied-aid program. It converted the loans to grants and dropped the formal distinction between tied and untied aid. This did not mean, however, that Danish aid was in fact no longer tied to Danish exports. The government maintained an informal tying arrangement and expanded the number of "cooperation countries" (in which bilateral grant aid had been concentrated in the past) to twenty "program countries," permitting tied aid to be spent in all of them. (This was an effort to reduce the total number of aid recipients to twenty, from the sixty that had been aided in the past.) The "program countries" would be chosen according to a number of criteria, including the level of their development and economic needs, the supply of aid from other donors and the capacity of the country to use the aid well, the possibility of promoting environmentally sustainable development and human and gender rights, and the opportunities for engaging Danish business in aiding the country.

What was happening here was an easing in the terms of Danish bilateral aid and a lessening of the obvious tying arrangements, consistent with DAC practices at the time. But tying nevertheless remained a part of that aid, and the government consistently stuck to that position. Along with the Japanese and the French, the Danes resisted pressures to untie its aid up through the end of the century, including scuttling an international agreement among aid-giving governments on untying aid that was almost reached in 2000.[10] This was pure domestic politics—the Danes were fearful of losing the support of the business community for their (relatively) large aid program and losing the six thousand to eight thousand jobs in Danish enterprises that were thought to depend on that aid.[11] Thus, while some aspects of Danish bilateral aid had become more accommodating to the development purposes of that aid during the period of "consolidation," aid's commercial goals, especially through tying, continued to be protected by the government, albeit those commercial purposes were increasingly constrained by development criteria.

Transition

The 1990s were a period of expanding purposes for Danish aid, as they were for many other aid-giving governments. But first of all, as part of a reorganization of the Ministry of Foreign Affairs in the wake of the end of the Cold War, it was decided fully to integrate DANIDA into the ministry. After 1991 there would be no separate department for DANIDA nor (apart from technical experts) even a separate career staff. The ministry was divided into "North" and "South," and DANIDA (now applied to activities rather than to an organizational entity) occupied much of what went on in the "South." At the same time, greater authority over aid decisions was decentralized to Danish embassies in the field, now also fully integrated to include both former DANIDA and Foreign Ministry staff. Perhaps to fortify the development purposes of Danish aid in light of the full merger of DANIDA into the Ministry of Foreign Affairs, in 1993 the government reestablished the post of minister of development cooperation (within the Ministry of Foreign Affairs).

In 1992, around the time of the United Nations Conference on Environment and Development in Rio de Janeiro, the Folketing voted (again against the government's wishes) to create a new Environment and Disaster Relief Facility and to fund it with a further increase in Danish aid by 0.5 percent of GNP by 2005. This facility, implemented by the Ministries of Environment and of Foreign Affairs, was in part stimulated by the Rio Conference and by the rising prominence both of environmental issues and problems of conflict in developing countries, especially in Africa. (The name of this facility was later changed to Environment, Peace and Stability Facility and eventually divided into an Environment Facility and a Peace and Stability Fund.) In the following year, a Secretariat for Environment and Sustainable Development was created to manage funds for these purposes. Though not acknowledged as such at the time, these initiatives were a de facto recognition of the increasing importance of two of the new purposes of aid in the 1990s—addressing global problems (which included the environment) and managing conflict.

It was also in 1992 that Denmark reached the target of aid as 1 percent of GNP. It is notable that to achieve this target, Danish aid increased rapidly in the early 1990s even though overall government spending declined. The priority ascribed to Danish aid was strong enough to protect it from budget cuts—in contrast to many other aid-giving countries during the early 1990s.

Changes also took place in the use of Danish aid for commercial purposes. One result of the shift in the way tied aid was managed in the late 1980s was a drop in the proportion of Danish aid spent on Danish goods and services. In an effort to offset that drop, the government undertook several initiatives in favor of Danish industry, including in 1993 a new "mixed-credit" program (in which aid monies were mixed with export credits to reduce interest charges and create attractive financing packages for Danish exporters).[12] The government also created a Private Sector Development program to support the establishment of partnerships between Danish firms and enterprises in developing countries, thus promoting Danish investments abroad as well as the development of the private sector in poor countries. While the business community at first resisted the shift away from tied aid (and, by implication, the use of aid to promote exports), by the end of the decade, Danish businesses and their umbrella organization, the Confederation of Danish Industries (Dansk Industri), had become enthusiastic about partnering with enterprises in developing countries to further private sector development there. (Such partnerships could also eventually help expand the demand for Danish exports, of which Danish industry was well aware.)

Giving more prominence to the use of aid for conflict management in 1993, Denmark initiated a program of Transitional Assistance for countries undergoing political change, whether from conflict or shift of political regime. Most of the recipients of this aid were countries emerging from conflict, such as Liberia, Cambodia, or Rwanda. Aid for political transitions in the poorer countries of the former socialist bloc—for example, Albania and Mongolia—was also included in this initiative. Denmark also began to provide assistance to support economic and political transitions in countries of Central and Eastern Europe. This aid was coordinated by the Ministry of Foreign Affairs and implemented by eighteen other government ministries and agencies. Finally, in 1990 the government set up a Democracy Fund to provide such support for Eastern Europe and the Baltic countries. (This fund's activities were later extended to developing countries as well.) Thus, by 1993, we can see in Danish aid signs of the new purposes also evident in the aid programs of other aid-giving governments: aid for global problems (mainly the environment); aid for democracy and for economic and political transitions; and the beginnings of aid for conflict management.

In 1994 the new Social-Democratic-led government produced a revised aid strategy document, entitled *A Developing World: Strategy for Danish Development Policy towards the Year 2000,* also known as *Strategy 2000.* In preparing this strategy, the ministry engaged the domestic "resource base" supporting foreign aid in an extended consultation. This process was as important to the government as a means of constituency strengthening as was the final policy document it produced. The document itself can be seen in part as a restatement of past aid policies—in particular, the emphasis on poverty reduction, with the added detail of how that goal would be accomplished (that is, concentrating aid in low-income countries and especially poor areas in those countries and financing activities in the social sector). However, this document can also be read as confirming the rise of newer purposes in Danish aid. Global problems—in particular, the environment and (after the UN conference on population) population issues—were highlighted. Gender equality and the importance of promoting human rights and democracy were also included.

Strategy 2000 reaffirmed the earlier decision to concentrate Danish aid in twenty "program countries" and called for an increased use of sector-wide assistance programs (SWAPs—the financing of approved investment budgets of particular ministries, such as health or agriculture, in developing countries), implying a move away from the funding of projects. This change, which was also adopted by a number of other aid agencies, was intended to improve the flexibility and effectiveness of Danish aid. Finally, *Strategy 2000* described Danish policies in international organizations as "active multilateralism"—signaling a more energetic engagement on the part of the government in pursuing the development objectives of its aid in multilateral aid agencies.

Six years later, in 2000, the government issued yet another new strategy paper, called *Partnership 2000.*[13] This paper reaffirmed past policy commitments but added several new priorities: addressing the problem of HIV/ AIDS (another element in what I have termed "global problems"); addressing the well-being of children and youth; and explicitly addressing the issue of conflict prevention and management. Global problems and conflict management, along with poverty reduction and human rights, were increasingly prominent among the priorities of Danish foreign policy.

To sum up the evolving profile of Danish aid during the twentieth century, three interesting trends stand out. One is the rapid rise in that aid throughout part of the 1970s to the end of the century, based on broad public support and the engagement of key elements of Danish society—especially NGOs and the business community—in the aid program. Aid for development was popular enough that the Folketing twice forced the government to accept higher levels of aid than it had planned or wanted.

Second, there was over time an increasingly explicit focus on poverty reduction as the stated main purpose of Danish aid. It would be mistaken, however, to conclude that in the competition for influence over Danish aid, NGO and development interests won out over commercial interests. There has been a conscious effort on the part of government toward compromise—in particular, to ensure that Danish commercial interests are protected in the Danish aid program, often offsetting changes in favor of poverty reduction with initiatives beneficial to business. Third, during the 1990s, when the rhetorical emphasis on poverty reduction as the core focus of Danish aid was the most explicit, other purposes were added.

The New Century: A Reorientation

The election of 2001 brought a significant shift in Danish politics, the victory of a right-of-center liberal-conservative alliance,[14] which included for the first time the Danish People's Party (DFP), a far right party. Because it was the third largest party in the Folketing, the Danish People's Party (albeit not a member of the government itself) was a critical member of the coalition in parliament on which the government relied to pass its legislation.

This shift toward the right in Danish politics reflected a growing dissatisfaction among the Danish population with liberal immigration policies and high taxes. (In fact, the two were linked in the election campaign of 2001.) Further, the Liberal Party campaigned on a promise to increase expenditures on health care and reduce foreign aid to fund them. It also said that it would no longer be bound by Denmark's policy of providing 1 percent of its GNP in foreign aid, though it promised that aid would still be above the 0.7 percent UN target.

Upon taking office, the new government proceeded to reduce Danish aid by 10 percent, bringing it down to 0.9 percent of GNP in 2002. It also reversed the earlier policy of putting aside an additional 0.5 percent of GNP for environmental, peace, and stability projects, reduced the budget for those projects by 50 percent, and transferred responsibility for them from the Ministry of Environment to the Ministry of Foreign Affairs. The government also reduced the number of its countries of concentration, canceled programs in several countries regarded as having a record of poor governance, and eliminated several advisory committees (though not the DANIDA Board). The government eliminated the post of minister of development (within the Ministry of Foreign Affairs).[15] The opposition Social Democratic party objected strongly to the cuts, arguing that "Our claim of being world leaders in foreign aid has been destroyed."[16] However, there was little public protest of the reduction in aid; in fact, half the public supported the reduction in foreign aid, with only 36 percent against.[17] Finally, the Social Democratic party found itself indirectly supporting the cut in aid in order to fund an increase in funding for health care at home, something on which it put a high priority.[18]

In 2002 the new government completed a review of Danish aid. It announced that "the Government wishes to break with the habitual thinking of years which dictates that if only assistance increases everything will be good."[19] It put considerable emphasis on democracy, human rights, and good governance as criteria for Danish aid, deciding to eliminate aid to Zimbabwe, Malawi, and Eritrea and to limit aid to other governments not meeting these criteria. It also put heightened emphasis on promoting the private sector in developing countries and promised to "boost the possibilities for Danish enterprises to contribute to the development of the private sector."[20] Later, in 2003, the government produced a white paper, *A World of Difference: The Government's Vision for New Priorities in Danish Development Assistance 2004–2008,*[21] that listed the priorities for Danish aid in the future. Poverty reduction was the "number one priority." Next came human rights, democratization and governance; stability, security, and the fight against terrorism; refugees, humanitarian assistance with a special emphasis on the countries from which refugees in Denmark originated; the environment; and social and economic development. It is worth noting that this list referenced the fight against terrorism and refugees—two issues that had not been priorities in the past. They were, in fact, linked and reflected the unease in Denmark about the influx of refugees and the growing resistance among the population to further immigration. If something could be done to stabilize and assist countries from whence the refugees came, it might be possible to stem the flow.

The question arose as to how far the new government would go in cutting and reorienting Danish aid. The general view in 2003, based on interviews with senior officials, was that the government would not cut the aid further (and it did not do so in the 2003 budget) and that it would not attempt fundamentally to reorient Danish aid away from its past emphasis on poverty reduction. The position of Denmark as a "front-runner" in aid-giving was too important to lose, and the support in Denmark for aid to reduce poverty was too widespread to ignore.[22] In a paper published in 2004, the government confirmed its intent to remain "in the forefront internationally [of development assistance] and this is to be maintained in the future. . . . Denmark's position in the forefront of the donor field provides clout and influence."[23]

That white paper also had the following language, however:

Since it came into office, the Government has worked to strengthen the effort to help refugees, the internally displaced and the permanently resident local populations in the refugees' regions of origin and areas marked by illegal migration. The activities in regions of origin will be strengthened in the coming years. Direct Danish region of origin assistance will continue to be developed in relation to activities and possible new countries of activity. . . .

. . . By means of the region of origin initiative, it should be possible to also improve conditions in the home regions of the refugees and internally displaced, giving them the possibility of returning home.

A link with the Danish national refugees effort must be established. What we do abroad and what we do at home must pull in the same direction.

This language reflected the concern of the ruling coalition regarding refugees within Denmark and its intent to use aid in the future to reduce refugee flows, above all by helping to improve conditions in their countries of origin. Further underlining the relationship between aid and reducing refugee flows was a government decision in August 2004 to re-create the portfolio of minister of development and give it to the new minister of immigration and integration (the latter term referring to the absorption of refugees into the Danish society and economy). This change did not mean that the management of Danish aid programs would be transferred to the new ministry. That responsibility remained in the Foreign Ministry. Only the responsibilities of the ministerial position (policy and public spokesperson on development) were shifted.

The combination of the development and immigration portfolios—even if only temporarily vested in the same person—was an unusual move. No other aid-giving government had moved to combine these two types of responsibilities. It appears that it was undertaken in part to please the conservative Danish People's Party (a key element in the government's parliamentary governing coalition), whose leader commented, "We've long supported pairing immigration policy and Third World Aid funds to provide help in neighboring refugee countries. And beyond that, I'm confident that refugee returns will be accelerated."[24] After the election of January 2005, the development portfolio was returned to the Ministry of Foreign Affairs.

The emphasis on reducing and even reversing the refugee flow to Denmark with foreign aid reappeared in the government's August 2005 report *Globalisation—Progress through Partnership: Priorities of the Danish Government for Danish Development Assistance 2006–2010.* Among the nine priorities for Danish aid was

> *Regions of origin—coherence home and abroad*
> The Government will strengthen Danish development assistance in regions of origin. The policy will aim to improve the living conditions of both displaced and local populations. An important goal will be that refugees and internally displaced persons as quickly as possible are given the opportunity to return and establish themselves either where they come from or close to their home areas. The government will increase the total funding allocated to efforts in regions of origin . . . and simultaneously work for the establishment of a global repatriation facility.[25]

These statements and shifts in responsibilities for the aid portfolio did not turn development aid into aid to reduce refugee flows and repatriate refugees already in Denmark. But it did demonstrate a readiness, at least among some Danish officials, to shift Danish aid in this direction (creating, in effect, a new purpose for Danish aid)—a tendency that seemed likely to gain momentum in the future, given the sensitivity of the refugee issue in the governing coalition and among the Danish public.

POLITICS

The profile of Danish aid raises three main questions that will guide my political analysis: What factors influenced the purposes of Danish aid? Why did the Danes decide to become and remain the largest aid donor relative to the size of their country's economy? And what do the changes in the new century tell us about the underlying politics of Danish aid and its likely future purposes?

Ideas

> It is difficult to be a Dane. Seen from the outside, most would say that the opposite was true: That being Danish is the easiest thing in the world. The country is well run, well organised, there is very little difference between

high and low, rich and poor, the social safety net is securely in place, etc., etc. Even so, we still feel that something isn't quite right. We don't, for example, travel abroad with the same air of nonchalance as a German or Swede or an American. We are a little more unassuming, we don't raise our voice in restaurants or other public places. Mentally, I suppose you could say we stand there with our hat in our hand, apologetic, a little self-effacing. Except when we do find a role we're comfortable with. . . .

Thus began a delightful essay entitled "Oh! To Be Danish," posted on the website of the Ministry of Foreign Affairs.[26] The tenor and tone of the essay capture the challenge to Denmark of finding a role for itself in the post–World War II world. As a small country on the edge of Western Europe, Denmark could not wield significant influence in the Cold War or even play a major role in European issues. Could it find a niche internationally where it could "punch above its weight"?[27]

One arena where it found that niche proved to be in development cooperation. Its high and rising (relative) aid levels and its policy emphasis on poverty reduction and development in poor countries were seen as providing the country with a role consistent with its size and values, while enhancing its status in the field of development cooperation. This generous aid policy created a reputation "of democratic and humanistic principles that contributes to the good international reputation and status of Denmark."[28]

Danish aid thus became a significant element in Denmark's foreign policy and its image of itself in the world as a leading "humane internationalist." This idea of its aid and its role in the world are understandable, given the constraints of size and geography on Danish foreign policy. But the choice of that role was by no means inevitable. Other small countries—for example, Austria, Canada, Finland, and Ireland—have chosen to provide much smaller amounts of aid as a proportion of their gross national income.[29] To understand this choice, we must dig deeper into the widely shared ideas held among Danes about the appropriate relationship between rich and poor and the role of the state in society.

Denmark has been among the most enthusiastic supporters of the welfare state[30] in the post–World War II world, offering a wide array of government services to the entire population, funded by relatively high taxes. Behind the broad acceptance of the welfare state in Denmark is a long history—of an emphasis on social justice and equality within Danish society and an acceptance that the state is an appropriate vehicle for realizing these goals. In the words of one observer: "The role of the state is the dominant element in the broad interpretation of the major features of Danish modern social history."[31] It was a short step for the Danes to view public aid for poverty reduction abroad as a logical extension of these widely accepted values and practices. Indeed, the same observer commented on "the very strong Danish tradition of support for forms of social development through public expenditure. This tradition has created a broad sympathy for the idea of transfer of resources from the rich North to the poor South, as an internationalization of the welfare state and the implied public support for social development."[32] Those views were reflected in high and rising public support for Danish aid over much of the period of this study—in 1998, for example, 84 percent of Danes thought that aid to developing countries was "important," and before the election campaign in 2001, a poll found that 70 percent of Danes thought that the relatively high level of Danish aid (over 1 percent of GNP) should "remain unchanged."[33]

There is one more idea that informed the Danish approach to foreign aid, contributing to the ability of the government to create and maintain broad public support for Denmark's relatively large aid program. That is the value in Danish culture placed on reaching compromises and consensus among differing views. As one of Denmark's experts on aid observed, "there is a tradition, within the political culture of Denmark, of political consensus."[34] The tendency toward political compromise is evident in the policy changes in Danish aid over time. For example, when commercial interests lost an advantage in one area (e.g., ending formally tied aid loans in 1988), they were given another (an expansion in the number of countries where "informally" tied aid could be spent). In another example, when a move to take DANIDA out of the Ministry of Foreign Affairs was rejected, DANIDA was elevated in status within the ministry; when DANIDA was fully integrated into the Ministry of Foreign Affairs, the post of minister of development cooperation was reestablished. Compromise as a cultural norm in Danish politics has undoubtedly been strengthened in the area of aid policies by the tactics of successive governments wishing to manage aid issues and debates in a way that retains the support of the aid "resource base" (that is, the constituencies supporting aid) and the public for foreign assistance.

These ideas provided frames, and behavioral norms may have *predisposed* Denmark to supporting large amounts of aid with an emphasis on development. However, it was interests and political institutions in Denmark that helped put aid and development, as well as other purposes, on the political agenda and helped decide the amount and direction of Danish assistance.

Institutions

Denmark is a constitutional monarchy based on a parliamentary system and proportional representation. This arrangement has produced a number of political parties—between eight and ten at most periods. It has also produced minority governments for most of the second half of the twentieth century, often involving a Conservative-Liberal bloc (somewhat more business oriented—the basis of the government in 2001 and again in 2005) or a Social Democratic–led bloc (somewhat more left oriented). Minority governments must maintain a coalition within the Folketing adequate to get their legislation passed. That can involve relying on an informal coalition of often small parties (not necessarily all of which are within the government). These parties, as the price of their support for government policies in parliament, can put their own issues—including development aid—on the national agenda. On occasion, groupings of parties in parliament can pass legislation even over the objections of government, thus forcing action on their favored issues. The tendencies toward minority governments have "given the Folketing and the political parties a quite extraordinary influence on the policies of changing governments, including North-South policy."[35]

When one minority party can make or break a coalition and, therefore, a government, the issues important to that party become important to the entire government. The Radical-Liberals—a relatively small party—were often the swing party in parliamentary coalitions during much of the period of this study. Foreign aid was one of their concerns, and they were thus able to ensure a high priority for generous aid for development in government policies, with the support of other left-leaning coalition parties.[36] It was this party that in 1985 proposed in the Folketing that the government adopt a target of 1 percent of GNP for Danish aid (over the opposition of the government at the time). Later, in 1992, they proposed the creation (again over government opposition) of the Environment and Disaster Relief Facility to expand aid yet further, which was also passed in the Folketing.

Thus, a combination of broad popular support for aid combined with the nature of Denmark's political institutions and parties led to high levels of aid and a focus on the development purpose of that aid. A third example of a party in the government's coalition pushing aid-related issues is the 2004 decision by the center-right government to shift the portfolio of minister of development to the new Ministry of Immigration, Integration, and Development. The speculation, noted above, was that it had much to do with placating the Danish People's Party—an important element in the government's coalition in parliament and one that was hostile to refugees in Denmark and saw development aid as a tool for reducing their numbers.

Another aspect of Danish political institutions is the active engagement in aid issues—even involving approval of specific projects—by the parliament, lending an unusual degree of transparency to Danish aid-giving. This has had two important consequences for Danish aid. First, the parliament—and by implication, the Danish public—has participated in periodic and extended debates on foreign aid, based on a series of reports and major legislative initiatives involving that aid. These debates, in turn, have helped inform parliamentarians and the public on aid matters and, because there were few attacks on the legitimacy or effectiveness of that aid, have served to develop a degree of understanding and support for Danish aid among the population and political elites (in the terms used earlier in this study—embracing the norm that affluent Denmark should provide substantial aid to poor countries). The consensus on high aid levels and their continuity over time did not prevent a substantial cut in Danish aid in 2001 with the assumption of power of a center-right government, but it appears to have limited that cut to a one-time phenomenon.

Interests

The major groups of interests engaged in Danish aid have been mentioned. Diplomatic and development interests tended to merge more in Denmark than in the other countries considered in this book. Within the government, these interests were located in the Ministry of Foreign Affairs. Outside the government, some two hundred NGOs of various kinds were involved in Danish aid as advocates, implementers, educators of the public, or all three: churches and missionary societies, cooperatives, unions, public interest groups, and several large relief and development-oriented organizations, including the Danish Red Cross, DanChurchAid, Mellemfolkligt Samvirke (Danish Association for International Cooperation), and numerous smaller ones. The relatively large number of NGOs with an interest in relief and development is part of a larger tradition of extensive and active civil society organizations in the country. In the words of one expert on Danish aid, "There is no doubt that the Danish NGOs . . . exerted considerable influence on selected parts of the Danish aid policy," in particular, with regard to the participation of the beneficiaries of development in determining how the aid was used, plus the importance ascribed to human rights, gender issues, and the environment. This same expert suggests, however, that the close relationship between the major NGOs and the government (and their reliance on government funding) led to their being "co-opted," reducing their willingness to criticize government policies.[37]

Danish industry, especially firms wishing to export abroad, has been active in Danish aid, primarily through the Confederation of Danish Industries, the organization representing the interests of Danish enterprises. While the goals of Danish business in engaging with foreign aid have shifted somewhat during the period of this study, from primarily export expansion to strengthening the private sector in developing countries, the importance of exports and of the jobs at home dependent on them has not vanished. It appears, for example, that in 2002 the new government was considering eliminating Danish aid for Vietnam along with several other country programs it canceled but decided not to do so because of the interests of Danish business in the sizable and promising Vietnamese market.[38] While not as prominent as the Danish Business Council, the Danish Agricultural Council, toward the end of the 1990s, also began to support the establishment and strengthening of similar organizations in developing countries.

Organization

Another important factor explaining the amount and purpose of Danish aid is the way the government was organized to manage its aid. Two characteristics of the organization of Danish aid make it quite unusual: one is that DANIDA has always been located within the Ministry of Foreign Affairs and by the end of the century, was fully integrated into that Ministry. The second is an institutional arrangement that gave the constituency for aid formal access and influence over the program—the DANIDA Board. Let us consider the impact of these arrangements on the purposes of Danish aid. Figure 7.2 shows in a highly simplified form the elements in the organization of Danish aid at the end of the twentieth century. In contrast to countries I've presented in the other cases, Danish aid is unified in one government ministry. Because of the influential role of the DANIDA Board and the

FIG. 7.2. THE ORGANIZATION OF DANISH AID, 2003

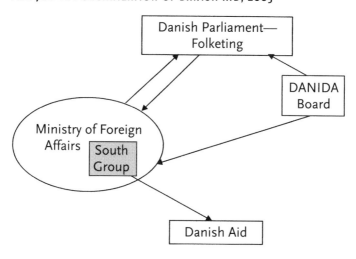

Source: DAC, Development Co-operation Review: Denmark (OECD, Paris, 2003), 18, http://www.oecd.org/dataoecd/23/63/2956543.pdf (accessed October 2005).

Folketing and the relationship between the two, however, I have shown them as part of the overall organization chart.

The location of DANIDA within the Ministry of Foreign Affairs gave Danish aid a prominence and importance in Danish foreign affairs (and an influence within government) that it would likely have lacked if DANIDA had been created as a subcabinet-level agency independent of the Ministry of Foreign Affairs, as was proposed and rejected in the early 1970s. This arrangement also gave DANIDA a measure of bureaucratic protection from temptations on the part of other ministries to try to influence the use of aid resources—a protection that it would not have had if it had been an autonomous agency. Finally, combining policy with implementation in the same organization provided DANIDA with an experienced, coherent voice on development aid within the ministry. And because the goals of Danish diplomacy seldom contradicted the developmental purposes of the aid, the often strong tensions between diplomatic and developmental purposes found in aid programs of other countries were little in evidence in Denmark. (What may be developing in Danish aid, however, are tensions between domestic policies favoring the repatriation of refugees in Denmark and the broader development goals of Danish aid. This emerging purpose of Danish aid can influence the country allocation and use of aid and these could conceivably undercut the development purpose, especially if countries of origin are poor development performers.)

A second unusual aspect of the organization of Danish aid was the DANIDA Board. The Board was established in the original law creating the Danish aid program, passed in 1962. Whether originally envisioned or not, the board came to perform several important functions vis-à-vis Danish aid. With representatives from various areas of Danish civil society, this Board in effect formalized access and ensured influence over Danish aid for its various constituencies. Thus, the Board became a vehicle for creating and maintaining a constituency within Denmark of sufficient size and strength to carry forward a relatively large aid program. The Board's ample representation from Danish civil society also ensured that even though DANIDA was part of the Ministry of Foreign Affairs, there was not undue diplomatic influence over the allocation and use of Danish aid. But what really gave DANIDA clout over Danish aid was the importance of its imprimatur for the parliament. Government typically would not send aid projects and proposals to parliament without the support of the DANIDA Board. (I am not aware of any other aid agency that has ceded as much authority to an external advisory board as has DANIDA.) Part of the "deal" in being on the board was to analyze and critique Danish aid proposals when they were first floated, but then to defend them to the board member's constituency and the public. The potential tensions among board members and other constituents of aid over the purposes of that aid—especially the development versus commercial purposes—were managed by ensuring that major elements of the constituency had a piece of the aid.

A third element is the role of the Folketing. It was the active engagement of this legislative body in Danish aid issues and its expectation that proposals (including specific aid projects) would be presented to it for consideration only after the DANIDA Board had approved them that gave the board its extraordinary influence over Danish aid.

This unusual organizational arrangement was stable over several decades. As with other aspects of Danish aid in early 2005, it is not clear whether these arrangements face fundamental change as the Danish parliament and government move to align Danish aid more with the refugee policies of the center-right governing coalition.

Summing Up

Why did Denmark become the largest donor relative to its gross national income and remain so over several years? The ideas shaping Danish aid supported such an approach and the Danish government framed the aid in terms of broadly shared values in Danish society—involving both the obligations of the rich to the poor and the role of Denmark in the world—to solidify public backing of a relatively large amount of aid. The institutions of the Danish political system encouraged a policy of generous aid-giving, especially the reliance on minority governments with a social democratic orientation, where small parties (with a particular interest in development and aid) could periodically exert considerable influence. Key interests inside and outside government (including, importantly, both diplomatic and development-oriented interests) reinforced one another in supporting the amount, country allocation, and use of aid. And the organization of Danish aid privileged the development orientation of that aid (through the DANIDA Board) and sought to engage commercial interests as well. The commercial engagement and orientation of Danish aid was a price paid for broad support.

Furthermore, the government proved adept at engaging public backing for foreign aid. Early on, the government undertook to inform its public on aid through its own activities and information but also through working with NGOs that supported aid. NGOs were urged to do their own "development education" with the Danish public through conferences on aid-related issues, exchanges of persons with developing countries, programs in the schools aimed at educating youth, and a host of other activities. In the 1990s the Danish government spent roughly $4 million per year on "development education" (rising to $10 million by the end of the decade)—double what the United States spent for a population over fifty times as large. All of these factors help explain both the high levels of Danish aid and the emphasis on development and related purposes. But then, how can we explain what at first seemed like a sudden and sharp shift in the amount and possibly the orientation of Danish aid after the election in 2001?

What this shift shows is, first, the importance of how the ideas justifying aid are presented to the public. In contrast to the Social Democrats, the Liberal-Conservative coalition that won election in 2001 did not talk about aid as an obligation of the rich to help the poor but reframed aid as trading off with domestic expenditures, especially on health, in a time of budget stringencies. Resource shortages at home were seen to have some relationship with high taxes and high levels of immigration (which itself brought high costs to Denmark in the social services provided immigrants). The reframing of aid-giving helps explain why public opinion, which had been so supportive of high levels of aid turned so quickly to support cuts in aid. Finally, the very political dynamic that supported high aid levels—the coalition politics associated with a parliamentary system based on proportional representation—can also produce the opposite result: that is, support within government for reducing aid levels based on center-right coalition politics.

However, the changes in aid-giving undertaken by the new government proved limited. Aid fell in 2001 and 2002 but rose again in 2003. Government statements on aid took on a more hard-headed tone, with more emphasis put on selectivity of recipients, the importance of results, and issues of national security, conflict, and terrorism. But poverty reduction remained at the top of the government's priorities for aid-giving. There was no major rupture in the purposes or amount of Danish aid despite the shift from a left-oriented to a right-oriented government (although there were ample signs of the rising importance of refugee management and repatriation as a purpose of Danish aid). Being a "front-runner" in aid-giving had become embedded in the Danes' image of themselves vis-à-vis the rest of the world and a genuine expression of their identities and norms. Further, the government, over many years, had built a broad "resource base" for high levels of aid-giving to fight poverty abroad. That base remained strongly supportive of development aid even though the political orientation of the government changed. And the voice for aid-giving inside the Danish government—the Ministry of Foreign Affairs—was an influential one. The inevitable conclusion is that, with foreign aid as with other public policies and programs, while political leadership can change dramatically, fundamental policies and broadly shared values, identities, and understandings do not shift so rapidly.

CHAPTER 8

Conclusions and Conjectures

This book has addressed the question "Why aid?" It has attacked the question at two levels — one describes the multiple and evolving purposes of aid-giving over the past half-century or so; the other digs into the political forces within five aid-giving countries that have shaped those purposes. It is the task of this final chapter to pull together the answers provided by the history of aid and the five case studies. I will do two additional things in this chapter: draw out several of the policy implications of my conclusions and, finally, peer into the future of foreign aid.

AID'S ORIGINS AND EVOLUTION

Foreign aid began as one thing and became another. It began as a realist response to the deepening Cold War between East and West. While continuing to be deployed in the service of national interests, aid eventually created the basis for a new norm in relations between states — that better-off states had an obligation to provide aid to less-well-off states to better the human condition in the latter. That norm did not exist in the middle of the twentieth century. It was widely accepted and unchallenged by the end of the century. For those of a theoretical bent, foreign aid must be understood through the lenses of both realism and constructivism. No one theory can adequately explain this twentieth-century innovation in relations between states.

Looking back, there is a political logic to the evolution of aid's purposes. Aid (apart from aid for relief) began in the United States in 1947 as a response to an external threat — it was a temporary expedient to bolster the economies of Greece and Turkey in the face of communist pressures. Without those pressures and the broader threat to security in Southwest Asia and the Middle East and later in Western Europe, the United States would not have begun an aid program then and, given the fiscal conservatism and isolationist tendencies in Washington, might not have begun one at all. Later, as the Cold War spread to the developing world, the US government put pressure on the governments of Western Europe, Canada, and Japan to create their own aid programs. These pressures played an important role—though not the only role—in persuading governments in Western Europe and Japan to establish or expand their own aid programs and to create government aid agencies to manage them in the 1960s. Most of these governments also had national interest reasons and, in some cases (like Denmark), domestic pressures for creating aid programs—managing decolonization, gaining access to strategic raw materials and export markets, reintegrating with the world community of states. The United States was pushing on an open door.

By the 1970s, aid had become a common element in relations between rich and poor countries. And during that decade and the one that followed, aid for development became increasingly prominent among aid's multiple purposes. For example, the portion of aid given to the least developed countries more than doubled between 1970 and the mid-1980s, the terms of aid-giving softened significantly, and the uses of aid shifted from funding economic infrastructure to social services and the more challenging problems of institutional and policy change. Further, during the 1990s and early years of the new century, aid-giving governments signed agreements to limit the commercial uses of aid, reducing the prominence of that purpose in aid-giving.

What led to the increase in priority for aid's development purpose? A key factor was the establishment within most donor countries of a political constituency for development aid. This constituency existed both inside and outside governments. Outside government, NGOs supporting aid grew in numbers and influence in most major aid-giving countries, at times acting in an informal alliance with government aid agencies. Inside government, aid agencies were set up, expanded their budgets and their staffs, strengthened their professional capacities, and increased their "development education" programs with their own publics. The importance of constituencies for development aid inside and outside government in influencing aid's purposes is underlined by the experience of those countries—Japan and France—where such constituencies were weak or lacked access and where, as a result, the development purpose of aid was the weakest.

Aid-giving governments also had pressures on them from outside their countries to elevate the amount of their aid and its development orientation. Some of these pressures came from other governments. Many emanated from a group of international development aid agencies, including the Development Assistance Committee of the OECD, the World Bank, the regional development banks, and the many UN agencies and organizations involved with aid issues (the UN Development Program, the Food and Agriculture Organization, other UN specialized agencies, the Economic and Social Council, and even the UN General Assembly), which, through a variety of means, pressed rich governments to increase the amount and quality of their development assistance. External pressures appear to have been most effective where they resonated with internal constituencies for development aid (e.g., in the Nordic countries) or, over the longer run, when they stimulated changes in those constituencies (e.g., urging the creation and strengthening of NGOs, as in Japan). But at a minimum, they succeeded in keeping development aid on the international agenda of all aid-giving governments and before the public and elites in those countries. External events, such as the two major famines in Africa in the 1970s and 1980s, raised the visibility in aid-giving countries of human suffering abroad—including problems of hunger as well as starvation and the role of aid in addressing those problems. They led both to an expansion of the constituency for development aid (that is, by stimulating the establishment of NGOs, which became advocates for development aid) and to strengthening the norm among publics and elites that governments had a responsibility to respond to human suffering abroad. (Humanitarian relief was highly motivating for the public in aid-giving countries, but humanitarian crises also often led into increased support for development aid—at least for several years in the aftermath of such crises—to deal with the underlying problems of human suffering.) The HIV/AIDS pandemic appears to have had a similar effect by the beginning of the new century. Thus, over a period of a half-century, publics and elites in rich countries came to accept the appropriateness and even the obligation of governments of rich countries to provide aid to governments and peoples in less-well-off ones.

Development-oriented NGOs and international organizations helped not only to promote an aid-for-development norm but sought to hold governments to account in fulfilling it. This does not mean that aid was not used for other purposes—such as Cold War containment, fighting terrorism, fortifying spheres of influence, or expanding markets for exports. These other purposes, tied to national security or economic interests, remained important and even essential to sustain high volumes of aid during the period of this study. But the development purpose of aid was no longer challenged as inappropriate, and, indeed, governments were increasingly forced to justify nondevelopment uses of their aid.

In the wake of the end of the Cold War in the 1990s, foreign aid fell in many donor countries, and the proportion of aid provided the poorest countries also fell, while the purposes for which aid was provided expanded to include promoting democracy, supporting economic and social transitions, addressing global issues, and mitigating conflict. The termination of the Cold War made foreign aid vulnerable to cuts in some countries, but two other factors played even more prominent roles in the drop in aid levels: economic and budgetary problems in donor countries and deepening doubts about the effectiveness of aid in spurring development, especially in sub-Saharan Africa.

The decreases in aid in the 1990s energized the constituency for development aid in many aid-giving countries to campaign for an increase in aid levels and a greater focus on development. Undoubtedly in part because of these efforts, public support in Europe and the United States for helping people in poor countries began to increase at the end of the twentieth and the beginning of the twenty-first centuries, as polls in the United States and European countries show.[1]

In the late 1990s and early years of the twenty-first century, governments in a number of aid-giving countries sought to reorganize their assistance to align it more closely with DAC development aid standards. These changes may have been hastened by the tragic events of September 11, 2001, and other terrorist attacks in Europe and elsewhere, which called the world's attention to problems of poverty, despair, and conflict in poor countries, but plans for aid increases and aid reforms preceded the terrorist attacks. Something more fundamental was at work—an embedded aid-for-development norm, supported by a growing domestic constituency. However, experience also suggests that an aid-for-development norm is not unconditional—it assumes that such aid is relatively effective and that economic conditions in aid-giving countries are sufficiently buoyant so that aid abroad is not seen as taking badly needed assistance away from people in distress at home. Within this broad historical pattern, each of this book's country case studies shows significant differences in the domestic political forces affecting the purposes of their aid—above all in the ideas and institutions shaping those purposes.

FINDINGS FROM COUNTRY CASE STUDIES

It is often thought that the main purpose of US aid is diplomatic—for most of the period of this study, fighting the Cold War. That impression is mistaken on two counts. Important among the diplomatic purposes of US aid has been peace-making, primarily in the Middle East. But more basically, roughly half of total US aid has been used for development and associated purposes. What has, in fact, marked US aid is its continuing dualism—the mix of diplomatic and development purposes. One reason for the dualism is found in the ideas shaping that aid, specifically the debate in the United States between libertarians, or classical liberals, on the political right, who argue that the role of the state in the economy should be limited and that foreign aid is an inappropriate or ineffective use of public resources, and the "humanitarians" on the political left, who argue that the United States should, as one of the world's richest countries, use its public resources generously to help the poor abroad. These arguments on the rightness of aid—not nearly so evident in other aid-giving countries—have been amplified by the adversarial nature of the US political system. They go a long way in explaining why aid has been so controversial in the United States, why support for foreign aid among the US public has been consistently lower than in any other major aid-giving country, and why, to garner enough support for annual aid appropriations, both diplomatic purposes (to gain the support or acquiescence of the conservative right or influential foreign affinity lobbies, especially that supporting the state of Israel) and development purposes (to obtain the support of the humanitarian left) have been essential. What will be interesting to watch in the future of US aid is whether the growing support of aid for humanitarian and development purposes from the Christian right will bring about a fundamental shift in the domestic politics and, ultimately, strengthen the development purpose of US foreign aid.

Japanese aid is often regarded as motivated primarily by commercial purposes—as a vehicle for expanding Japan's exports. Commercial interests were important in the first two decades of Japanese aid-giving, but even then they were nested in broader diplomatic purposes of the Japanese government. What was missing in Japan's aid was a major development focus, even after commercial purposes declined. Why was this so? Because Japanese traditions, in contrast to much of the West, put a low priority on public charity (families were supposed to take care of their needy), and the emphasis on a strong state and family left little room for civil society and, by implication, the nongovernmental organizations that populate the political landscape of aid-giving in the United States and Europe. As a result, the values and political constituencies sustaining public resources for development in other countries were weak in Japan (though over time and with international pressures, this began to change). The thing to watch in the future of Japanese aid is whether an emerging constituency for development outside government will eventually prove influential enough to strengthen the development focus of Japan's aid, overcoming, or forcing reforms in, the fragmented organization of Japanese aid within government.

France presents yet another combination of domestic political factors affecting its aid. French aid is often interpreted as primarily driven by postcolonial policies of maintaining a sphere of predominant influence, primarily in sub-Saharan Africa. This is true as far as it goes. But why did France choose to use its aid for so long in this way, even in the face of rising domestic criticisms that its aid was being wasted or helping corrupt dictators stay in power? Much of the answer has to do with widely shared ideas about France's rightful role in world politics, together with a highly centralized and not very transparent government (the National Assembly had little involvement in or even knowledge of the details of French aid, and development-oriented NGOs had little access to government decision-making) with an internal organization, reinforced by informal private networks, that privileged the use of French aid for diplomatic purposes. This system is beginning to break down with the passing of the Gaullist generation of politicians in Paris and the criticisms of younger political elites not tied to *Françafrique*. Whether reforms in the organization of French aid— highly fragmented like that of Japan—will lead to a more coherent, accountable, development-oriented program of aid is still in question and is the key thing to watch for in the future.

German aid shows a trend of diminishing diplomatic and commercial influences and an increasing concentration of responsibilities for aid policies in its Ministry of Development. Set up as a result of coalition politics in 1961, the ministry was initially a shell with few responsibilities for aid. But over time, its existence provided a political logic for successive ministers to argue successfully for greater control over German aid. That aid decreased dramatically during the economic stresses of the 1990s—especially the costs of absorbing East Germany—but it rebounded at the beginning of the new century, supported by a sizable and active NGO constituency for development aid and an activist minister of development who was also vice chairman of the Social Democratic Party—the leading party in the government coalition. Germany is committed to a substantial increase in its aid in coming years. The thing to watch is whether aid is of sufficient priority to the government for it to fulfill this commitment.

Denmark offers yet another contrast in the domestic politics of aid. Its embrace of social democratic ideas that the rich should assist the poor and that government was an appropriate vehicle for that assistance at home translated relatively easily to acceptance of development aid abroad. Its parliamentary system based on proportional representation reinforced the prominence of development aid as successive governments had to bargain with small political parties—some of which put development aid at the top of their political priorities—to create governing coalitions that raised the amount and development orientation of Denmark's aid. The government's need to create an adequate "resource base" (i.e., domestic constituency) for aid led it to allocate a significant portion of its aid initially to promote Danish commercial interests abroad, but this use was gradually limited over time as development criteria increasingly governed the allocation and use of this aid.

Denmark illustrates yet other interesting aspects of the domestic politics of aid. That country's growing backlash against immigration and heavy government taxes led to the election in 2001 of a center-right coalition that reframed foreign aid—portraying it not as an extension of social democratic values abroad but as an expenditure abroad that traded off against needed health expenditures at home. The new government cut Danish aid by 10 percent, dropping that country to second place in relative generosity. But the government did not attempt to cut Danish aid further, possibly because such a move would have collided with considerable domestic resistance. Public support for aid, although declining after the election in 2001 (reflecting the reframing of aid in terms of domestic norms and preferences), was still strong. The thing to watch in Denmark is the extent to which the reelected center-right government will try to reorient Danish aid toward reducing the number of immigrants in the country and keeping others at home. Two elements in Danish identity appear to be in conflict when it comes to Denmark's aid: its long tradition of caring for the poor at home and abroad versus guarding an ethnically and culturally homogeneous country that seems to many Danes to be threatened by a sizable number of immigrants and refugees from very different cultures and countries. Given the sensitivities in many European countries to sizable immigrant populations within their borders, Denmark may show us one of the future faces of aid in that part of the world.

FURTHER INSIGHTS FROM THE CONCEPTUAL FRAMEWORK

The conceptual framework of this study—including ideas, institutions, interests, and organization—was intended to provide a basis for analyzing the politics of aid in five countries. But the framework itself invites us to consider more general insights regarding the domestic politics of aid-giving.

First, norms are important in shaping and sustaining aid-giving. But how aid is framed in terms of those norms is also important. The impact of norms and framing is evident in a number of my cases—especially in the United States, where prominent members of the Christian right, previously skeptical about foreign aid, have begun to reframe certain kinds of aid as "Christian duty." (This view of aid has long been held by Christian Democratic parties in Europe but not so prominently in the United States, perhaps because of the prevalence there of classical liberal views on the political right, which in general strongly favor a minimal role of government in society and oppose public welfare programs.) What has led to this reframing of aid in the United States? It seems likely that the emergence of a more educated, activist, and internationalist Christian right, led by elements of the evangelical community (which has increasing numbers of missionaries in developing countries), together with the rapid growth of local evangelical movements in Latin America and sub-Saharan African, have fed this trend, both through learning and the experience of poverty and deprivation abroad. The support for increased aid from the evangelicals and the Christian right facilitated passage through the US Congress of significant increases in US aid proposed by the Bush administration (though this was not the only factor supporting the increase in US aid).

The case of Denmark provides another illustration of the power of the way aid is framed—in this case, by center-right parties linking it directly and indirectly to the contentious issues of immigration, high taxes, and inadequate expenditures on domestic health services. Support for aid in Denmark fell when the center-right parties made these links in their electoral campaign, preparing the ground for a cut in Danish aid when the center-right took power in 2001. Both of these cases illustrate that aid can be framed and reframed in terms of a number of domestic norms, and effective framing can have significant and immediate consequences for the amount and orientation of foreign aid and, over time, for the purposes of aid. The case of Denmark also suggests, however, that there may be limits, based on widely shared societal values extended over a considerable period, on how much change in aid levels and possibly aid's purposes can be implemented through reframing. The center-right coalition refrained from cutting aid below the initial 10 percent, anticipating significant resistance to further cuts from the public and the Danish aid lobby.

The case studies confirm the argument, suggested at the beginning of the book, that the structure of governments, combined with electoral rules, can influence the purpose of aid. The need to create governing coalitions led to enhanced aid for development as a price of coalition building and maintenance, affecting the organization of aid in Germany and the amount of aid and aid's purposes in Denmark up to 2001.[2] This dynamic does not work in the winner-take-all presidential system of the United States, which discourages the formation of small political parties favoring niche issues (even though there might well be an adequate constituency base for such parties in the United States if electoral rules were based on proportional representation and the system were a parliamentary one).

The case of Denmark illustrates the proposition that informed and engaged legislatures can affect aid's purposes. The Folketing often debated aid issues and was long a vehicle for education and consensus-building among political elites and the public on Danish development aid. The opposite case is found in France and Japan, where the legislatures played no role in aid—they were mostly uninformed and seldom debated aid issues, leaving aid policies and decisions opaque and not subject to public scrutiny or influence. Where legislatures do not hold the executive branch to account, the public may strongly support aid, but it may be little informed about the actual uses of that aid and have little impact on them. The public and political elites can also turn sharply against aid when scandals erupt involving the use of aid for commercial or political purposes, as they have in the less transparent aid systems of Japan and France.

The importance of a constituency for development aid and its degree of access to government is well confirmed by my cases. Where that constituency was weak or lacking in access—as in Japan and France, respectively—the development purposes of aid were weak. Where that constituency was strong and well connected to government decision-makers, as in the case of Denmark, aid's development purposes were much more prominent. However, the cases of the United States and Denmark suggest an amendment to this proposition. A constituency with access to government may ensure that aid's development purpose is prominent, but it is not usually adequate to ensure that development is aid's *only* purpose. In both countries, other interests influence the purposes of aid—in Denmark, commercial interests, and in the United States, diplomatic ones. And these other interests proved essential to carrying sizable aid budgets forward year after year in these political systems.

Fifth, the case studies also demonstrate a relationship between the way a government organizes its aid and the priority of development in aid's purposes. Development has gradually become a more prominent purpose in German aid as the Ministry of Development has increasingly gained responsibilities over Germany's aid programs. The fragmented aid organizations in France and Japan have contributed to the weak development purpose in those government's aid programs, and the stickiness of these systems has impeded efforts to elevate that purpose through government reorganization.

The bureaucratic location of aid also matters, though the relationship between location and aid's development purposes is not as simple or straightforward as aid practitioners have often assumed. One would expect that a ministerial level development aid agency would carry more influence in government than a subcabinet-level aid agency. The case of Germany, compared to that of the United States, would seem to validate this prediction. But the case of Denmark—where aid has been fully merged into the Ministry of Foreign Affairs—suggests a caveat. The development purpose of Danish aid has not been overwhelmed by Denmark's diplomatic policies, because those policies regarding developing countries are consistent with furthering development. In contrast, for the United States, in a position of world leadership, diplomatic goals (e.g., peace-making in the Middle East, containing communism, fighting terrorism) have a high priority in the mission of the Department of State and can collide with development purposes when aid is needed to reward regimes, even corrupt and incompetent ones, which support US policies. The potential inconsistency between development and diplomatic goals was at the heart of the conflict on the issue of merging USAID into the Department of State in the 1990s and remains alive at the time of this writing.

One further lesson on aid organization is suggested from the case studies. Even though aid systems are difficult to reform where such reforms involve major changes in government bureaucracies, change can occur through the creation of entirely new agencies—as in the case of the Millennium Challenge Corporation in the United States. This approach avoids costly confrontations with existing agencies and the interests they represent but has the downside of further fragmenting the overall organization of aid.

A final comment needs to be made about the interaction of domestic and international factors in shaping aid's purposes. If domestic political forces are so important in influencing foreign aid, why has there been an obvious convergence in the purposes of aid over the past decade and a half among different aid-giving governments? Part of the answer is that external pressures, sustained over time, can change the fundamental determinants of aid's purposes. Prolonged external pressures on governments of rich countries to provide more and better aid for development have affected the way publics, and particularly political elites within aid-giving governments, think about what the purposes of aid should be and how their government measures up. They have, as in the case of Japan, encouraged governments to support the establishment and strengthening of development-oriented NGOs that, in turn, become lobbies for aid for development. External pressures have put development issues on the political agendas in many aid-giving countries over a period of time, helping to inform their publics on aid-giving and development needs abroad. In some cases, where governments have claimed a major world role in development aid—as in Japan, France, and Denmark—criticisms from abroad have provoked criticisms at home and have eventually motivated governments to bring their policies more into alignment with international norms for development aid.

Many of the factors leading to a convergence in aid's purposes in the 1990s and early years of the twenty-first century relate to events within aid-giving countries rather than external pressure or events: the passing of a generation in France that cleared the way for new approaches to aid-giving; the beginnings of greater accountability in Japanese political institutions; the resistance to immigration in Denmark; the rise of the evangelicals in US political life. International events, trends, and pressures are important sources of change, but they often work through domestic political forces, and those forces also produce change, independent of what is going on beyond their borders.

IMPLICATIONS FOR POLICY

It was not the purpose of this book to generate policy recommendations. But there are two implications of this study that stand out as obvious, compelling, and little addressed by policy-makers. "Aid effectiveness" has almost always been defined as "developmental effectiveness," and assessments of aid's impact on growth have often found aid to be ineffective. Yet one of the lessons from this study is that aid's purposes have always been mixed, related in significant part to the domestic political forces influencing the amount, allocation, and use of aid. And it seems likely that, despite an aid-for-development norm, aid's purposes will continue to be mixed in the future. It is, therefore, irrational and potentially highly misleading to evaluate *all aid* according to only one of its purposes. What has long been missing is an effort to identify in detail and evaluate those other purposes of aid and to apply development criteria only to that aid that is primarily directed at development purposes.[3] Roughly half of US bilateral aid might fall into the category of "aid primarily for nondevelopment purposes"—much of it tied to diplomatic purposes of various kinds—which should be evaluated as to whether it achieved those purposes. For example, was US aid for peace-making in the Middle East effective in helping to further peace between Israel and its neighbors? To what extent was aid successful in resisting the expansion of communism in Europe in the 1940s and 1950s and Central America in the 1980s? How effective has French aid been in fortifying a sphere of influence in Africa? To my knowledge, there has been no effort on the part of any aid donor at any time to provide a rigorous evaluation of its aid programs for purposes other than development.

This lack of a comprehensive effort to evaluate aid effectiveness in terms of its various purposes is not just a problem of bureaucratic untidiness. It is highly relevant to the future of development aid. The increases in aid during the early years of the twenty-first century have been justified in part on the promise that aid will be more effective in the future than it has been in the past, based on greater selectivity of recipients, better "ownership" on the part of recipients, and improved aid management through an emphasis on results. Yet aid is still provided for mixed purposes. If evaluations of aid's impact in the future continue to apply development criteria indiscriminately to all aid rather than distinguish among aid's different purposes and if future evaluations find that aid's impact on development is still disappointing, there could well be an unjustified backlash against aid in general among the public and political elites in aid-giving countries. It is important to take the full range of aid's purposes into account in making our evaluations, and we are not there yet.

A second policy implication involves aid effectiveness. All the donor governments in this study have committed themselves to increase their aid for development substantially throughout the remainder of the first decade of the twenty-first century. If they should seek to fulfill that commitment (which is not guaranteed), most of them lack the organizational capacity to manage dramatic increases in aid. The fragmented systems of the United States, Japan, France, and even Germany will make policy coordination within aid-giving governments, the design and implementation of greatly expanded development-aid programs and projects, and their monitoring and evaluation very challenging. Yet major increases in aid will have to be allocated and disbursed quickly; large and growing pipelines will lead legislatures to go slowly on approving increases in aid, as the US Congress has done with the Millennium Challenge Account. But moving large amounts of aid quickly, especially in fragmented donor aid systems, risks using it poorly, compelling donor governments to transfer the bulk of it to the governments of poor countries (rather than using NGOs and other intermediaries, for example, for small, community-based activities), which themselves lack the capacity to use aid well and the systems to ensure it is used for the purposes intended. If rapidly rising amounts of aid are wasted or fuel corruption in recipient countries, public support for aid in donor countries could erode and lead to a drop in aid in the future. Organization—and capacity—matters more than ever, both among donor and recipient governments.

CONJECTURES ABOUT THE FUTURE OF AID

Looking forward into the twenty-first century, diplomatic uses of aid will remain, especially for the United States, as it continues to pursue a role of global leadership. Peace-making will still demand resources, as will efforts to eliminate terrorism, weapons of mass destruction, crime, and drugs. Demands on aid for diplomatic purposes will likely increase if major international tensions arise—for example, from a Europe attempting to create a balance of power against the United States, or from a China asserting its influence in Asia and beyond. Global problems, such as climate change, the international transmission of disease, and shortages of water and energy, are likely to intensify with expanding world population and increased incomes and these will bring greater demands for aid to address them.

But from the perspective of 2006, it appears that the main purpose of aid will remain the challenge of development and poverty reduction. And this challenge will be increasingly concentrated in sub-Saharan Africa. At the heart of this challenge will be figuring out how to strengthen the performance of institutions—the rule of law, the responsible and competent functioning of governments and their leaderships, and the behavior of markets. We are still far from understanding why governments have performed so poorly in much of Africa and how to help them improve their performance—not just their capacities but their probity as well—and what to do about it. Where governments do not perform to meet the minimal needs of their populations, they can fail—their societies can dissolve into civil conflict. And this tendency, evident not just in Africa but in parts of Asia and even Latin America, is already leading aid-giving governments to create a new purpose of aid: preventing state failure and civil conflict. At the time of this writing, a number of aid agencies—USAID in the United States, the Department for International Development in the United Kingdom, and the Japan International Cooperation Agency—were beginning to think through the meaning and causes of state failure and the possible use of aid to respond to that failure.[4] It will likely evolve into a new purpose of aid once we can gain a better grasp on how to address it.

This is the bad news regarding the future context of aid. There promises to be much good news as well in the world of 2010 and beyond, with implications for the future of foreign aid. First, China and India—if they continue to grow—will further reduce world poverty. There are hundreds of millions of people still desperately poor in those countries, but steady growth over a decade or more could make a major difference, as it has already done in China over the past several decades. However, that growth will carry costs as well—costs to the world environment, pressures on food production (as better-off Chinese and some Indians shift from grain to protein consumption), and pressures on water resources, already scarce in both countries. These consequences of success may increase the priority of addressing global problems with aid resources in the future.

There is another set of trends, already evident in the world of the early twenty-first century, that could bring good news for the world's poor as well as challenges for aid-giving. First is the rapid aging of the populations in Europe and Japan (and even, China). If these countries are to maintain their standards of living, they may be forced to open up to immigration, largely from poor countries. Immigration could lead to large remittance flows (even larger than the nearly $100 billion per year in remittances during the first half of the 2000s) that could provide much enlarged resources to families and communities in poor countries. But there is a major challenge for host countries in managing immigration without provoking a backlash from their own citizens (one that is already evident in Europe and has even begun to affect the amount and use foreign aid, for example, in Denmark).

Development in the Twenty-First Century: A World of "Many-to-Many"

Then there is the emerging world of "many-to-many" in aid-giving just as in telecommunications. For much of the period of this study, foreign aid was the principal source of concessional development finance from rich countries to poor countries, and that finance was often delivered on the basis of one-to-one (government to government, sometimes via international organizations). With the increase in NGOs working in developing countries, aid began to look like one-to-many—provided to central governments, to local governments, and to local NGOs and even private enterprises to promote economic and social progress. But public aid remained the predominant source of external concessional financing in development in poor countries. What has become evident at the beginning of the new century is that private giving of all kinds, aimed at development and reducing poverty, has begun to increase substantially. In addition to the world's major foundations, such as Ford, Rockefeller, and Sasakawa, large amounts of funds have been provided from individuals through their own newly created foundations—for example, the Gates Foundation, the Open Society (funded by George Soros), and other, often substantial, private donors.

Further, corporations have begun to expand their funding of development activities in poor countries, from their own company foundations, from their marketing divisions, or from individual giving programs located within corporations. Some of these private development transfers are in the form of "venture development" or "venture philanthropy"—investments by rich individuals and venture capital–type firms in organizations (NGOs, businesses) in poor countries for socially beneficial and often profit-making activities—what are called "double bottom-lines." Some are transfers to social entrepreneurs—individuals with a vision and energy to bring about beneficial change in their communities but without the intention of making a profit. A number of organizations have sprung up in the United States and Europe to encourage social entrepreneurs and bring them together with funders. Ashoka, an NGO in the United States, has long sought out social entrepreneurs to support them. The Schwab Foundation in Switzerland, established in 1998, has undertaken similar activities, as have the Kellogg Foundation in the United States and many others elsewhere. Internet-based firms have begun to create portals in which individual and corporate givers can transfer funds directly to NGOs working in poor countries to further their activities.

It seems likely that by 2010 the amount of private giving and the number of organizations and individuals funding and being funded to better the human condition in the developing world will be far larger than it was in 2005. It promises to be a dynamic world of many-to-many. If even a portion of this activity proves effective, it could make a major change in poor countries, not just improving the quality of life at the community level but educating and energizing local groups to become active in pursuing their own interests with their governments. And should that happen, governments—even in Africa—will be forced to become more accountable to all their peoples and eventually become the promoters of development rather than the obstacles that so many of them have been in the past.

But this world of many-to-many will challenge aid agencies—what will be the impact of a world of many-to-many on foreign aid—especially aid for development? What opportunities and challenges will it present?

We can only speculate on the answer, but several consequences seem likely. First, the more individuals and groups there are engaged in bettering the human condition abroad, the stronger the norm will become that rich countries should assist poor countries to develop. Experiencing directly problems of poverty, conflict, disease, and environmental degradation can change norms and ideas and could not only strengthen the aid-for-development norm in rich countries but expand the constituency for development aid. But a world of many-to-many will create organizational and management challenges for aid-giving governments. Most basically, it can create coordination challenges beyond those that already exist among aid-giving institutions. And it will challenge the leadership of public aid agencies in the field of development: if they are to work effectively with the widening variety of private development actors, they will need to be much more flexible, nimble, and collaborative than they have been in the past. There are some signs that aid agencies are waking up to these challenges and opportunities—USAID, for example, created a new program sponsoring "public-private partnerships," and other agencies have begun to look for such partnerships as well.

The experience of a half-century of the "innovation in . . . foreign policy" identified by Hans Morgenthau and cited at the beginning of this book suggests that foreign aid—and the norms and constituencies created around it—will remain a common and familiar element in relations between countries in the rapidly changing world of the twenty-first century. Its purposes will continue to be mixed—with human betterment at its core, but with diplomatic goals still important, especially to the United States and other governments aspiring to leadership roles in the world. New and at present unforeseeable purposes are likely to be added as the pace of technological change—especially information technologies—accelerates and as the world of many-to-many evolves. For all that, domestic political forces—themselves increasingly influenced by trends beyond their borders—will remain key factors in the future of foreign aid.

INTERVIEWS

The interviews below were conducted in 2002 and 2003. The interviewees are listed according to their position at the time they were interviewed. I conducted only one formal interview in the United States, because of continuous opportunities to gather information for my research from practitioners in government, NGOs, and the academy in Washington, DC.

UNITED STATES

Andrew Natsios, Administrator, USAID

JAPAN

Eigo Azukizawa, JBIC, Tokyo
Hideki Esho, Professor, Hosei University, Tokyo
Yasuo Fujita, JBIC Institute, Tokyo
Takeshi Fujitani, Asahi Shimbun
Junichi Hasegawa, JBIC, Tokyo
Ryokichi Hirono, Professor Emeritus, Seikei University, Tokyo
Fukada Hiroshi, JICA, Tokyo
Kato Hiroshi, JICA, Tokyo
Masatoshi Honda, Associate Professor, National Graduate Institute for Policy Studies (GRIPS), Tokyo
Shinsuke Horiuchi, Japan Institute of International Affairs, Tokyo
Satoshi Iijima, JBIC Institute, Tokyo
Katsuji Imata, CSO Network, Tokyo
Juichi Inada, Professor, Shenshu University, Tokyo
Naoko Ishii, Ministry of Finance, Tokyo
Hiroshi Kadota, Nippon Keidanren, Tokyo
Kaori Katada, CSO Network, Tokyo
Nobuhiko Katayama, World Vision, Tokyo
Fukunari Kimura, Professor, Keio University, Tokyo
Hirohisa Kohama, Professor, University of Shizuoka, Tokyo

Tetsuo Konaka, JBIC, Tokyo

Chimaki Kurokawa, Japan Platform, Tokyo

Tadashi Maeda, JBIC, Tokyo

Kosuke Nakahira, Vice Chair, Institute for International Economic Studies, Tokyo

Takashi Nakamura, JBIC Senior Representative, Washington, DC

Izumi Ohno, Professor, GRIPS, Tokyo

Kenichi Ohno, Professor, GRIPS, Tokyo

Kotaro Otsuki, Economic Cooperation Bureau, Ministry of Foreign Affairs, Tokyo

Mami Sakuma, JBIC Institute, Tokyo

Yasutami Shimomura, Professor, Hosei University, Tokyo

Ishii Sumie, Japan Organization for International Cooperation in Family Planning, Tokyo

Keiichi Tango, Executive Director, JBIC Institute, Tokyo

Takao Toda, JICA Representative, Washington, DC

Toru Tokuhisa, Director General, JBIC Institute, Tokyo

Ichita Yamamoto, Member, House of Councillors, Tokyo

Motohide Yoshikawa, Deputy Director General, Economic Cooperation Bureau, Ministry of Foreign Affairs, Tokyo

Yakashi Yoshimura, Nippon Keidanren, Tokyo

Yukio Yoshimura, World Bank, Tokyo

FRANCE

Richard Carey, Development Assistance Committee, OECD, Paris

Michel Doucin, Paris

Jean-Jacques Gabas, President, GIS Economie Mondiale Tiers-Monde Développement, Paris

Francois Gaulme, Agence Française de Développement, Paris

Jean-Marie Hatton, Haute Conseil de la Coopération Internationale, Paris

Jean-Francois Lanteri, Ministere des Affaires Etrangères, Paris

Anne de Lattre, Advisor to Agence Française de Développement, Paris

Richard Manning, Chair, Development Assistance Committee, OECD, Paris

Hunter McGill, Development Assistance Committee, OECD, Paris

Serge Michailof, Agence Française de Développement, Paris

Emile-Robert Perrin, Haute Conseil de la Cooperation Internationale, Paris

Sheherazade Semsar, Development Institute International, Paris

GERMANY

Friedrich Beimdiek, Ministry of Development, Berlin

Michael Bohnet, Ministry of Development, Bonn

Michael Dauderstadt, Friedrich Ebert Stiftung, Berlin

Dieter Dettke, Friedrich Ebert Stiftung, Washington, DC

Franziska Donner, GTZ, Frankfurt

Hansjorg Elshorst, Transparency International, Berlin

Erhard Eppler, former minister of development, Bonn

Albrecht Graf von Hardenberg, GTZ, Frankfurt

Asche Helmut, GTZ, Frankfurt

Hans Hielscher, Journalist
Ernst-J. Kerbusch, Friedrich Ebert Stiftung, Bonn
Adolf Kloke-Lesch, Ministry of Development, Bonn
Stephan Klingebiel, German Development Institute, Bonn
Doris Kohn, KfW, Frankfurt
Martin Lutz, Ministry of Foreign Affairs, Berlin
Uwe Optenhogel, Friedrich Ebert Stiftung, Berlin
Uwe Otzen, German Development Institute, Bonn
Ludger Reuke, Germanwatch, Bonn
Hans-Helmut Taake, German Development Institute, Bonn
Reinold Thiel, Editor, E + Z, Frankfurt
Adelheid Troscher, Bundestag, Berlin
Jurgen Wiemann, German Development Institute, Bonn
Doris Witteler-Stiepelmann, Ministry of Development, Berlin

DENMARK

Ole Winckler Andersen, Ministry of Foreign Affairs, Copenhagen
Holger Bernt-Hansen, Chair, DANIDA Board, Copenhagen
Torben Brylle, Ministry of Foreign Affairs, Copenhagen
Niels Dabelstein, Ministry of Foreign Affairs, Copenhagen
Poul Engberg-Pedersen, Centre for Development Research, Copenhagen
Steen Folke, Center for Development Research, Copenhagen
Bjorn Forde and Lars Engberg, Mellemfolkeligt Samvirke, Copenhagen
Jorgen Hansen and Hans Peter Slente, Dansk Industri, Copenhagen
Nanna Hvidt, Ministry of Foreign Affairs, Copenhagen
Jesper Jespersen, Journalist, Copenhagen
Peter Lysholt Hansen, Ministry of Foreign Affairs, Copenhagen
Gorm Rye Olsen, Centre for Development Research, Copenhagen
Anne Sorensen, Journalist, Copenhagen
Carsten Staur, Ministry of Foreign Affairs, Copenhagen
Finn Tarp, Centre of African Studies, Copenhagen
Lars Udsholt, Mellemfolkeligt Samvirke, Copenhagen
Michael Zilmer-Johns, Ministry of Foreign Affairs, Copenhagen

OTHER COUNTRIES

Rob D. van den Berg, Ministry of Foreign Affairs, Netherlands
Helge Pharo, Professor, University of Oslo, Norway

ABBREVIATIONS, ACRONYMS, AND FOREIGN TERMS

AFD. Agence Française de Développement (French Agency for Development)

AFL-CIO. American Federation of Labor–Congress of Industrial Organizations

AIPAC. American-Israel Public Affairs Committee

ASEAN. Association of Southeast Asian Nations

BMZ. Bundesministerium für Wirtschaftliche Zuzamenarbeit und Entwicklung (Federal Ministry for Economic Cooperation and Development, Germany)

CCCE. Caisse Centrale de Coopération Economique (Central Bank for Economic Cooperation, France)

CFA. Communauté financière africaine (African Monetary Union, France)

CICID. Interministerial committee on international cooperation and development (France)

DAC. Development Assistance Committee of the OECD

DANIDA. Danish International Development Agency

EPA. Economic Planning Agency (Japan)

ESF. Economic Support Fund (United States)

GNI. Gross national income

GTZ. German Corporation for Technical Cooperation

HCCI. High Council for International Cooperation (France)

IDA. International Development Association

IDCA International Development Cooperation Agency (US)

IMF. International Monetary Fund

JBIC. Japan Bank for International Cooperation

JICA. Japan International Cooperation Agency

KfW. Kreditanstalt für Wiederaufbau (Bank for Reconstruction, Germany)

LDP. Liberal Democratic Party (Japan)

MCA. Millennium Challenge Account (United States)

METI. Ministry of Economics, Trade and Industry (Japan)

MITI. Ministry of Trade and Industry (Japan)

MOF. Ministry of Finance (Japan)

MOFA. Ministry of Foreign Affairs (Japan)

NEPAD. New Partnership for Africa's Development

NGO. Nongovernmental organization

OA. Official assistance

ODA. Official development assistance

OECD. Organisation for Economic Co-operation and Development

OECF. Overseas Economic Cooperation Fund (Japan)

PL480. Public Law 480 (United States)

PRC. People's Republic of China

PRSP. Poverty reduction strategy paper

SWAP. Sector-wide assistance program

TICAD. Tokyo International Conference on African Development (Japan)

UNDP. United Nations Development Program

USAID. United States Agency for International Development

VENRO. Verband Entwicklungspolitik Deutscher Nichtregierungs-Organisationen (Association of German Development Nongovernmental Organizations)

JAPANESE TERMS

Diet. Japanese parliament.

gaiatsu. External pressures.

Keidanren. Japan Federation of Economic Organizations.

naiatsu. Internal pressures.

FRENCH TERMS

besoin de rayonnement. Need for influence (said of the French culture and language).

cooperants. French citizens who taught in the schools of former French colonies and performed other technical assistance.

Françafrique. Network of French and African political leaders.

pays du champ. Concentration countries.

pays hors champ. Countries not of special concern.

GERMAN TERMS

Bundestag. Lower house of the German parliament.
Länder. The sixteen German states.

DANISH TERMS

Folketing. Danish parliament.

NOTES

CHAPTER ONE

1. Hans Morgenthau, "A Political Theory of Foreign Aid," *American Political Science Review* 56, no. 2 (June 1962): 301.

2. Private charity through nongovernmental organizations such as Save the Children or from private foundations such as the Ford Foundation or Rockefeller Foundation to fund good works abroad was well established before World War II and may have provided a model for transferring public funds abroad for some. But on the whole, private charity was generally regarded as quite distinct from using public funds for similar activities. Governments had long used public concessional resources to bribe one another, to subsidize friendly individuals and groups in foreign countries, or to fund tributes from less powerful to more powerful governments. But these transfers are quite different from foreign aid as we know it today and as I shall analyze it here.

3. Development Assistance Committee (DAC), Organisation for Economic Cooperation and Development (OECD), "International Development Statistics (IDS) Online," http://www.oecd.org/dac/stats/idsonline (accessed October 2005). This figure is net of repayments, in current dollars, and includes "official development assistance" (ODA) for poor countries and "official assistance" (OA) to better-off developing countries and countries in transition from socialism. For more on the definitions of ODA and OA, see n. 15. Unless otherwise noted, the data on foreign aid in this study are from DAC, "International Development Statistics (IDS) Online," at the URL noted above. Users of this data source must register, but access is easy and free.

4. Ibid. In constant 2003 dollars, the total would exceed $2.5 trillion. This does not include private aid through nongovernmental organizations.

5. One of aid's most prominent advocates at the time of this writing is Jeffrey Sachs, professor of economics at Columbia University, who has argued that aid should be doubled. See, for example, his book *The End of Poverty* (New York: Penguin, 2005). Challenging that view is William Easterly in his book *The White Man's Burden* (New York: Penguin, 2006).

6. What follows here is a review of aid literature relevant to aid's purposes. But this is not the only literature on foreign aid. There is the "literature of passion"—paeans of praise for aid (usually advocating greatly increased aid levels) or jeremiads attacking aid, typically arguing that aid is a waste of money or worse and urging that aid be terminated or fundamentally reformed. An example of literature attacking aid is Graham Handcock's *Lords of*

Poverty (London: Macmillan, 1989). This literature tends to emit more heat than light. Second is the normative literature on foreign aid, arguing for or against aid on philosophical and ethical grounds. See, for example, Deen Chatterjee, ed., *The Ethics of Assistance* (New York: Cambridge University Press, 2004); Thomas Pogge, *World Poverty and Human Rights* (Cambridge, UK: Polity, 2002); Henry Shue, *Basic Rights* (Princeton, NJ: Princeton University Press, 1980); Stanley Benn, *A Theory of Freedom* (Cambridge: Cambridge University Press, 1988); and Onora O'Neill, *Faces of Hunger* (London: Allen & Unwin, 1986). Finally, there is the growing literature on aid effectiveness. The many evaluations, studies, books, and articles in this category focus almost entirely on the success or failure of aid to achieve one of its purposes—promoting development. This is an important subject but not the focus of this study.

7. George Liska, *The New Statecraft* (Chicago: University of Chicago Press, 1960), 14. See also Lloyd Black, *The Strategy of Foreign Aid* (Princeton, NJ: Van Nostrand, 1968). For a more recent statement of realist thinking, see Nicholas Eberstadt, *Foreign Aid and American Purpose* (Washington, DC: American Enterprise Institute, 1988).

8. See, for example, Steven Hook, *National Interest and Foreign Aid* (Boulder, CO: Lynne Rienner, 1995).

9. See Leonard Dudley and Claude Montmarquette, "A Model of the Supply of Bilateral Foreign Aid," *American Economic Review* 66, no. 1 (1976): 132–42; R. D. McKinlay, "The Aid Relationship: A Foreign Policy Model and Interpretation of the Distributions of Official Bilateral Economic Aid of the United States, the United Kingdom, France and Germany, 1960–1970," *Comparative Political Studies* 11, no. 4 (1979): 411–63; Alfred Maizels and Machiko Nissanke, "Motivations for Aid to Developing Countries," *World Development* 12, no. 9 (1984): 879–900; Paul Mosley, "The Political Economy of Foreign Aid: A Model of the Market for a Public Good," *Economic Development and Cultural Change* 33, no.2, 373–94; Bruno Frey and Friedrich Schneider, "Competing Models of International Lending Activity," *Journal of Development Economics* 20 (1986): 225–45; James Lebovic, "National Interests and US Foreign Aid: The Carter and Reagan Years," *Journal of Peace Research* 25, no. 2 (1988): 115–35; Peter Schraeder, Steven Hook, and Bruce Taylor, "Clarifying the Foreign Aid Puzzle: A Comparison of American, Japanese, French and Swedish Aid Flows," *World Politics* 50, no. 2 (1998): 294–323. While these studies and others like them are helpful as a first effort to identify and compare broad donor motivations, their efforts to create models and employ measurable indicators have often produced simplistic and, at times, misleading results—poorly specifying indicators, conflating correlation with causality, ignoring key motivations where they were difficult to disentangle and measure quantitatively, and failing to capture changing purposes of aid-giving. On the other hand, quantitative studies have made a valuable contribution to understanding foreign aid where they have taken on the less complicated task of testing whether donors have lived up to particular commitments in aid-giving. For example, to what extent have donors honored their commitments to reward democratization, penalize corruption, and embrace selectivity (i.e., rewarding good governmental performance)? In the early 1990s, they did reward democratizing countries; from 1970 to 1995, they did not penalize corrupt ones; and in the 1990s, aid donors did become more selective in their aid allocations—except the United States and France. See Alberto Alesina and David Dollar, "Who Gives Foreign Aid to Whom and Why?" *Journal of Economic Growth* 5 (2000): 33–63; Alberto Alesina and Beatrice Weder, "Do Corrupt Governments Receive Less Foreign Aid?" (working paper 7108, National Bureau for Economic Research, May 1999); David Dollar and Victoria Levin, "The Increasing Selectivity of Foreign Aid, 1984–

2002" (working paper 3299, World Bank Research Department, May 1, 2004), http://econ .worldbank.org/view.php?type=5&id=35475 (accessed December 2004).

10. See, for example, James Cockcroft, Andre Gunder Frank, and Dale Johnson, *Dependence and Underdevelopment* (New York: Anchor Books, 1972); or Walter Rodney, *How Europe Underdeveloped Africa* (Washington, DC: Howard University Press, 1974). For a more recent version of this argument, part of a broader discourse deconstructing power and dominance in international affairs, see Arturo Escobar, *Encountering Development* (Princeton, NJ: Princeton University Press, 1995). Efforts to explain foreign aid through this prism also include Teresa Hayter, *The Creation of World Poverty* (London: Pluto Press, 1981); and Teresa Hayter and Cathrine Watson, *Aid: Rhetoric and Reality* (London: Pluto Press, 1985).

11. David Halloran Lumsdaine, *Moral Vision in International Politics* (Princeton, NJ: Princeton University Press, 1993), 3.

12. See Cranford Pratt, ed., *Internationalism under Strain: The North-South Policies of Canada, the Netherlands, Norway and Sweden* (Toronto: University of Toronto Press, 1989). Another study of the role of ideas (though not norms of altruism or social democracy) in influencing foreign aid (and US foreign policy) is *Liberal America and the Third World* by Robert Packenham (Princeton, NJ: Princeton University Press, 1973). Packenham's study analyzes the thinking behind US aid between 1947 and 1970 in its use to promote political and economic modernization abroad and ties this thinking to the broader ideas associated with the liberalism of the political left in the United States.

13. Some structural realists, like Kenneth Waltz, downplay the role of domestic politics. But there is a considerable literature on domestic politics and foreign policy (though not on foreign aid). Among the best-known works that examine domestic politics are Graham Allison and Phillip Zelikow, *Essence of Decision: Explaining the Cuban Missile Crisis* (New York: Longman, 1999), for bureaucratic politics; Peter Katzenstein, *Small States and World Markets: Industrial Policy in Europe* (Ithaca, NY: Cornell University Press, 1985), for institutions and interests; Michael Brown, Sean Lynn-Jones, and Steven Miller, eds., *Debating the Democratic Peace* (Boston: MIT Press, 1996), for the impact of democracy on war. For a treatment of the role of domestic politics in international negotiation, see Peter Evans, Harold Jacobson, and Robert Putnam, eds., *Double-Edged Diplomacy: International Bargaining and Domestic Politics* (Berkeley: University of California Press, 1993). On the role of ideas, see Judith Goldstein and Robert Keohane, eds., *Ideas and Foreign Policy: Beliefs, Institutions and Political Change* (Ithaca, NY: Cornell University Press, 1993). On the impact of international politics on domestic politics, see Peter Gourevitch, "The Second Image Reversed: International Sources of Domestic Politics," *International Organization* 32 (1978): 881–912. The best single example of an examination of some of the domestic elements influencing aid's purpose is Vernon Ruttan, *United States Development Assistance Policy: The Domestic Politics of Foreign Economic Aid* (Baltimore: Johns Hopkins University Press, 1996).

14. In addition to allocations that do not entail any repayment at all, the grant element of an aid program includes a measure of the degree to which any loans are concessional (i.e., below the market cost of borrowing the funds). The grant element of a loan is usually expressed as a percentage of the original face value. There is no magic minimum grant element that makes a public transfer of resources "foreign aid." I am using the DAC 25 percent level in this study because I am relying on DAC data for much of my discussion of aid flows.

15. The Development Assistance Committee of the Organisation for Economic Co-operation and Development was created in 1959 (and initially called the Development Assistance Group) as an international club of aid-giving governments in North America, West-

ern Europe, and Japan. (No international organizations or NGOs are members.) It produces the most comprehensive data on aid-giving by its members as well as nonmembers. (Like most data on foreign aid, its numbers have their flaws, but they are the best available, especially for comparative purposes.) The DAC defines official development assistance (ODA) as grants or loans to poor countries and territories in Part 1 of the DAC list of aid recipients—countries whose per capita incomes have averaged below $9,200 in 2001 dollars for three years or more. Aid to the "more advanced" eastern European and developing countries on Part 2 of the DAC list is recorded separately as official assistance (OA). These countries have been above the World Bank high-income-country threshold for three consecutive years. ODA is restricted to concessional resource transfers from governments or international institutions with promotion of economic development and welfare as the main objective. The terms of the transfers must have a grant element of at least 25 percent. Technical assistance and debt forgiveness, mainly for ODA debts, are included in ODA data. In fact, the DAC's definition of development is expansive, including humanitarian relief and a variety of other purposes loosely associated with development. Further, the DAC does not make judgments as to whether development is the main objective of aid-giving when it counts ODA; it just needs to be one of the purposes.

16. Recently, Amartya Sen has defined development even more broadly, as "freedom"—that is, the capacity on the part of all individuals in society to choose a fulfilling life. See Amartya Sen, *Development as Freedom* (New York: Anchor Books, 2000).

17. For example, "development" typically aims at bringing about beneficial change in a particular country. It is country focused, and its ultimate goal is to reduce poverty there. "Addressing global issues" aims at dealing with particular problems of a transnational scope, such as the international transmission of disease. The latter activity may involve working in a developing country but on a particular type of problem (e.g., disease eradication) and aims not at bringing about beneficial change throughout that society or reducing poverty there but at resolving a problem on a global scale. Democracy promotion may be a means to the end of furthering development—at least in the view of some practitioners—but it is also an end in itself, a separable purpose distinct from bringing about economic and social progress in poor countries. Similarly, "conflict mitigation" may be important to furthering development, but it is also an end in itself and involves activities quite different from those intended to produce economic and social changes.

18. Aid can expand activities other than those to which the aid is tied, because it is fungible—that is, aid can replace planned expenditures for activities governments have already intended to fund (e.g., childhood inoculations), and governments can then switch planned funds to other purposes, such as purchasing arms. For this reason, it is often difficult to be sure what foreign aid is really financing.

19. GNP and GNI are virtually the same but may differ slightly when goods and services have been sold but not yet paid for. I use GNP in this study up to 2001, when GNI became the denominator.

20. See, for example, David Cingranelli and Thomas Pasquarello, "Human Rights Practices and the Distribution of US Foreign Aid to Latin American Countries," *American Journal of Political Science* 29, no. 3, 539–63; David Carleton and Michael Stohl, "The Role of Human Rights in US Foreign Assistance Policy: A Critique and Reappraisal," *American Journal of Political Science* 31, no. 4, 1002–18; James McCormick and Neil Mitchell, "Is US Aid Really Linked to Human Rights in Latin America?" *American Journal of Political Science* 32, no. 1, 231–39.

21. See Goldstein and Keohane, *Ideas and Foreign Policy;* and Peter Katzenstein, ed., *The Culture of National Security* (New York: Columbia University Press, 1996), 54.

22. For a review of the literature on the influence of political institutions on policies, see Stephan Haggard and Mathew McCubbins, eds., *Presidents, Parliaments, and Policy* (New York: Cambridge University Press, 2001).

23. See, for example, Markus Goldstein and Todd Moss, "The Surprise Party: An Analysis of US ODA Flows to Africa" (working paper 30, Center for Global Development, Washington, DC, July 30, 2003), http://www.cgdev.org/content/publications/?expert=2713. One place where a change in political parties in government has had an impact has been in the United Kingdom, where Conservative governments have put UK aid programs in the Foreign Office and Labour governments have taken them out of the Foreign Office and created either a separate aid agency or a ministry of development (e.g., the Department for International Development, existing at the time of this writing). But even these organizational changes do not appear by themselves to have had a major effect on the purposes of UK aid. See Owen Barder, *Reforming Development Assistance: Lessons from the UK Experience* (Center for Global Development, October 5, 2005), http://www.cgdev.org/content/publications/detail/4371/ (accessed November 2005).

24. There is a small but interesting literature examining the way aid agencies operate, with a particular focus on the behavioral incentives embedded in the organizational structure of those agencies and their effect on aid effectiveness. See, for example, Judith Tendler, *Inside Foreign Aid* (Baltimore: Johns Hopkins University Press, 1975); and Clark Gibson, Krister Andersson, Elinor Ostrom, and Sujai Shivakumar, *The Samaritan's Dilemma* (New York: Oxford University Press, 2005). What these studies do not include is consideration of the broader political context within which aid is provided and the behavioral incentives created by that context.

25. For an analysis of the operation of the UK aid system, see Owen Barder, *Reforming Development Assistance.*

CHAPTER TWO

1. Even relief aid had antecedents, going back to antiquity—though not many. I am grateful to Michael Clemens of the Center for Global Development for the following observation on the ancient history of relief aid: "The earliest documented instance I've seen is from 226 BC, when a huge earthquake hit Rhodes, toppling the famous colossus. Rhodes was a main clearing house for Mediterranean trade—something like an ancient Singapore. Led by Ptolemy III of Egypt, several nations around the Mediterranean immediately sent food aid and other assistance to the quake victims" (personal correspondence, December 2004).

2. See, for example, Charles Bohlen, "Economic Assistance in United States Foreign Policy," *Department of State Bulletin,* March 28, 1960; and David Baldwin, *Economic Development and American Foreign Policy* (Chicago: University of Chicago Press, 1966).

3. See William Adams Brown, Jr., and Redvers Opie, *American Foreign Assistance* (Washington, DC: Brookings Institution, 1953), 21.

4. Alain Noel Pratt and Jean-Philippe Therein, "From Domestic to International Justice: The Welfare State and Foreign Aid," *International Organization* 49, no. 3 (1995): 523–55.

5. Olav Stokke, "The Determinants of Norwegian Aid Policy," in *Western Middle Powers and Global Poverty,* ed. Olav Stokke (Uppsala: Scandinavian Institute of African Studies, with the Norwegian Institute of International Affairs, 1989), 163.

6. See J. A. Nekkers and P. A. M. Malcontent, introduction to *Fifty Years of Dutch Development Cooperation, 1949–1999*, ed. J. A. Nekkers and P. A. M. Malcontent (The Hague: SDU Publishers, for the Ministry of Foreign Affairs, 2000), 27.

7. Domestic politics—at least those that were observable by scholars and others outside of the Soviet government—appear to have played much less of a role in Soviet aid than they did in Western aid. As of this writing even the size of Chinese aid is a state secret, and decisions appear to be made entirely within the bureaucracy and Communist Party (based on interviews with Chinese aid officials and experts, Beijing, November 2005).

8. The term *nongovernmental organizations* (NGOs) is used here to mean not-for-profit organizations. They may have a grassroots membership (often also called "private voluntary organizations" in the United States) or simply work as a professional organization specialized in a particular field—e.g., relief, development, environmental conservation, or family planning. They may concentrate entirely in the delivery of services, act solely as political advocacy organizations for their particular causes, or do both. They may be entirely independent of other organizations or related to them, such as church-affiliated NGOs.

9. Some attribute this quote to Lao Tzu. See, for example, http://www.brainyquote.com/quotes/quotes/l/laotzu121559.html.

10. US NGOs have often been advocates on issues of direct relevance to them—the amount of foreign aid appropriations and legislative earmarks directing a portion of aid toward their particular types of activities. European NGOs have tended to be advocates for high levels of aid, the use of aid for development and on broader issues of political empowerment and change in developing countries. See Brian Smith, *More than Altruism: The Politics of Private Foreign Aid* (Princeton, NJ: Princeton University Press, 1990), 134–35.

11. Ibid., 79. Smith and others have observed that the nature of NGO activism in Europe and the United States differ somewhat. European NGOs are often much more critical of their governments' policies regarding development aid and other international concerns. US NGOs tend to be less critical publicly of US government policies but more active in lobbying for aid, development, and their particular programs within the broader development field. A number of observers have attributed these differences to the fact that US NGOs are much more dependent on government funding for their activities abroad than European NGOs. Another reason for the difference is that NGOs in the United States can lobby the Congress—a powerful player in aid and other government spending programs—with some effect, whereas efforts to lobby European parliaments tend to have far less political access in shaping their governments' aid programs. The country case studies on aid's purposes provide more detail on the different role of legislatures in policy-making.

12. For an insightful history of the evolution of population and family-planning policies in the United States, see Peter Donaldson, *Nature against Us* (Chapel Hill, NC: University of North Carolina Press, 1990). See also Phyllis Piotrow, *World Population Crisis: The United States Response* (New York: Praeger, 1973).

13. James P. Grant, "Development: The End of Trickle Down?" *Foreign Policy*, Fall 1973, 43.

14. For a history of the logical framework, see Richard Ray Solem, "The Logical Framework Approach to Project Design, Review and Evaluation in AID" (AID working paper 99, April 1987), http://www.dec.org/pdf_docs/PNABE999.pdf.

15. See Basil Cracknell, *Evaluating Development Aid* (London: Sage, 2000), 44.

16. World Bank, *The McNamara Years at the World Bank* (Baltimore: Johns Hopkins University Press, 1981), 6.

17. A "soft" loan is one with highly concessional terms—for example, a forty-year repayment period with ten years' grace (during which no repayments have to be made) and a 1 percent or less interest rate or service charge. (These are the types of terms used by the World Bank for its soft loans.) Such loans have a high gift component in them compared to harder, market-based terms associated with international commercial lending.

18. At this time, a number of reports by prominent individuals and international commissions were issued, most of which urged that aid through multilateral institutions be increased, in large measure to improve its developmental focus. For a review of these reports, see Robert Asher, "Development Assistance in DD II: The Recommendations of Perkins, Pearson, Peterson, Prebisch and Others," *International Organization* 25, no. 1 (Winter 1971): 97–119.

19. DAC, "International Development Statistics (IDS) Online" (accessed October 2005).

20. Asher, "Development Assistance in DD II," 99.

21. These newly independent countries were Armenia, Azerbaijan, Belarus, Estonia, Georgia, Kazakhstan, Kyrgyzstan, Latvia, Lithuania, Moldova, Russia, Tajikistan, Turkmenistan, Ukraine, and Uzbekistan.

22. See Stockholm International Peace Research Institute (SIPRI), "Patterns of Major Armed Conflicts, 1990–2001," appendix 1A in *SIPRI Yearbook 2002*, http://editors.sipri.se/pubs/yb02/app01a.html (accessed October 2004).

23. In the United States, the end of the Cold War rationale *caused* a search for other, compelling purposes for foreign aid. During my own period as deputy administrator of USAID in the early 1990s, we consciously sought to redefine our mission and purposes in terms of prevailing diplomatic themes—such as "sustainable development" or conflict prevention. "Sustainable development" was left intentionally vague (it could mean environmentally sound development, financially strong development, politically supported development, and a host of other things) in order to garner maximum relevance and support for aid-giving. The adoption of the theme of "conflict prevention" was basically an effort to gain greater relevance with the State Department and White House, even though at that time there were no particular ideas about how to prevent conflict except to continue funding those activities USAID had always funded.

24. See Samuel Huntington, *The Third Wave: Democratization in the Late Twentieth Century* (Norman: Oklahoma University Press, 1991), 3.

25. See DAC, *DAC Policy Statement on Conflict, Peace and Development Co-operation on the Threshold of the 21st Century* (OECD, Paris, May 6, 1997), http://www.oecd.org/findDocument/0,2350,en_2649_34567_1_119820_1_1_1,00.html (accessed October 2004).

26. These calculations are based on data from DAC, OECD, "International Development Statistics (IDS) Online" (accessed March 2006). They are no more than rough estimates, because a significant portion of bilateral aid is not included in sectoral categories like these. Nor is most bilateral aid broken down by these sectors.

27. It is not clear how much of a reorientation actually took place in World Bank lending. The Bank's own data show a 20 percent increase in annual lending for "human capital development" between 1990 and 1999, but human development lending as a proportion of total IDA lending over that period increased only 3 percent. See World Bank, "Lending to Selected Sectors, Fiscal Year 1999," http://www.worldbank.org/poverty/wbactivities/lend/1999.htm. For a recounting of the World Bank under the leadership of Wolfensohn, see Sebastian Malaby, *The World's Banker: A Story of Failed States, Financial Crises, and the Wealth and Poverty of Nations,* Council on Foreign Relations Books (New York: Penguin, 2004).

28. World Bank, *Assessing Aid: What Works, What Doesn't, and Why* (New York: Oxford University Press for the World Bank, 1998). Published by the world's most prominent aid agency and a major advocate for development aid, this report proved quite controversial with economists and econometricians. See, for example, Henrik Hansen and Finn Tarp, "Aid Effectiveness Disputed," in *Foreign Aid and Development: Lessons Learnt and Directions for the Future,* ed. Finn Tarp (New York: Routledge, 2000). See also Michael Clemens, Steve Radelet, and Rikhil Bhavnani, "Counting Chickens before They Hatch: The Short-Term Effect of Aid on Growth" (working paper no. 44, Center for Global Development, Washington, DC, July 22, 2004), http://cgdev.org/Publications/?PubID=130 (accessed October 2005). This paper also challenges the methodology and findings of *Assessing Aid.*

29. For an excellent account of managing for results, see Annette Binnendijk, DAC Working Party on Aid Evaluation, "Results Based Management in the Development Co-operation Agencies: A Review of Experience" (OECD, Paris, February 14, 2001), http://www.dac.org (accessed October 2004).

30. See Dollar and Levin, "Increasing Selectivity of Foreign Aid."

31. DAC, "International Development Statistics (IDS) Online" (accessed October 2004).

32. See the topic "Poverty Reduction Strategies" on the World Bank website, http://www.worldbank.org/poverty/.

33. See World Bank Operations Evaluation Department, *The Poverty Reduction Strategy Initiative: An Independent Assessment of the World Bank's Support through 2003* (Washington, DC, 2004), 46, http://www.worldbank.org/ieg/prsp/ (accessed February 2006). See also Laure-Helene Piron, with Alison Evans, "Politics and the PRSP Approach: Synthesis Paper" (working paper 237, Overseas Development Institute, London, March 2004), http://www.prspsynthesis.org/ (accessed February 2005).

34. World Bank, "Millennium Development Goals," www.developmentgoals.org (accessed March 2005). The base year for measuring progress toward these goals is 1990.

35. See Shanta Devarajan, Margaret Miller, and Eric Swanson, "Goals for Development: History, Prospects, and Costs" (World Bank policy research working paper, Washington, DC, April 2002). The UN Millennium Project (led by Jeffrey Sachs) recommended even higher levels of additional ODA: by 2006, $70 billion above the level of ODA in 2002 (nearly a doubling in ODA alone), rising to $130 billion above 2002 ODA levels by 2015. See UN Millennium Project, *Investing in Development: A Practical Plan to Achieve the Millennium Development Goals* (London: Earthscan, 2005), 250, http://www.unmillenniumproject.org/documents/MainReportChapter17-lowres.pdf (accessed February 2006).

36. The Jubilee 2000 campaign developed into a "coalition of Christian denominations, Jewish and Muslim faiths, the trades unions, Black community groups in Northern countries, women's groups, and celebrities" in the words of one of its main originators, Ann Pettifor. It grew rapidly to establishing organizations in some forty countries and engaged in an active and coordinated lobbying effort to persuade creditor governments and international organizations to cancel the debts owed them by developing countries at the millennium. See Ann Pettifor, "The Jubilee 2000 Campaign," http://www.sedos.org/english/pettifor.htm (accessed March 2005), for her brief account of the history of Jubilee 2000.

37. Resistance to reducing the large debts owed multilateral institutions was based on the idea that if concessional loan repayments were canceled, the revenues accruing to

these institutions would fall, forcing them to cut back on future loans to poor countries and, in effect, penalizing those which had repaid their debts. However, debt relief for heavily indebted poor countries was financed by contributions from bilateral aid agencies, covering the costs of loan repayments to the World Bank, thus not affecting revenues from past lending.

38. DAC, "International Development Statistics (IDS) Online" (accessed October 2005). The data for 2004 are provisional.

39. This estimate is based on US government data, including the request level to Congress for 2005. The figures do not include exceptional funding for reconstruction in Iraq, insofar as I could identify the levels of that funding in US government data, and thus should reflect the underlying trend in US aid-giving. (See chapter 3 on US aid for more details and sources.) DAC data on US aid (which includes aid associated with the wars in Iraq and Afghanistan and their aftermath) shows an increase between 2000 and 2003 of 42 percent.

40. Evidence for a greater readiness on the part of the US public to use aid to address poverty abroad is contained in a poll done in November 2001 assessing the US public's reaction to the terrorist attacks, in which nearly 80 percent of those polled said they would strongly favor or somewhat favor "building goodwill toward the US by helping poor countries develop their economies." While foreign aid was not mentioned in the question, it would seem to be implied in it. The 80 percent favorable rating contrasts with traditional US polls regarding aid, where just over half of the population has supported it. See Program on International Policy Attitudes (PIPA), "Americans on the War on Terrorism: A Study of US Public Attitudes" (November 13, 2001), 9, http://www.pipa.org/OnlineReports/Terrorism/WarOnTerror_Nov01/WarOnTerror_Nov01_rpt.pdf (accessed February 2006).

41. James Wolfensohn, "Fight Terrorism and Poverty," *Development Outreach,* October 2001, www1.worldbank.org/devoutreach/fall01/special.asp (accessed March 2005).

42. This publication, beginning in 1993, is a product of the Reality of Aid Project, supported by EUROSTEP, the Latin American Association of Development Organizations, and a coalition of NGOs. It usually includes short chapters on the aid programs of DAC aid-giving countries and several topical issues.

CHAPTER THREE

1. Morgenthau, "Political Theory of Foreign Aid," 301.

2. Dean Acheson, *Present at the Creation* (New York: Norton, 1969), 293.

3. For the entire speech, see the Truman Library, http://www.trumanlibrary.org/whistlestop/50yr_archive/inaugural20jan1949.htm.

4. Ruttan, *United States Development Assistance Policy,* 71.

5. The president said so in his speech to Congress in 1954 on foreign economic policy. Cited in W. W. Rostow, *Eisenhower, Kennedy, and Foreign Aid* (Austin: University of Texas Press, 1985), 92. For more on this period, see Kimber Charles Pearce, *Rostow, Kennedy, and the Rhetoric of Foreign Aid* (East Lansing: Michigan State University Press, 2001).

6. While foreign aid was provided to governments to secure their support, participation in alliances, and militarily useful facilities, the use of that aid was tied to economic concerns—stabilizing economies, easing balance of payments and budgetary constraints on arms purchases (though not directly to fund those purchases), and funding development

projects. Aid provided directly to fund military expenditures on the part of the recipient is not included in the definition or data on "foreign aid" in this study.

7. Cited in Louise Tillin, "India and Russia's Common Past," BBC News, World Edition, December 4, 2002, http://news.bbc.co.uk/2/hi/south_asia/2542431.stm.

8. For a full exposition of Rostow's ideas, see his *Stages of Growth,* (New York: Cambridge University Press, 1960).

9. Not with everyone, however. Rostow's conception of the process of growth and modernization was criticized by many scholars as far too simplistic, too focused on the United States, and, in the end, just plain wrong. But for a time at least, his theory provided a compelling frame for politicians to use as a guide and justification for increasing and reorienting US foreign aid. As an epilogue to Rostow's impact on the US policy community, he came to be identified later with the aggressive pursuit by the United States of the war in Vietnam and thus became unpopular among many in the policy and academic communities, with the result that both his stages of growth theory and his prowar policies became discredited.

10. In theory, food aid was not supposed to replace normal commercial imports. But this was difficult to ascertain and, in any case, the program was often justified as doing just that.

11. H. Field Haviland, "Foreign Aid and the Policy Process: 1957," *American Political Science Review* 52, no. 3 (September 1958): 709.

12. John F. Kennedy, "Special Message to the Congress on Foreign Aid," March 22, 1961, http://www.jfklink.com/speeches/jfk/publicpapers/1961/jfk90_61.html (also available through http://www.presidency.ucsb.edu).

13. It was widely believed at this time that economic development would lead to political development or democracy; thus, furthering one would promote the other. See Packenham, *Liberal America and the Third World.*

14. USAID, *US Overseas Loans and Grants* (also known as the *Greenbook;* accessible from USAID's website or at http://qesdb.cdie.org/gbk/). I use USAID data in this chapter unless otherwise noted.

15. See Department of State, Office of the Historian, *Foreign Relations of the United States, 1961–63,* vol. 9, *Foreign Economic Policy* (Washington, DC: Government Printing Office, 1995), section 84 (available online at http://dosfan.lib.uic.edu/ERC/frus/frus61–63ix/06 _Section_6.html).

16. For a brief history of the DAC, see Seymour Rubin, *The Conscience of the Rich Nations: The Development Assistance Committee and the Common Aid Effort* (New York: Harper & Row, for the Council on Foreign Relations, 1966).

17. Michael Clemens of the Center for Global Development, Washington, DC, dug this information out. Clemens recounts that "On March 22, 1961, Kennedy sent a special message to Congress proposing the creation of USAID and calling the 1960s the 'development decade,' asking them to appropriate $4 billion in aid. He didn't mention any 1 percent targets in this message, but does say that the funds he was asking for are 'the rock-bottom minimum of funds necessary to do the job' and hopes that the new US commitment will 'demonstrate the seriousness of our intentions to other potential donors.'" Kennedy's speech can be found at the sites listed in note 12 above.

18. Despite these cuts, the total level of US aid expenditures rose in 1962. This is because aid expenditures typically take place with a lag—often of a year or more because of the time needed for project preparation, negotiations with recipient governments, and so on—from

the time they are appropriated by Congress. Thus, the cuts in 1962 did not show up in expenditures until the following years.

19. See Otto Passman in "The Report of the Clay Committee on Foreign Aid: A Symposium," *Political Science Quarterly* 78, no. 3 (September 1963): 348. It is unusual for chairpersons of congressional committees responsible for particular programs to rant against those very programs. But this has occurred a number of times on foreign aid, reflecting its controversial position among members of Congress and the public.

20. See Committee to Strengthen the Security of the Free World, US Department of State, "The Scope and Distribution of United States Military and Economic Assistance Programs; Report to the President of the United States," (Washington, DC: Government Printing Office, 1963).

21. Kennedy, "Special Message to the Congress."

22. For a more detailed look at this process, see Manlio DeAngelis, "Foreign Aid: The Transition from ICA to AID, 1960–61," in *Commission on the Organization of the Government for the Conduct of Foreign Policy* [the "Murphy Commission"], vol. 10 (Washington, DC: Government Printing Office, June 1975).

23. There has never, to my knowledge, been an effort by scholars or public officials to separate out the countries aided primarily for diplomatic purposes and evaluate the aid on that basis. For a critique of the mix of these purposes in US foreign aid, see Robert Zimmerman, *Dollars, Diplomacy and Dependency* (Boulder, CO: Lynne Rienner Publishers, 1993).

24. See Department of State, "Report of Task Force on Foreign Aid" [the Perkins Committee Report], in *Foreign Relations of the United States, 1964–1968,* vol. 9, *International Development and Economic Defense Policy; Commodities,* by the Office of the Historian (Washington, DC: Government Printing Office, 1997), document 70, http://www.state.gov/www/about_state/history/Vol_IX/61_84.html (accessed March 2006). See also "Report to the President from the Task Force on International Development" [the Peterson Report], in *US Foreign Assistance in the 1970s: A New Approach* (Washington, DC: Government Printing Office, 1970).

25. In theory, all US government spending programs must be periodically authorized and appropriated by (separate) congressional committees. Authorization involves legislative permission to function; appropriations provide the funds with which to function. In the case of foreign aid, authorization legislation was typically required every two years and appropriations legislation, every year. In practice, the requirement for authorizing legislation has been waived since 1985, given the difficulty of getting members of Congress to pass it without putting so many amendments on it that it became unacceptable to the executive branch, which threatened to veto it, and given the reluctance of members of Congress to vote for foreign aid when not absolutely necessary (as it is for appropriations).

26. For an excellent detailed recounting of this period and the evolution of these ideas, see Ruttan, *United States Development Assistance Policy,* chap. 6.

27. See Richard M. Nixon, "Foreign Aid: The President's Message to Congress, May 28, 1969," Richard Nixon Library, Archives, May 1969, http://www.nixonfoundation.org/clientuploads/directory/archive/1969_pdf_files/1969_0218.pdf (accessed March 2006).

28. See Louis Harris and Associates (for the Chicago Council on Foreign Relations), "Public Opinion and US Foreign Policy," December 14, 1974; Market Opinion Research for the Presidential Commission on World Hunger, "World Hunger and US Role," December

1979; Gallup Organization (for the Chicago Council on Foreign Relations), "Attitudes of Public and Leaders on Foreign Policy," January 1979. Another set of polls also suggest a modest easing in public skepticism regarding foreign aid, though there is no direct evidence that concern about world hunger played a role in this change. During the 1970s, Roper asked whether the US spending on foreign aid was too much, too little, or about right. In 1973, 76 percent responded "too much." By 1976 this number had dropped to 67 percent. It remained around 60 percent during the remainder of the decade. See Roper Organization, 1973, 1976, 1977, 1978, 1980.

29. Jimmy Carter, "Human Rights and Foreign Policy," speech given at Notre Dame University, June 1977, http://usinfo.state.gov/usa/infousa/facts/democrac/55.htm.

30. It would be possible to argue that promoting human rights became a new purpose of US aid. I have not done so here because this value-based goal had limited influence on the allocation of US aid and little aid was used directly to further human rights in recipient countries. See, for example, Lars Schoultz, "US Foreign Policy and Human Rights Violations in Latin America: A Comparative Analysis of Foreign Aid Distributions," *Comparative Politics* 13 (1981): 149–70; Michael Stohl, David Carleton, and Steven Johnson, "Human Rights and US Foreign Assistance from Nixon to Carter," *Journal of Peace Research* 21 (1984): 215–26. The general consensus among these and other articles is that there was little relationship between human rights concerns and the allocation of US aid.

31. It is often assumed that levels of aid to Israel and Egypt were set in the Accords. I could find no evidence of that in my research. When I asked William Quandt and Anthony Lake, who were senior officials in the Carter administration and both involved in the Accords negotiations, whether they recalled any concrete commitments of aid as part of the Accords, they had no memory of such commitments.

32. USAID, *Greenbook,* http://qesdb.cdie.org/gbk (accessed November 2005).

33. I recount this incident largely from memory, because I was the State official who provoked the review of the aid budget by the Policy Planning Staff. I had recently served in the Office of Management and Budget and still carried my sense of righteous indignation at what appeared to be poorly justified, excessive spending proposals. My memos criticizing the aid budget opened the door for senior State Department officials to seize control of the final stages of the USAID budget process and put their mark on the budget before it went to the White House. The incident was, in effect, a mild form of takeover. Outrage on the part of USAID officials was neither surprising nor unjustified (since the budget had already been negotiated between State and USAID officers at working levels). However, there are, to my knowledge, no published materials on Senator Humphrey's motivations at this time and one of Senator Humphrey's former key staffers—Richard McCall—does not recall complaints from USAID staff about the new involvement of State in USAID's budget as a motivation of Senator Humphrey's initiative. Nevertheless, the general tendency in Washington politics and in the politics of aid for agency staffs to complain to sympathetic congressional staffs when they feel their policy and organizational interests are threatened may have been at work here.

34. For a recounting of this incident, see David Stockman, *The Triumph of Politics: How the Reagan Revolution Failed* (New York: Harper & Row, 1986).

35. DAC, "International Development Statistics (IDS) Online" (accessed March 2006).

36. The US government had long been aware of global problems. For example, President Nixon mentioned them—the environment, "population control," and international

crime — in his 1971 report to Congress, *Building for Peace* (February 1971). But they were not yet significant purposes of US aid, except for family planning programs, which served purposes of promoting development and addressing what was in the 1960s increasingly regarded as a global problem.

37. See Richard Holbrooke, *To End a War,* rev. ed. (New York: Modern Library, 1999), 36. Holbrooke mentions discussion of the $500 million in preparations for the negotiations. It is my memory (I was deputy administrator of USAID at the time) that the $500 million was actually part of the incentives offered to the warring parties to make peace. In the end, more than that amount was spent in Bosnia-Herzegovina for reconstruction.

38. See, for example, Heritage Foundation, *Index of Economic Freedom* (Washington, DC: Heritage Foundation, 1995); and World Bank, *Assessing Aid.*

39. For a critical account of Wolfensohn's efforts to reduce NGO criticisms of the World Bank and the subsequent increase in influence of those organizations on how the Bank does business, see Malaby, *World's Banker.*

40. Not surprisingly, some of the greatest enthusiasts for merger were located in the State Department's Global Affairs Bureau, where responsibility for managing the diplomacy of global issues was lodged, but with little funding to back up that diplomacy. These efforts to merge USAID with the Department of State have not, to my knowledge, been documented in print. I am drawing on my personal experience, since I was actively involved in these issues from 1994 to 1996.

41. See Steven Kull and I. M. Destler, "Foreign Aid," chap. 5 in *Misreading the Public* (Washington, DC: Brookings Institution, 1999).

42. See, for example, Madeline K. Albright, "The Testing of American Foreign Policy," *Foreign Affairs* 77, no. 6 (November/December 1998): 50–65; and Richard Gardner, "The One Percent Solution: Shirking the Cost of World Leadership," *Foreign Affairs* 79, no. 4 (July/August 2000): 11.

43. The first announcement was made in a speech to the InterAmerican Bank on March 14, 2002, to be later repeated in Monterrey, Mexico, at the UN Conference on Financing Development. See http://www.whitehouse.gov/infocus/developingnations /millennium.html.

44. See White House, *The National Security Strategy of the United States of America,* September 2002, http://www.whitehouse.gov/nsc/nss.pdf.

45. The US invasion and occupation of Iraq added a further $2 billion in 2003 and another $18 billion in 2004.

46. Cited in Bruce Stokes, "Monterrey Morass?" *National Journal* 34, no. 11 (March 16, 2002): 803.

47. For more on the role of the Christian right and evangelicals in US politics, see William Stevenson, ed., *Christian Political Activism at the Crossroads* (Lanham, MD: University Press of America, 1994); Christian Smith, *Christian America?* (Los Angeles: University of California Press, 2000); Bryan Le Beau, *The Political Mobilization of the New Christian Right,* http://are.as.wvu.edu/lebeau1.htm (accessed October 2004).

48. Jesse Helms, "We Cannot Turn Away," *Washington Post,* March 24, 2002, B7.

49. Dennis Hoover, "What Would Moses Do? Debt Relief in the Jubilee Year," *Religion in the News* 4, no. 1 (Spring 2001), http://www.trincoll.edu/depts/csrpl/RINVol4No1/jubilee _2000.htm. One of the extraordinary elements in Helms's change of heart was the rock star Bono. An active Christian himself, Bono apparently inspired Helms and a number of other

influential US senators with his arguments and quotations from scripture in favor of debt relief, aid to fight HIV/AIDS, and development assistance. At Helms's behest, the president met with Bono before deciding to increase development aid significantly, and Bono apparently played a role in the size of that increase, which the president announced at the UN Conference on Financing Development in Monterrey, Mexico, in March 2002. See Miles Pomper, "Conservative Firebrand Helms Tempers His Image in Final Term," *Congressional Quarterly,* March 30, 2002, 875–76.

50. See Library of Congress, *A Century of Lawmaking in the New Nation: US Congressional Documents and Debates, 1774–1875, Annals of Congress,* 3rd Congress, 1st Session, 172, http:// memory.loc.gov/cgi-bin/ampage?collId=llac&fileName=004/llac004.db&recNum=83.

51. Library of Congress, *A Century of Lawmaking,* "Elliot's Debates—On the Memorial of the Relief Committee of Baltimore, for the Relief of St. Domingo Refugees," House of Representatives, January 10, 1794, http://memory.loc.gov/cgi-bin/query/r?ammem/hlaw: @field(DOCID+@lit(ed00423)):.

52. The use of the term *liberal* in US political discourse can be confusing. I have used *political liberal* to refer to those on the left of the political spectrum, supportive of a larger, more active government role in society. *Classical liberal* is used to refer to those who, taking their inspiration from John Locke and others, have emphasized the importance of personal liberty and a limited role for government in society—in effect, the position of "political conservatives" in the United States.

53. *Congressional Globe,* US Senate, 29th Congress, 2nd Session, 512.

54. Ibid., 430.

55. For a brief history of US public aid for relief, see the *Congressional Record,* vol. 43, parts 1–4, 60th Congress, 2nd Session, 1909, 453.

56. Barry Goldwater, *The Conscience of a Conservative* (Shepardsville, KY: Victor Publishing, 1960), 95. Italics are Goldwater's.

57. Arthur Schlesinger, Jr., *The Politics of Hope* (Boston: Riverside Press, 1962). See also Louis Hartz, *The Liberal Tradition in America* (New York: Harcourt Brace, 1955). Hartz argues that the "liberal consensus" evident in US history was related to the absence of feudalism in the United States, obviating the need, so apparent in Europe, to fight against it (often exacerbating fundamental social cleavages and civil violence and increasing the popularity of radical doctrines like socialism). Thus, the continuing effect of this historical absence differentiates American political thought and even social habits from those of Europe.

58. See Bruce Bartlett, "End Foreign Welfare," *National Review Online,* March 18, 2002, http://www.nationalreview.com/nrof_bartlett/bartlett031802.asp. For an examination of these complex views regarding domestic welfare programs (which were echoed in opinions regarding foreign aid), see Martin Gilens, *Why Americans Hate Welfare* (Chicago: University of Chicago Press, 1999).

59. Richard Rahn, "Turn Off Foreign Aid?" (Cato Institute, September 2003), http:// www.cato.org/dailys/09–14–03.html.

60. Ibid. This PIPA poll also found that these attitudes were consistent over time, being in evidence in their earlier polls in the 1990s. Another major source of polling on US attitudes regarding foreign aid is John Rielly, ed., *American Public Opinion and US Foreign Policy, 1999* (Chicago: Chicago Council on Foreign Relations, 1999). (Also see earlier years in this series.) For a summary of polling on US attitudes, see Ian Smillie, "The United States," in

Public Opinion and the Fight against Poverty, ed. Ida McDonald, Henri-Bernard Solignac Lecompte, and Liam Wegimont (Paris: Development Center, OECD, 2003).

61. The Gallup Poll, *Public Opinion 1935–1971,* vol. 2, *1949–1958* (New York: Random House, 1972), 1546. The poll was taken in 1958 and 51 percent of those polled were "for" foreign aid. A number of polls came up with similar percentages (e.g., the Chicago Council on Foreign Relations polls, cited above). However, Steven Kull, polling for PIPA, found in 1995 that over 80 percent of the US population agreed with the statement that "the United States should be willing to share at least a small portion of its wealth with those in the world who are in great need." See Steven Kull, *Americans and Foreign Aid* (College Park, MD: Program on International Policy Attitudes, School of Public Affairs, University of Maryland, 1995), 3. Again, the differences in these results undoubtedly reflect the differences in the way the polling questions are asked. Kull's question is framed in strongly ethical terms. Other questions typically include the term "foreign aid," which often elicits a negative reaction based on all the factors I have described.

62. Marc Stern, *Development Aid: What the Public Thinks* (New York: United Nations Development Program, 1998), 15, http://www.undp.org/ods/pub-working.html.

63. For an account of these men, their backgrounds, and their impact on American foreign policy, see Walter Isaacson and Evan Thomas, *The Wise Men: Six Friends and the World They Made* (New York: Touchstone, 1986).

64. Recounted to me by David Obey, Democratic member of the House of Representatives from Wisconsin. It is likely that Obey was not bluffing (he is not usually a bluffer), and the White House knew it. President Reagan sent a letter to the Congress stating that a vote for the aid budget was a vote for the president's program and thus dampened Republican criticisms of those voting for aid.

65. Presidents can advocate for aid in public speeches—mainly in their annual address to the UN General Assembly, in their annual State of the Union speech, or in speeches dedicated to foreign aid. In all these cases, presidential mentions of foreign aid were much less frequent in the 1980s and 1990s than they were decades earlier, suggesting the lessening priority of aid issues together with the potential political costs of raising them.

66. It is not well known how many times Mrs. Clinton, who was a strong supporter of foreign aid and of USAID, quietly intervened with the president on foreign aid issues. She was, from our point of view in USAID, practically our only friend in the White House. A Republican official in USAID in both Bush administrations recounted to me how in the Bush administration in the early 1990s, he created an informal alliance with Mrs. Quayle—the vice president's wife—on issues of humanitarian relief, in which she had an interest, and was thus able to fend off unwanted pressures from other agencies on those issues.

67. USAID stopped publishing data on the proportion of aid used to purchase US goods and services in 1996. The Congressional Research Service cites a figure of 81 percent of USAID procurement being spent on US products and services in 2002–2003. See Curt Tarnoff and Larry Nowels, "Foreign Aid: An Introductory Overview of US Programs and Policy" (Congressional Research Service, Library of Congress, April 2004), http://fpc.state .gov/fpc/c12172.htm (accessed October 2004). (These reports, usually done at the request of members of Congress, are often quite insightful and objective but not normally available directly from the Congressional Research Service. Those relating to foreign affairs are now available on the Department of State website.) Aid tying has long been a means for USAID to fend off pressures for a more direct allocation of aid for export promotion. At the begin-

ning of the 1990s, USAID was exceptionally weakly led and thus in poor repute within the executive branch and with Congress. At that time several senators (and their staffs) began to pressure USAID to shift its funding to support large infrastructure projects as a way of benefiting US firms. This effort to direct foreign aid increasingly toward promoting US exports was gathering momentum when the Clinton administration took office. In 1993, an internal report on the purposes of US aid led by the State Department resulted in a decision to eliminate export promotion as a goal of foreign aid. Subsequently, the Export-Import Bank set up its own "tied aid" war chest to be used to help US firms facing unfair competition abroad and the pressures eased—but not the tying of aid.

68. Both *Fortune* magazine and the Aspen Institute ranked AIPAC as one of the most effective lobbyist organizations in Washington. See Susan Rees, "Effective Nonprofit Advocacy" (Washington, DC: Aspen Institute, 1998); and *Fortune*, "Power 25," May 28, 2001.

69. In late 1995, when the Congress was appropriating funds (in "continuing resolutions") adequate to cover only a few weeks of USAID expenditures at a time, the administration urged Congress not to appropriate the entire annual level of aid to Israel (which was usually paid in a cash transfer on the first day of the new fiscal year, beginning in October) for fear that once all the aid money for Israel had been appropriated, Congress would have no more incentive or inclination to appropriate aid for the rest of the year. The importance of aid to Israel in aid appropriations is cited in Paul Findlay, *They Dare to Speak Out* (Chicago: Lawrence Hill Books, 1989). However, US economic aid to Israel is set to be eliminated by 2010, according to an agreement between the US and Israel governments. Economic aid to Israel fell by nearly half between 1998 and 2002, with some offset in increases in military aid. The political implication of this important change is not yet clear but could involve a lessening in support for economic aid from pro-Israeli groups, which could translate into reduced support in Congress for economic aid generally.

70. USAID does not publish the amount or portion of its aid channeled through NGOs. It is likely to be substantial, however. When I was in USAID in the early to mid-1990s, the policy office found that around 25 percent of development assistance (one of the types of US bilateral aid) was implemented by NGOs, translating into approximately 10 percent of US bilateral ODA. In 1995, Vice President Gore, at USAID's urging, announced that in the future 40 percent of that aid would be channeled through NGOs. See "Remarks of Vice President Al Gore at the UN World Summit for Social Development," March 12, 1995, Copenhagen, Denmark (Department of State website, archives), http://dosfan.lib.uic.edu/ERC/intlorg/WS_Social_Dev/950312.html. This commitment was a tactic, among other things, to persuade NGOs to support USAID in its fight against merger with the Department of State. It is not clear that USAID ever reached that goal.

71. Management problems were reflected in USAID's inability for a number of years to produce the information required for an annual audit of its financial activities. See, for example, "Statement of Everett L. Mosley, Inspector General, USAID, to the House of Representatives, Committee on Government Reform, Subcommittee on National Security, Veterans Affairs and International Relations," March 15, 2001.

72. See Bureau of International Labor Affairs, US Department of Labor, *Faces of Change: Highlights of US Department of Labor Efforts to Combat International Child Labor* (2003), 20, http://www.dol.gov/ilab/media/reports/iclp/faceschange/facesofchange.pdf.

73. For one effort to estimate some of these expenditures, see Benjamin Nelson, "International Affairs: Activities of Domestic Agencies," Testimony before the Task Force on

International Affairs, Committee on the Budget, US Senate, General Accounting Office, GAO/T-NSIAD-98-174, June 4, 1998.

74. As of March 2006, the MCC had proven very slow to begin operations and disbursements of aid funds, creating doubts about its effectiveness over the long term. Meanwhile, the secretary of state proposed creating a position in the Department of State—a director of development—that would be filled by the administrator of USAID. While the intent of this move was to align and rationalize USAID's work with that of the Department of State, it looked very much like part of the general tendency for the Department of State to take over many of USAID's traditional activities and now quite possibly direct control of the agency. It would be ironic if at the same time the Bush administration had elevated both the rhetorical prominence of development in US foreign policy and the volume of aid for development, it ended up in fact undercutting its support for development abroad by creating a new and weak development agency (the MCC) while hastening the absorption of USAID into the State Department with the very real likelihood that the development mission of USAID would be overwhelmed by the diplomatic imperatives of the larger and more powerful Department of State.

75. By 2004 the Association of Evangelical Relief and Development Organizations (set up in 1978) had forty-eight members. By the beginning of the twenty-first century, the growing activism of the evangelical movement was being noted in the US media. See, for example, Peter Waldman, "Evangelicals Give US Foreign Policy an Activist Tinge" (MSNBC), http://msnbc.msn.com/id/5068634/ (accessed March 2006).

CHAPTER FOUR

1. See, for example, Eisuke Sakakibara, *Structural Reform in Japan: Breaking the Iron Triangle* (Washington, DC: Brookings Institution Press, 2003).

2. In this history of Japanese aid, I use "MITI" until 2001, when the name of the ministry was changed to Ministry of Economics, Trade and Industry, or METI.

3. David Arase, *Buying Power: The Political Economy of Japan's Foreign Aid* (Boulder, CO: Lynne Rienner, 1995), 31.

4. Ibid., 39–40.

5. MOFA, "Japan's ODA Budget (FY2003 and 2004 Budget)," http://www.mofa.go.jp/policy/oda/budget/2004_0.html (accessed June 2004).

6. Interviews with JBIC personnel, October 2003, Tokyo.

7. Arase, *Buying Power*, 55.

8. DAC, "International Development Statistics (IDS) Online" (accessed March 2006).

9. See DAC, *Development Co-operation 1973* (OECD, Paris, 1973), 191.

10. Robert M. Orr, Jr., *The Emergence of Japan's Aid Power* (New York: Columbia University Press, 1990), 55. Aid was used to *ensure access* rather than *simply to develop* and expand the quantity of raw materials produced—a subtle but important difference. The former goal was highly diplomatic in nature; the latter was more strictly commercial.

11. Dennis Yasutomo, "Why Aid? Japan as an 'Aid Great Power,'" *Pacific Affairs* 62, no. 4 (Winter 1989–90): 490–503; Tomoko Fujisaki et al., "Japan as Top Donor: The Challenge of Implementing Software Aid Policy," *Pacific Affairs* 69, no. 4 (Winter 1996–97): 519–39.

12. See Dennis Yasutomo, *The Manner of Giving: Strategic Aid and Japanese Foreign Policy* (Lexington, MA: Lexington Books, 1986). He points out that the report on which this "pol-

icy" was based was quite ambiguous about the precise role of Japanese ODA in this framework. This suggests that there may have been more packaging than substance in this effort to locate ODA in Japan's broader foreign policy.

13. See Ministry of Foreign Affairs (MOFA), "History of Development Assistance" (1994), http://www.mofa.go.jp/policy/oda/summary/1994/1.html (accessed November 2005), which cites MOFA, "The Philosophies of Economic Cooperation: Why Official Development Assistance?" (1980).

14. DAC, "International Development Statistics (IDS) Online."

15. DAC, *Development Co-operation 1983* (OECD, Paris, 1983), 195.

16. An anonymous reader of this chapter from JBIC points out that what was tied was the use of contractors—they had to be Japanese firms. The commodities used by those firms for Japanese aid projects could be purchased in other countries. (This was not the case with US tied aid.) Similarly, the 2004 DAC Peer Review of Japan points out that grant aid from MOFA is tied to Japanese firms but those firms are not required to purchase Japanese goods and services. The Japanese government therefore reports its grant aid as "untied." These reporting practices on the part of the government of Japan are inconsistent and confuse the issue of how much Japanese aid is really tied. See DAC, *Peer Review of Japan* (OECD, Paris, 2004), 62.

17. See, for example, Margee Ensign, *Doing Good or Doing Well? Japan's Foreign Aid Program* (New York: Columbia University Press, 1992).

18. Robert Orr, Jr., "Collaboration or Conflict? Foreign Aid and US-Japan Relations," *Pacific Affairs* 62, no. 4 (1989–90): 481.

19. For background and analysis of the growth of the internationally oriented NGO movement in Japan, see Kim DoHyang Reimann, "Riding the International Wave: Sustainable Development, Advocacy NGOs and Official Development Assistance (ODA) Policy in Japan in the 1990s," 42nd International Studies Association Annual Convention, Chicago, 2001; Kaori Kuroda, "Japan-Based Non-governmental Organizations in Pursuit of Human Security," *Japan Forum* 15, no. 2 (2003): 227–50; Kaori Kuroda and Katsuji Imata, "Shifting Paradigms for International NGOs and Constituency Building: Evolving Scene from Japan," paper presented to ARNOVA Annual Conference, Montreal, November 2002, http://www.csonj.org/report/pdf/Arnova2002.pdf.

20. While I was in USAID in the early 1990s, there were internal discussions of what our strategy should be with our Japanese counterparts, with whom we met periodically. One of the goals we considered was pressing the Japanese government to engage their NGO community more seriously in development discussions and the implementation of aid projects. This was intended as a means of encouraging the government to shift its aid more in the direction of technical assistance and institution-building as a means of poverty reduction—in effect, aligning its aid more with DAC norms of aid-giving. I also met with Japanese NGOs while on an official visit to Japan—another way of signaling the US government's support for an expanding role for them in Japanese aid. In interviews with Japanese NGO officials for this book, I was told that external pressures—*gaiatsu* again—did play a role in changing Japanese government policies vis-à-vis NGOs.

21. In contrast to most other governments from developed countries, the Japanese government refused to put NGO representatives on its delegation to the UN Conference on Environment and Development in Rio in 1992—for which it was strongly criticized by other governments and international NGOs. Thereafter, it changed its policies on NGO repre-

sentation. See Reimann, "Riding the International Wave"; Kuroda, "Japan-Based Non-governmental Organizations," 235.

22. See Kuroda and Imata, "Shifting Paradigms for International NGOs," 8. Only eight out of eight thousand nonprofit organizations had been approved for tax breaks as of 2002.

23. See DAC, "Statistical Annex of the 2005 Development Co-operation Report," http://www.oecd.org/document/9/0,2340,en_2649_201185_1893129_1_1_1_1,00.html, which gives ODA statistics for 2003.

24. Some saw the kickbacks as part of a broader set of linkages. The construction industry received the corrupt payments and was a major contributor to LDP politicians. These politicians, in turn, were known to lobby bureaucrats on behalf of their constituents and funders. The Japanese government persuaded the new Aquino government in Manila to stop leakage of documents involving Japanese aid practices so as to avoid further embarrassment. See Orr, "Collaboration or Conflict?" 82.

25. MOFA, "Japan's ODA Annual Report (Summary) 1994," section 3, http://www.mofa.go.jp/policy/oda/summary/1994/3.html (accessed March 2006).

26. World Bank, *The East Asian Miracle* (New York: Oxford University Press, for the World Bank, 1993).

27. Indeed, one critic of Japanese aid, Prof. Seiji Maehara from the Minshuto Party, has asserted that "The only clear foreign policy it [Japan] has pursued is its goal to gain a permanent UN Security Council seat. Japan's generous ODA has been part and parcel of that effort" ("Matters of Opinion: Should Japan Curtail ODA Spending?" *Daily Yomiuri On-line*, October 18, 2003). One Japanese official involved in the first TICAD conference told me that the government never intended to hold successive conferences but acceded to pressures from the Africans to do so.

28. I was the US representative at the DAC at a meeting in the mid-1990s when the exercise that produced this document began. The idea behind it came from Hiryoshi Hirabayashi, then Director General of the Economic Cooperation Administration of the Japanese Ministry of Foreign Affairs.

29. See MOFA's annual report on ODA for 1994, "Japan's ODA Annual Report (Summary) 1994," section 3.1, http://www.mofa.go.jp/policy/oda/summary/1994/3.html#1 (accessed March 2006).

30. The phrase "human security" figured prominently in the government of Japan's report "Japan's Medium-Term Policy on Official Development Assistance" (February 4, 2005), 2ff, http://www.mofa.go.jp/policy/oda/mid-term/policy.pdf (accessed February 2005). Its main emphasis was on the needs of "individual human beings."

31. DAC, "International Development Statistics (IDS) Online."

32. DAC, "Statistical Annex of the 2005 Development Co-operation Report," Table 14, "The Flow of Financial Resources to Developing Countries and Multi-Lateral Organizations" (OECD, Paris, 2006), http://www.oecd.org/dataoecd/52/9/1893143.xls (accessed March 2006). The data are in commitment terms.

33. Steven Hook and Guang Zhang, "Japan's Aid Policy since the Cold War: Rhetoric and Reality," *Asian Survey* 38 (November 1998): 1051–66.

34. DAC, *Development Co-operation Review Series: Japan, 1999*, no. 34 (OECD, Paris, 1999), 17–18. The same criticisms were mentioned in the DAC review of Japan's aid in 2004, though in much gentler form. For a summary of that review, see OECD, "Japan (2003),

DAC Peer Review: Main Findings and Recommendations," 2004, http://www.oecd.org/document/10/0,2340,en_2649_34603_22579914_1_1_1_1,00.html.

35. DAC, *Peer Review: Japan (2004)* (OECD, Paris, 2004), 26, http://www.oecd.org/dataoecd/43/63/32285814.pdf.

36. Kenichi Ohno, *East Asian Growth and Japanese Aid Strategy* (Tokyo: GRIPS Development Forum, National Graduate Institute for Policy Studies, 2002), 21. A number of Japanese scholars and experts on aid complained about the weakness of Japanese leadership in the field of development assistance in interviews with them.

37. There has been a long debate on the nature of the Japanese state vis-à-vis the rest of the world. Some Japanese and Western scholars have argued that in foreign policy generally, Japan has tended to be a "reactive" state, responding to pressures from abroad rather than taking its own initiatives internationally. If an accurate theory regarding Japanese foreign policy, it could help explain Japan's weak leadership role in foreign aid, which may relate to more basic aspects of Japanese politics and culture. See Kent Calder, "Japanese Foreign Economic Policy Formation: Explaining the Reactive State," *World Politics* 40 (July 1988): 517–41. However, the "reactive state" theory is contested by many other scholars. For a review of this debate, see Akitoshi Miyashita, "*Gaiatsu* and Japan's Foreign Aid: Rethinking the Reactive-Proactive Debate," *International Studies Quarterly* 43 (1999): 695–732. My impression of the Japanese government in the foreign aid area, based on observation over several years, is that it was both reactive and proactive. Japanese officials (primarily MOFA officials) did respond to external pressures, especially from the United States, *and* they also sought to develop and further their own initiatives internationally. However, even though many officials were extremely competent, their influence remained limited because their peripheral engagement in international aid debates, their limited experience in aid activities on the ground, and the organization of their aid system inhibited the acquisition of such experience by those officials and made government-wide initiatives on foreign aid difficult.

38. Based on net aid, including ODA and OA. DAC, "International Development Statistics (IDS) Online." For aid levels in 2004 and 2005, see "Japan's ODA General Account Budget by Ministry," March 2005, http://www.mofa.go.jp/policy/oda/budget/2005–3.html.

39. See Purnendra Jain, "Japan's Troubled Foreign Aid Policy," *Asian Times,* July 30, 2002, http://www.atimes.com.

40. Eric Altbach, "Japan's Foreign Aid Program in Transition: Leaner, Greener—with More Strings Attached?" *JEI Report,* no. 5, February 6, 1998, 2.

41. DAC, *Peer Review: Japan (2004),* 19.

42. Interview with Ishita Yamamoto, member of the Diet and chair of the Foreign Relations Committee of the upper house, October 8, 2002, Tokyo. See also DAC, *Peer Review: Japan (2004),* 25.

43. Kiroku Hanai, "Fair, Transparent Foreign Aid," *Japan Times,* April 28, 2003.

44. See Tatsuya Watanabe, "Muted Celebrations for 50 Years of Japanese Aid," in *Reality of Aid 2004,* by Reality of Aid (London: Zed Books, 2005), 254–58; available online at http://www.realityofaid.org/ (accessed June 2004).

45. See Takeshi Fujitani, "Japan ODA Needs Substantial Reform, Experts Say," *Asahi Shimbun,* November 2, 2002. See also Policy Research Council of the Liberal Democratic Party, Commission on Foreign Affairs, Research Commission on Foreign Affairs, Special Committee on External Economic Cooperation, "The Direction of ODA Reform; Interim Report (tentative translation)," October 29, 2002, photocopy.

46. See DAC, "Japan (2003): DAC Peer Review: Main Findings and Recommendations," 2004, 2, http://www.oecd.org/document/10/0,2340,en_2649_34603_22579914 _1_1_1_1,00.html.

47. Makoto Iokibe, "Japan's Civil Society: An Historical Overview," in *Deciding the Public Good: Governance and Civil Society in Japan*, ed. Yamamoto Tadashi (Tokyo: Japan Center for International Exchange, 1999), 76.

48. Yoshida Shin'ichi, "Rethinking the Public Interest in Japan: Civil Society in the Making," in *Deciding the Public Good*, ed. Yamamoto Tadashi (Tokyo: Japan Center for International Exchange, 1999), 47.

49. One scholar of Japanese aid points out that "Japanese society is group-oriented and thus people tend to give mutual assistance within their own groups (usually the family or company) before extending such assistance to others. In particular, the Japanese concept of *uchi* (inside) and *soto* (outside) discourages anyone from assisting those who do not belong to his or her own group." Keiko Hirata, "Whither the Developmental State? The Growing Role of NGOs in Japanese Aid Policy Making," *Journal of Comparative Policy Analysis* 4, no. 3 (2002): 177.

50. MOFA, "Japan's Official Development Assistance Charter" (June 30, 1992), *Japan's ODA Annual Report 1999*, http://www.infojapan.org/policy/oda/summary/1999/ref1.html.

51. Orr, "Collaboration or Conflict?" 27.

52. Opinion Survey on Foreign Affairs, Cabinet Office, Government of Japan, "What Role Japan Should Play in International Society" (survey date: October 6–16, 2005), http://web-japan.org/stat/stats/220PN43.html (accessed March 2006). Not all public opinion polls were consistent in their findings, however. Saori Katada cites a 1999 survey undertaken by the prime minister's office that found nearly half of the Japanese public thought Japan should provide aid because, as a rich country, it should help poor countries on humanitarian grounds. Saori Katada, "Japan's Two-Track Aid Approach," *Asian Survey* 42, no. 2, 341.

53. MOFA, "Japan's ODA Annual Report (Summary) 1997" (1997), http://www.mofa.go.jp/policy/oda/summary/1997/index.html.

54. The Constitution of Japan, chap. 2, "Renunciation of War," article 9, http://www.solon.org/Constitutions/Japan/English/english-Constitution.html#CHAPTER_II. Even though the Japanese constitution was drafted by US advisors to the US occupation force after World War II, the pacifist elements in it appear to have been widely embraced by the Japanese population in the postwar period.

55. T. J. Pempel, "Japanese Foreign Economic Policy," in *Between Power and Plenty*, ed. Peter Katzenstein (Madison: University of Wisconsin Press, 1978), 142.

56. Up to the reform of 1993, there were multiple-member constituencies. The shift to single-member constituencies enhanced public influence over who was sent to parliament and thus increased the importance of public opinion in Japanese electoral politics and on public issues generally.

57. The term is used by Bradley Richardson in his book, *Japanese Democracy* (New Haven, CT: Yale University Press, 1997). In fact, the LDP lost power in 1993 but returned as part of a government coalition in 1994 and then again led the government from 1996.

58. Orr, "Collaboration or Conflict?" 10.

59. Orr points out that many members of the Diet are former bureaucrats, some of whom have considerable knowledge of foreign aid and can lobby their former colleagues on

issues and projects of special interest. There are also among Diet members "parliamentary friendship leagues" related to particular countries that these leagues favor and for which they often urge higher levels of aid. Orr judges their influence to be limited, however. Orr cites another expert who found that factions within the LDP favored certain countries for aid, but LDP members did not credit them with much influence. "Collaboration or Conflict?" 23. These and other, sometimes less savory, ties—as between commercial interests and particular recipient governments—are often mentioned (including by foreign diplomats and aid officials with an opportunity to observe them in action), but because data on them do not exist, it is difficult to gauge the extent of their influence.

60. One of the limitations on greater engagement in policy-making on the part of parliamentarians is the lack of information available to them about government programs. Some who have served in government can access needed information easily through their past network of contacts. But for those who do not have such networks, it can be more difficult. This lack of access to information could place limits on future policy activism in the LDP and the Diet.

61. Keiko Hirata, "New Challenges to Japan's Aid: An Analysis of Aid Policy-Making," *Pacific Affairs* 71, no. 3, 319.

CHAPTER FIVE

1. See, for example, Hubert Deschamps, "France in Black Africa and Madagascar between 1920 and 1945," in *Colonialism in Africa 1870–1960*, ed. L. H. Gann and Peter Duignan, vol. 1 of *Cambridge History of Africa* (New York: Cambridge University Press, 1982).

2. Teresa Hayter, *French Aid* (London: Overseas Development Institute, 1966), 28.

3. Cited in ibid., 29.

4. These included Côte d'Ivoire, Benin (then called Dahomey), Togo, Niger, Mali, Senegal, the Central African Republic, Chad, Cameroon, Gabon, Djibouti, the Republic of the Congo (Brazzaville), Upper Volta (later Burkina Faso), and Madagascar.

5. For analyses of the diplomatic goals of French aid, see John Chipman, *French Power in Africa* (London: Basil Blackwell, 1989); Peter Schraeder, "From Berlin 1884 to 1989: Foreign Assistance and French, American, and Japanese Competition in Francophone Africa," *Journal of Modern African Studies* 33, no. 4 (1995): 539–67.

6. See, for example, Philippe Leymaire, "Malaise dans la cooperation entre la France et l'Afrique," *Le Monde diplomatic,* June 2002, 19.

7. DAC, "International Development Statistics (IDS) Online" (accessed March 2006).

8. Hayter, *French Aid,* 49.

9. Pierre Pean, *L'Homme de l'Ombre* (Paris: Fayard, 1990), 294; my translation. See also Philippe Gaillard, *Foccart Parle: Entretiens avec Philippe Gaillard,* vols. 1 and 2 (Paris: Fayard, 1997).

10. Countries in this category included France's former African territories, other francophone African countries, and several other, small African countries: Benin, Burkina Faso, Burundi, Cameroon, Cape Verde, the Central African Republic, Chad, Comoros, Congo (Brazzaville), Côte d'Ivoire, Djibouti, Gambia, Equatorial Guinea, Gabon, Guinea-Bissau, Guinea, Lesser Antilles, Madagascar, Mali, Mauritania, Mauritius, Niger, Rwanda, Sao Tome, Senegal, Seychelles, Togo, and Zaire.

11. The percentage of French bilateral aid in the form of loans was 13 percent in 1978–80, rising to 22 percent by 1989. This reflected the increasing amounts of aid handled by

the Caisse Centrale de Développement and the Ministry of Finance as opposed to the Ministry of Cooperation. See DAC, *Chairman's Report 1990* (OECD, Paris, 1990), 256.

12. DAC, *DAC Peer Review France* (OECD, Paris, 1994), 18.

13. Overseas Development Institute, *French Aid: The Jeanneney Report (an Abridged Translation of La Politique de Coopération avec les Pays en Voie de Développement)* (London: Overseas Development Institute, 1964), 21.

14. Ibid.

15. For a description of the contents of the Gorse Report, see Richard Robarts, *French Development Assistance: A Study in Policy and Administration*, Administrative and Policy Studies Series, no. 03–017, vol. 2 (Beverly Hills, CA: Sage, 1994).

16. For Cot's version of this story, see Jean-Pierre Cot, *L'epreuve du pouvior: le tiers-mondisme ou quoi faire?* (Paris: Le Seuil, 1984). See also Jean-Francois Bayart, *La Politique Africaine de François Mitterand* (Paris: Karthala, 1984).

17. Stephane Hessel, "Le Relations de la France avec les pays en développement," report to the prime minister (mimeograph, Paris, 1990).

18. Jean-Jacques Gabbas, "French Development Co-operation Policy," in *Perspectives on European Development Co-operation*, ed. Olav Stokke and Paul Hoebink (London: Routledge, 2005).

19. See, for example, Philippe Leymaire, "'Françafrique' a l'ancienne," *Le Monde diplomatique*, March 2001, 10. See also Stephen Smith and Antoine Glaser, *Ces messieurs Afrique: Le Paris-village du continent noir* (Paris: Calmann-Lévy, 1992), 209.

20. The informality, secretiveness, and assumed (nefarious) influence of this network has been the subject of much gossip, a considerable amount of criticism, and a number of exposés in the French media and books on French aid and France's relationships with African governments in particular. See, for example, Francois-Xavier Vershave, *La Françafrique: Le plus long scandale de la Republique* (Paris: Stock, 1998). Because so many of the critiques of French aid—especially the exposés—lack footnotes, it is hard to gauge their reliability. Insiders familiar with the workings of French aid have told me that *Françafrique* had in fact influence over a relatively small amount of the aid managed by the Ministry of Cooperation and almost none over French aid located in other government agencies.

21. See Victor Chesnault, "Que faire de l'Afrique noire?" *Le Monde,* February 28, 1990; my translation.

22. See Serge Michailof, ed., *La France et l'Afrique* (Paris: Karthala, 1993), 483. Michailof was a senior official in the French government when the book (originally another government report on aid) was written, with the approval of the then Minister of Cooperation, Edwina Avice. In 1992, she was fired by President Mitterand after deciding to cut off aid to Zaire because of human rights abuses by Mobutu's government (without consulting the president). The government then decided to suppress the report. Michailof published it anyway as a book and left France for a job with the World Bank.

23. Part of the problem in exposing the positive results of France's aid is that government evaluation efforts were limited and dispersed among a variety of agencies, and those evaluations that were undertaken were often confidential and thus not available to the public. Further, the government made little effort to inform its public about the impact of its aid in development education and other programs.

24. While in Paris interviewing for this book, I visited an old friend who had been one of President de Gaulle's advisors and to a degree involved with France's African policies. In 2003 this proud and able member of France's postwar political elite confessed that he had

become ashamed of France's policies in Africa, including its aid policies. If he is anything to go by, such feelings must now be widespread even among the older generation of the best of France's civil servants.

25. While French aid to Togo did decline both absolutely and relative to the overall falling amount of France's bilateral aid, its aid to Cameroon—a government that had manipulated elections and had a reputation for corruption—continued to be relatively generous. This suggests that the French government put more emphasis on human rights abusers—which the Togolese government was and the government of Cameroon less so— than on progress toward democracy. Further, Togo was a small and not very significant country; Cameroon was considerably larger and better off, giving it more importance in Paris.

26. Claud Freud, *Quelle Coopération?* (Paris: Karthala, 1986), 29–30.

27. This decline in aid would have been even more dramatic if debt relief were not counted, which averaged $1.4 billion per year between 1994 and 2004. DAC, "International Development Statistics (IDS) Online," 2004 (accessed March 2006).

28. See Michel Roussin, *Afrique Majeure, Pouvoir et strategie* (Paris: France-empire, 1997), 66; my translation. Michel Roussin had also been charged and briefly jailed for corruption, though the charges did not involve his stint at the Ministry of Cooperation.

29. See "Interview du Premier ministre par G. Schneider (RFI), B. Stern (Le Monde) et P. Dessin (TUS)," Paris, February 4, 1998, http://www.archives.premier-ministre.gouv.fr/jospin_version2/pm/d040298.htm.

30. DAC, "Development Co-operation Review: France," *DAC Journal* 1, no. 3 (2000), http://www.oecd.org/dataoecd/17/25/29424648.pdf.

31. The DAC report also observed that diplomatic and development purposes are "not necessarily contradictory." DAC, *Peer Review: France,* (OECD, Paris, 2004), 20, http://www.oecd.org/dataoecd/31/40/32556778.pdf.

32. Ibid., 29.

33. Ibid., 14.

34. One observer of French bureaucratic politics, tartly observed with regard to the AFD's task of working harmoniously both with the Ministry of Finance and the Ministry of External Affairs: "The Quay d'Orsay [the Ministry of External Affairs] and Bercy [the Ministry of Finance] have never worked together" See Francois-Xavier Verschave, "Du rapport Tavernier au discourse de la 'reforme,'" in *Rapport 1999,* ed. Observatoire Permanente de la Coopération Française (Paris: Karthala, 1999), 56. The writer goes on to remark that "The 'Treasury-types' continue to govern the major part of development assistance. They clearly have no idea about or experience with the fight against poverty" (my translation).

35. The AFD was ably led, with Jean-Michel Severino, a former World Bank vice president, appointed as director general in 2002 and with other capable and experienced senior officials. One of them remarked to me that the AFD was still "organizing its opacity"—presumably through enacting extensive regulations or complicated decision-making processes or providing only partial information on what an agency is doing. This is a common tactic of relatively weak aid agencies in their dealings with stronger agencies or ministries to provide themselves with political space and to protect their autonomy by preventing other agencies from figuring out how to raid their budgets and control their programs. (It was long a tactic used by USAID—quite effectively at times—to keep the Department of State and others in the dark about how to influence decisions on the allocation and use of development assistance.)

36. However, the HCCI, by encouraging and publishing on its website and in books reflections and criticisms on French aid, did give somewhat greater transparency to that aid.

37. See Marc Pilon, "La reforme de la cooperation française: institutionelle ou politique?" in *Rapport 1998*, ed. Observatoire Permanent de la Coopération Française (Paris: Karthala, 1998), 30.

38. See INRA, *Europeans and Development Aid*, Eurobarometer 50.1, report for Directorate-General VIII of the European Commission, February 8, 1999, 2.

39. For an excellent recounting of the postwar period in France and the role in it of Charles de Gaulle, see Jean Lacouture, *DeGaulle: The Ruler 1945–1970* (New York: Norton, 1992).

40. See, for example, Eduardo Cue, "French Judges Target the Politically Powerful," *Christian Science Monitor*, February 2, 2001, http://search.csmonitor.com/durable/2001/02/05/fp8s1-csm.shtml.

41. Ibid., 45. See also Smith and Glaser, *Ces messieurs Afrique.*

42. See Euforic, "Advisory Structures for Development Cooperation Policy in France," http://www.euforic.org/fr/advis_fr.htm.

43. Jean-Marie Hatton, "Le panorama des associations françaises de solidarite internationale," extract from *L'Etat et les ONG: pour un partenariat efficace*, by Commissariat general du Plan (Paris: la Documentation française, 2002), http://www.hcci.gouv.fr/lecture/synthese/sy007.html.

44. The absence of such a think tank has been noted and lamented by senior French officials. See, for example, Jean-Michel Severino, "Modes d'elaboration de la pensee française," in *Cooperer au debut du XXIe siecle*, by Haut Conseil de la Coopération Internationale (Paris: Karthala, 2003). In fact, the AFD has begun to undertake development research, convene development conferences, and become, in effect, France's principal think tank on aid and development issues.

45. Benoit Cyrille (pseudonym), "La Politique Française de Coopération," *Projet*, no. 241 (Spring 1995): 45.

46. See "Interview du Premier ministre."

47. In a poll done in 2001, French respondents were asked which three priorities (from a list of twelve) they favored for providing aid. One-third supported reducing hunger, a quarter mentioned development in poor countries, and slightly under a quarter mentioned fighting HIV/AIDS. See BVA Actualité, *Les Français Face a L'enjeu de la Lutte contre La Faim dans Le Monde*, October 2003, 4, http://www.coordinationsud.org/IMG/doc/BVA-actu_CCFD.doc.

48. One scholar of French-African relations has also noted emerging changes in those relationships, but also observes that the old *reseaux* still have an influence. See Tony Chafer, "Franco-African Relations: No Longer So Exceptional," *African Affairs* 101 (2002): 343–63. Another scholar also notes a trend toward "normalization" of Franco-African relations, but views President Chirac (seen as part of the old Gaullist policies toward Africa) as the main impediment to more rapid change. See Gordon Cumming, "Modernization without 'Banalisation': Towards a New Era in French African Aid Relations?" *Modern & Contemporary France* 8, no. 3 (2000): 359–370. Several French scholars have noted the change in some of the underlying forces shaping France's Africa policies and, as a consequence, its aid policies. Jean-Francois Medard has noted the "erosion of Françafrique," observing that "If Chirac disappears from the political scene, most of the covert aspects of Françafrique should disappear with him," but not necessarily the networks that Medard and others worry have

become "criminalized." See "French African Policy: The End of 'Françafrique'?" paper (in outline) for research workshop Africa and the Great Powers, Copenhagen, April 2002, 1, 3, photocopy. Another French scholar of French aid made the following observation: "France is trying to extract itself from the image it portrayed in the 1990s, of a *France-Afrique* based on networks of military, political and financial influences stemming from the colonial period, with attendant actions in several countries . . . that did not seem beyond reproach. . . . Can France erase this image? It is difficult to say 'yes,' but apparently the habits and actions of old, like those so strongly castigated, the Foccart's type actions, have disappeared: information is serving to rein in excess, democracy is making inroads (admittedly not all at the same pace), but interference is strongly condemned and French public opinion is very much against this type of influence. Parliament is asking the government more and more questions." Gabbas, "French Development Co-operation Policy."

CHAPTER SIX

1. Jurgen Simon, "Administration of Development Assistance Projects in the US Agency for International Development (AID) and the German Federal Ministry for Economic Cooperation (BMZ): A Comparative Study of Organizational Effectiveness" (PhD diss., Indiana University, 1982), 122 (available from University Microfilms International).

2. See Jurgen Dennert, *Entwicklungshilfe geplant oder verwaltet?* (Bielefeld: Bertelsmann Universitätsverlag, 1968), 93.

3. Jurgen Simon, "Administration of Development Assistance Projects," 125.

4. For an effort to survey the aid activities of German ministries, see Walter Eberlei and Christoph Weller, "Deutsche Ministerien als Akteure von Global Governance," *Report* (Institut für Entwicklung und Frieden der Gerhard-Mercator-Universität, Duisburg), vol. 51 (2001).

5. DAC, "International Development Statistics (IDS) Online" (accessed March 2006).

6. Ibid.

7. Interview with Erhard Eppler, May 9, 2003, Berlin, Germany.

8. BMZ, *Die entwicklungspolitische Konzeption der Bundesrepublik Deutschland* (Bonn, January 11, 1971).

9. Burghard Claus and Hans H. Lembke, "The Development Cooperation Policy of the Federal Republic of Germany," in *Development Cooperation Policies of Japan, the United States and Europe,* ed. Ippei Yamazaqa and Akira Hirata (Tokyo: Institute of Developing Economies, 1992), 240.

10. Ibid.

11. Until the end of the Cold War, Germany did require that governments receiving its aid recognize that West Berlin was associated with West Germany. Several governments—for example, Angola and Mozambique—refused to adhere to this requirement and did not, therefore, receive German aid during this period.

12. Claus and Lembke, "Development Cooperation Policy," 240.

13. In 1995, at the urging of the BMZ (which found dealing with a wide variety of NGOs challenging), national NGOs and NGO networks working in development came together to form an umbrella organization—VENRO—which took the lead in strategic planning for advocacy and relating to the government and the Bundestag.

14. Cited in DAC, *Development Co-operation Review: Germany* (OECD, Paris, 2001), 13.

15. Claus and Lembke, "Development Cooperation Policy," 266–67.

16. The DAC, in its peer reviews of German aid, has remarked on the high proportion of that aid spent on infrastructure and equipment—often a sign that commercial interests are having some influence on the use of the aid. However, it is not possible to observe this trend in the DAC data on the sectoral distribution of German aid, because, by 2003, a whopping 43 percent of that aid is classified as "other" with no hint of what it funded. The high portion of infrastructure financing likely reflects the organization of German aid, with the role played by KfW, which provides credits for capital projects—natural candidates for infrastructure and equipment funding (in contrast to the emphasis on technical assistance in aid—largely grants—from the GTZ). In this organization and its ensuing rigidities, the German aid system resembles that of Japan.

17. This proposal surfaced during the election in 1994, but it caused such a backlash of criticism from NGOs that it was dropped. It surfaced again in the election of 2002, but with little effect. Not surprisingly, the idea appears to have had some traction in the Foreign Office.

18. The BMZ document *Crisis Prevention and Conflict Settlement* (http://www.bmz.de/en/service/infothek/fach/spezial/spezial018/), with its broad and encompassing generalities, reflects the early stage of thinking on the difficult and complex issues involving the causes of conflict and how external governments can act to help prevent conflicts from breaking out.

19. Cited in DAC, "Development Co-operation Review: Germany," *DAC Journal* 2, no. 4 (2001): 45, http://www.oecd.org/dataoecd/20/62/1934046.pdf.

20. German aid in 2002 was at 0.27 percent of GNI. See Guido Ashoff, "German Development Co-operation since the Early 1990s," in *Perspectives on European Development Cooperation,* ed. Paul Hoebink and Olav Stokke (London: Routledge, 2005), 16. Several German aid officials suggested that the Minister of Development, who strongly supported an increase in German aid, used the EU to create a commitment to do so which her government then had to accept.

21. DAC, *Statistical Annex of the 2005 Development Co-operation Report,* table 7, "Burden Sharing Indicators," http://www.oecd.org/dataoecd/52/9/1893143.xls (accessed March 2006).

22. Germans vote twice in federal elections. One is a vote for an individual representing a constituency. The candidate in a particular constituency obtaining the majority of votes is elected. The other is for a "Land list," or party list, the outcome of which is based on the proportion of votes each party receives (based on a complicated formula). The latter vote determines the representation of political parties in the Bundestag and is thus the more important of the two votes.

23. Jurgen Wiemann, *German Development Assistance* (Bonn: German Development Institute, 1996), 15.

24. DAC, "Development Co-operation Review: Germany" (2001), 21; and DAC, "Development Co-operation Review: Germany" (2006), 25. Opinion surveys are not published by the German government, but the peer reviewers of German aid for the DAC had access to their findings. Further, an opinion poll by the European Commission published in 2005 showed that 91 percent of Germans thought it important or very important "to help people in poor countries develop"—the same percentage that the poll found for the EU as a whole. See Public Opinion Analysis, European Commission, *Special Eurobarometer: Attitudes towards Development Aid* (European Commission, February 2005), 28, http://europa.eu.int/comm/public_opinion/archives/ebs/ebs_222_en.pdf (accessed March 2005).

25. This section is based on confidential interviews with German officials from the Foreign Office and the BMZ, in Berlin and Bonn, undertaken in September 2002.

26. See, for example, Thomas Fues, "Germany," in *The Reality of Aid 1996*, by Reality of Aid (London: Earthscan, 1996).

27. Guido Ashoff, "The Coherence of Policies towards Developing Countries: The Case of Germany," in *Policy Coherence in Development Co-operation*, ed. Jacques Forster and Olav Stokke (London: Frank Cass, 1999), 170.

28. Birgit Dederichs Bain, "Germany," in *The Reality of Aid 1997–1998*, by Reality of Aid (London: Earthscan, 1997), 70. Nearly 40 percent of bilateral German ODA was reportedly tied to the purchase of German goods and services. By 2001 German financial aid (primarily from the KfW) was officially untied, while technical assistance (mainly from the GTZ) was often tied. Germany has signed the various international agreements, mentioned in chapter 2, on untying its aid.

29. Ibid., 59.

CHAPTER SEVEN

1. Olav Stokke has defined humane internationalism thus: "(i) the acceptance of an obligation to alleviate global poverty and to promote social and economic development in the Third World; (ii) a conviction that a more equitable world would be in the best long-term interests of the Western, industrial nations; and (iii) the assumption that meeting these international responsibilities is compatible with the maintenance of a socially responsible national economic and social welfare policy." See Olav Stokke, "Determinants of Aid Policies: Introduction," in *Western Middle Powers and Global Poverty*, ed. Olav Stokke (Uppsala: Scandinavian Institute of African Studies, with the Norwegian Institute of International Affairs, 1989), 11. The designation of Denmark as a "front-runner" came from the Development Assistance Committee (DAC) in its various peer reviews and commentaries on Danish aid.

2. Ellen Hanak and Michael Loft, "Danish Development Assistance to Tanzania and Kenya, 1962–85: Its Importance to Agricultural Development," in *Aid to African Agriculture: Lessons of Two Decades of Experience*, ed. Uma Lele (Baltimore: Johns Hopkins University Press, 1991), 171.

3. DAC, "International Development Statistics (IDS) Online" (accessed March 2006).

4. The increase was even greater in terms of Danish kroner — nearly quadrupling in value.

5. Hanak and Loft, "Danish Development Assistance," 177. Isak Dinesen's best-known book on Kenya is *Out of Africa* (New York: Random House, 1938).

6. Lester Pearson, *Partners in Development*, Report of the Commission on International Development (created by the World Bank) (New York: Praeger, 1969).

7. Cited in Knud Erik Svendsen, "Denmark: Social Development and International Development Cooperation" in *Welfare, Development and Security: Three Danish Essays* (Copenhagen: Danish National Institute of Social Research, 1995), 47.

8. See Patricia Bliss McFate, "To See Everything in Another Light," *Daedalus*, Winter 1984, 48.

9. One observer of Danish aid speculates that the benefit to the Social Liberals of this initiative is that "the party could raise its profile on the North-South issue at no cost; because the government, which the party supported in other respects, did not resign." See

Gorm Rye Olsen, "Danish Development Policy: The Art of Compromise," *Forum for Development Studies*, no. 1–2 (1994): 283.

10. See "Rich Nations Block Aid Accord," *Guardian* (Manchester), June 23, 2000, www.guardian.co.uk.

11. Cited in Gorm Rye Olsen, "Danish Aid Policy in the Post Cold War Period: Increasing Resources and Minor Adjustments" (working paper 02.15, Center for Development Research, Copenhagen, 2002), 5.

12. These credits, however, were permitted only in countries where commercial financing would not be available and for approved development activities, in accord with the 1992 Helsinki Arrangement on mixed credits, agreed to by OECD member states.

13. See Ministry of Foreign Affairs of Denmark, "Danish Development Policy," edited September 27, 2005, http://www.um.dk/en/menu/DevelopmentPolicy/DanishDevelomentPolicy/Partnership2000/ (accessed March 2006).

14. The "Liberal" party in Denmark started life many decades ago as a left-wing party but became a right-wing party over time, reflecting commercial interests, among others.

15. These are the major changes made by the new government affecting Danish aid. For more details, see DAC, *Development Co-operation Review: Denmark* (OECD, Paris, 2003), http://www.oecd.org/dataoecd/23/63/2956543.pdf (accessed March 2006).

16. "Aid Cuts," *Copenhagen Post*, September 5, 2002, http://www.cphpost.dk.

17. "Public Support for Aid Cuts," *Copenhagen Post,* February 19, 2002.

18. "Support for Private Health Bill—and Aid Cuts," *Copenhagen Post*, March 15, 2002.

19. See Ministry of Foreign Affairs of Denmark, "Danish Development Policy," http://www.um.dk/en/menu/DevelopmentPolicy/DanishDevelopmentPolicy (accessed November 2004).

20. Ibid.

21. See DANIDA, Ministry of Foreign Affairs of Denmark, "A World of Difference: The Government's Vision for New Priorities in Danish Development Assistance 2004–2008" (Copenhagen, 2003).

22. A public opinion poll by Aalborg University and A.C. Nielsen AIM in 2003 found that 68 percent of the public were opposed to any further reductions in Danish aid. Cited in DAC, *Development Co-operation Review: Denmark,* 21.

23. DANIDA, Danish Ministry of Foreign Affairs, "Security, Growth—Development: Priorities of the Danish Government for Danish Development Assistance 2005–2009" (August 2004), 3, 22, http://www.um.dk/nr/rdonlyres/c1ef2855-a885–49b8–96a0–5d3ac7b22912/0/securitygrowthdevelopment.pdf.

24. There was also some speculation that the new Minister of Development, Immigration and Integration was awarded the development portfolio as compensation for not having been appointed as Denmark's EU commissioner. See "Minister Primed for Broader Role," *Copenhagen Post*, August 12, 2004, http://www.cphpost.dk/get/80785.html. There was even some speculation that this move was an effort to shield development aid from pressures from the right-wing People's Party to use it for reducing and repatriating refugees.

25. Ministry of Foreign Affairs of Denmark, *Globalisation—Progress through Partnership: Priorities of the Danish Government for Danish Development Assistance 2006–2010* (August 2005), 4, http://www.um.dk/en/menu/DevelopmentPolicy/DanishDevelopmentPolicy/PrioritiesOfTheDanishGovernmentForDanishDevelopmentAssistance/ (accessed October 2005).

26. See Klaus Rifbjerg, "Oh! to Be Danish: An Essay" (Ministry of Foreign Affairs of Denmark), http://www.um.dk/Publikationer/UM/English/Denmark/kap8/8.asp (accessed March 2006).

27. This is a phrase a number of commentators on Danish foreign policy have used. See, for example, Hans-Henrick Holm, "Danish Foreign Policy Activism: Rise and Decline" (Danish School of Journalism, n.d.), http://www.djh.dk/pdf/forskning/decline.pdf (accessed March 2006).

28. In response to a question in the Folketing, cited in Holm, "Danish Foreign Policy Activism," 22. This characterization of the ideas behind Denmark's aid policy—the image and status it accorded the country—is not to suggest that Copenhagen did not take a hard-headed look at its national interests and pursue them vigorously in Scandinavia, the Baltic, Europe, and NATO and at the UN. Denmark put considerable value on maintaining a close, supportive relationship with Washington, while viewing Europe as a main focus of its foreign policy efforts. Development cooperation was only one of Denmark's preoccupations in the world.

29. In 2004 Denmark gave 0.85 percent of its GNI. Austria gave 0.2 percent, Canada gave 0.27 percent, Finland gave 0.35 percent, and Ireland gave 0.39 percent. The most generous country that year was Norway, providing 0.87 percent of its GNI in aid; the least generous was Italy at 0.15 percent. See DAC, "International Development Statistics (IDS) Online" (accessed March 2006).

30. By 2003 the Danes were avoiding the term "welfare state," having replaced it with "welfare society" in an effort to expand the responsibilities for social welfare to society and individuals within it. This change in terminology reflected a backlash against the welfare state (and its heavy tax burden) that helped carry the center-right coalition to power in 2001 and to reelection in 2005.

31. Svendsen, "Denmark," 37.

32. Ibid.

33. Olsen, "Danish Aid Policy"; "Public Support for Aid Cuts," *Copenhagen Post,* February 19, 2002.

34. Olsen, "Danish Development Policy," 282.

35. Ibid.

36. Hans Lembke, "Denmark's Development Cooperation Policy" (photocopy, German Development Institute, Bonn, 1985); and Knud Erik Svendsen, "Danish Aid: Old Bottles," in *Western Middle Powers and Global Poverty,* ed. Olav Stokke (Uppsala: Scandinavian Institute of African Studies, with the Norwegian Institute of International Affairs, 1989), 91–116.

37. Olsen, "Danish Aid Policy," 18–19. The new government installed after the election of 2001 decided to reduce the concentration of Danish aid on a handful of major NGOs and announced it would be dispersed much more widely among those and the many smaller NGOs as well.

38. Confidential interview, Copenhagen, November 2003.

CHAPTER EIGHT

1. See PIPA, "Americans on Foreign Aid and World Hunger" (February 2001), http://65.109.167.118/pipa/pdf/feb01/ForeignAid_Feb01_rpt.pdf (accessed March 2005); and see Public Opinion Analysis, European Commission, *Special Eurobarometer: Attitudes towards*

Development Aid (European Commission, February 2005), 5, http://europa.eu.int/comm/ public_opinion/archives/ebs/ebs_222_en.pdf (accessed March 2005).

2. The history of Dutch aid shows a similar pattern. See J. A. Nekkers and P. A. M. Malcontent, eds., *Fifty Years of Dutch Development Cooperation, 1949–1999* (The Hague: SDU Publishers, for the Ministry of Foreign Affairs, 2000).

3. For one effort to assess the impact of aid intended to promote growth on that growth, see Clemens, Radelet, and Bhavnani, "Counting Chickens before They Hatch." This paper separated emergency aid, aid for purposes that might affect growth over the long term (e.g., for the environment or democracy promotion), and aid aimed at promoting growth and found a high correlation of aid for growth with growth.

4. See, for example, USAID, "Fragile States Strategy" (Washington, DC, January 2005), http://www.usaid.gov/policy/2005_fragile_states_strategy.pdf (accessed March 2005); Department for International Development, *Why We Must Work More Effectively in Fragile States* (London: Government of the United Kingdom, January 2005), http://www.dfid.gov .uk/pubs/files/fragilestates-paper.pdf (accessed March 2005). See also Center for Global Development, *On the Brink: Weak States and US National Security,* Report of the Commission on Weak States and US National Security (Washington, DC, 2004), http://www.cgdev.org/ doc/weakstates/Full_Report.pdf.

INDEX